D0521533

INSIDE MICROSOFT® WINDOWS® CE

BY

JOHN MURRAY

Microsoft·Press

Inside Microsoft Windows CE

Published by Microsoft Press
A Division of Microsoft Corporation
One Microsoft Way
Redmond, Washington 98052-6399

Library of Congress Cataloging-in-Publication Data
Murray, John, 1959-
    Inside Microsoft Windows CE / John Murray.
      p.   cm.
    Includes index.
    ISBN 1-57231-854-6
    1. Microsoft Windows (Computer file)   2. Operating systems
(Computers)   I. Title.
    QA76.76.O63M8665 1998
    005.4'469--dc21   98-28532
                                         CIP

Printed and bound in the United States of America.

2 3 4 5 6 7 8 9 QMQM 3 2 1 0 9 8

Distributed in Canada by ITP Nelson, a division of Thomson Canada Limited.

A CIP catalogue record for this book is available from the British Library.

Microsoft Press books are available through booksellers and distributors worldwide. For
further information about international editions, contact your local Microsoft Corporation office or contact Microsoft Press International directly at fax (425) 936-7329. Visit our
Web site at mspress.microsoft.com.

Acquisitions Editor: Eric Stroo
Project Editor: Victoria Thulman
Technical Editor: Jim Fuchs

---◆---

For John O and the Lake Washington H.S. Class of '98

---◆---

CONTENTS

CONTRIBUTORS

Foreword

Over the past 30 years, I've watched the computer business go from the mainframe era to the minicomputer era to the personal computing era, and now to the *very personal computing* era. I find it very gratifying to be part of that transition.

When we started work on Microsoft Windows CE for embedded applications, we decided to focus on 32-bit, virtual memory–capable microprocessors. We believed that Moore's Law would continue to function and that this hardware platform would become economical as we popularized Windows CE for the next generation of intelligent appliances.

Our goal was to bring the more sophisticated software environment of today's personal computer into the embedded world. We didn't go back and try to capture the style and capabilities of traditional real-time embedded systems but instead focused on adding modularity and real-time features to this new, componentized Microsoft Windows operating system.

Today we have microprocessors going into automobiles whose memory capacity and performance are basically equivalent to what I designed into supercomputers in 1982. The ability to apply this level of computing performance at very low cost to benefit people who want to live "the web lifestyle," as Bill Gates calls it, represents a radical step forward in the role that computing devices and software play in support of our daily lives.

One of the great things about Microsoft is that we have Bill Gates's leadership. Our continuity of management enables us to invest and persevere in our development efforts over long periods of time. As computing has evolved, this continuity has allowed us to begin introducing computers to the devices that people find to be mission-critical for their daily lives, such as televisions, telephones, radios, and cars, as well as other support systems, such as home, building, and traffic automation.

We launched the PC Companion line with the Handheld PC; now we are shipping the Palm-size PC, bringing the Auto PC on line, and collaborating with Sega to use Windows CE as part of the Dreamcast home video game system. As part of the digital TV efforts, we are reconstructing the

WebTV client as a form of digital television that runs on Windows CE, and we are using Windows CE in the advanced digital set-top box that TCI will deploy. To produce as many products as the Windows CE team has in a short period of time is a real testimony to the individuals and to the team.

We hope that facilitating interconnection between these devices will be a major benefit of Windows CE. Windows CE allows us to bridge traditional personal computing and intelligent appliances, and its scalability allows us to make these devices ubiquitous.

Connectivity will be the single biggest differentiator between the universe of devices today and the universe of devices 10 years from now. It will require a new communications infrastructure, including radio, wireline communications, satellites, and digital TV transmission mechanisms, as well as new standards. To succeed, we in this industry have to operate at a macroscopic technical, economic, and political level because no one company—not even Microsoft—can effect all the changes by itself.

We see a lot of momentum behind the current Windows CE products, but we also recognize the huge opportunity for the hundreds of thousands of people who design specialty systems and who welcome the arrival of a small but powerful networking-capable, Internet-aware operating system. The creativity of this development community—the people who read this book—will invent new ways to use this technology.

Craig Mundie,
Senior Vice President,
Consumer Platforms Division,
Microsoft Corporation

Preface

With Windows CE, Microsoft is extending its franchise to televisions, telephones, and other "intelligent" devices that can incorporate cheap, powerful, 32-bit microprocessors and communicate with one another. This book is a survey of the Windows CE operating system—its architecture, some design details, and ways to think about it—in the words of the Microsoft developers who created it. If you are an embedded systems developer, Win32 programmer, or entrepreneur, you will benefit from the instant expertise to be gained from their tutorials.

I spent a year and a half with the Windows CE team, writing developer documentation, sample code, and white papers, then took my video camera or tape recorder around and asked the developers to explain their pieces of the system. Sometimes I said, "Imagine that you are explaining the architecture to a new hire who will be taking over your code." I basically asked variations of three questions:

- What is new or different about the Windows CE design compared to other Microsoft Windows operating systems?

- What parts of Windows CE can other developers replace, customize, or configure?

- Where have developers been asking the most questions?

I then edited and arranged the interviews into a sequence that provides a workable survey of the entire system. Every one of the chapters can be expanded into a complete book, but I wanted to produce a single book that you could read on a cross-country plane flight. By the time you pick up your luggage on the other coast, you will understand the Windows CE vision and know where to find more detailed information.

Many books in Microsoft Press's *Inside* series describe new programming interfaces, but Windows CE is based on the existing, well-known Win32 programming interfaces, and dozens of excellent introductory books and training programs are already available. (Even the new programming interfaces unique to Windows CE are already featured in *The Windows CE Programmer's Guide,* which I helped write, and Doug Boling's forthcoming book, *Programming Microsoft Windows CE*). Accordingly, code or pseudocode appears here only for material that does not appear in the first edition of *The Windows CE Programmer's Guide.* This book focuses on the vision and architecture of the system.

About the approach to this book: I like two kinds of computer books, those that are concise and those that reveal the personalities of the developers. Kernighan's and Ritchie's *The C Programming Language* and Helen Custer's *Inside Windows NT* fall into the first category, and Patrick Naughton's appendix in *The Java Handbook* and the passages about the Microsoft developer in Fred Moody's *I Sing the Body Electronic* fall into the second. With this book, I tried to achieve both concision *and* personality, and employed oral history as the technique to get there. This book aims for a balance between solid technical information and the developers' stories. The title *Inside Microsoft Windows CE* suggests a blend of system architecture details and a look at what it is like to be inside a development team working on a new Microsoft OS.

Overall, the book captures the developers' personalities with only a slight additional cost: it could have been more terse, but preserving the context and integrity of each interview meant allowing some redundancy. On the other hand, because I did eliminate almost all of the redundancy, I am obliged to offer a few impressions from my 50 interviews and 18 months behind the scenes with the Windows CE team:

- ◆ Nearly every interview started with a recap of overall product goals before moving to the architecture of an individual area. The same product vision was repeated, almost verbatim, in interview after interview. Also, nearly every team member recited a genealogy of Microsoft product teams leading to the Windows CE team (which usually included one of the predecessor teams, WinPad or Pulsar). Many expressed a strong and deep sense of loyalty, even to teams long since disbanded.

- ◆ People who are not inside Microsoft can't fully appreciate the fierce rivalries and pitched battles that take place *within the company itself.* I spoke with the survivors on both sides of three major design wars. These stories, told to me independently by many

different people, shared underlying themes: the importance of each individual contributor and the belief that each individual should take risks and compete for his or her vision.

◆ At some point almost every developer, unprompted, tempered a discussion of a successful design by mentioning trade-offs or even initial failures or flaws in their work that had to be corrected. This honesty and humility is a trait that I appreciate and often find in engineers.

◆ While oral history can accurately portray team members' perceptions, it can also provide conflicting and inaccurate accounts. I contacted the Intel Corporation and the Microsoft Legal department to obtain official statements regarding the termination of the WinPad project, but they were either unwilling or unable to provide these details before the book went to press. The material in this book, therefore, cannot be viewed as a complete and objective portrayal of the WinPad project. It must instead be interpreted only as a subjective description that explains the team's motivation to design Windows CE as a portable system.

The development team was articulate and engaging. I have tried to preserve the "sleazy hacks," the "weird and complex beast," "the civil libertarian palette model," the "rock, paper, scissors arrangement," "the unified field theory people," "Roland's rule of thumb," "the beautiful scenario," "Yoo-hoo, HTML control," and the many other vivid phrases that embody the spirit of this important new operating system.

ABOUT THIS BOOK

Chapter 1, "Setting the Stage," introduces the goals of the development team by walking through a proposed mission statement: "Windows CE is a new, portable, real-time, modular operating system that features popular Microsoft programming interfaces and that is supported by tools that enable rapid development of embedded and dedicated systems." Chapter 1 also helps explain the context in which team members worked by describing the roles on a typical Microsoft development team.

Chapter 2, "Overview of Windows CE," offers a longer high-level discussion of the embedded markets and Microsoft's strategy with Windows CE. Windows CE assumed its current form as a modular operating system, suitable for a variety of different devices, with the 2.0 release. Each subsequent release offers a set of tested configurations. This chapter explains the componentization model and offers a block diagram of a system that includes all of the available components. Subsequent chapters examine these individual blocks in detail.

Chapter 3, "The Kernel," describes the innermost part of the operating system. The kernel supports the standard Win32 process and thread model and provides round-robin, priority-based thread scheduling. This chapter also describes the virtual memory system and the use of protected server libraries (PSLs) to enhance performance and minimize memory use. The kernel is written to provide low latency times, thus making it appropriate for use in real-time systems.

Chapter 4, "Data Storage," describes the three components of the object store: the file system or systems, the registry, and Windows CE property databases. Many Windows CE devices do not offer a physical hard drive but instead provide persistent storage in RAM built on top of an underlying subsystem, called the internal heap. This chapter describes the heap in detail, including its built-in compression and its support for transactioning, which ensures data integrity on low-power devices. It also describes how embedded developers can add their own extensible file systems.

Chapter 5, "The GWE Subsystem," describes the graphics, window manager, and event manager subsystem, subsets of the standard Windows Kernel32, User32, and Gdi32 libraries. The chapter also describes the Windows message-based programming model from the point of view of the Windows CE components that manage user applications. It shows how the GWE design separates event management and graphics, allowing the smallest possible system size while still supporting Windows programs—even on devices without display hardware.

Chapter 6, "Porting to New Hardware," dives down to the lowest levels of the system to explain the porting layer and the device driver models that tie Windows CE to the device hardware. This chapter explains the OEM Adaptation Layer and the native and stream interrupt device drivers. This chapter also walks through the interrupt model, showing the interactions between the kernel, the interrupt service routine (ISR), and the device driver's interrupt service thread (IST).

Chapter 7, "Communications," describes the complete set of options available to communicate with the desktop, the Internet, and other Windows CE devices. Windows CE supports a wide variety of Win32 communication APIs that support modems, networking cards, and serial and infrared communications. The block diagram shows the relationship between the communications protocols and the standard higher-level Win32 programming interfaces supported by Windows CE. This chapter also describes the desktop synchronization model, ActiveSync, and Mobile Channels, a high-level scripting interface for the Palm-size PC that is built on top of the other communications interfaces.

Chapter 8, "User Interface and Shell Services," provides an overview of the challenges in user interface design for new information appliances and offers suggestions for designers working with smaller input and display areas. Windows CE supports a variety of shell options, ranging from custom minimum shells produced independently by embedded developers to shells that are similar to the Microsoft Windows 98 look and feel. Some devices, such as the Auto PC and Palm-size PC, support alternate forms of user input, such as voice input and handwriting input.

Chapter 9, "Testing Your Embedded System," describes some of the challenges facing developers building embedded systems and applications, especially the new challenges that differ from those faced by developers of the traditional PC platform. The Microsoft software engineers who managed the Windows CE QA efforts provide suggestions on how to approach testing, from specific practices and tools through management and communications strategies. The device driver tests and test harness developed by the QA team are provided to embedded developers in the Device Driver Test Kit (DDTK).

Chapter 10, "Development Tools," describes the wide variety of development kits and tools offered for Windows CE and provides overviews of the programming interfaces. The Windows CE development kits build on standard Microsoft IDEs, such as Microsoft Visual C++, adding emulation and remote debugging tailored for Windows CE devices. The tools support Win32, COM, ActiveX, MFC, ATL, Microsoft Visual Basic, and Microsoft Visual J++ programming.

Chapter 11, "A Look at Some Windows CE Configurations," looks at how Microsoft and other embedded customers are configuring Windows CE for their markets. In addition to discussing Windows-based terminals, the Sega Dreamcast home video game system, the Auto PC, the Palm-size PC, and the Handheld PC, this chapter notes that embedded developers are creating new devices and putting applications on existing platforms to create vertical or dedicated devices based on Windows CE.

Chapter 12, "The Future of Windows CE," taps the experience of some of the Windows CE group's senior managers (and other senior Microsoft architects) to discuss future technology, future user interfaces, and future devices based on Windows CE.

Acknowledgments

This book owes its existence to the current and past members of the Microsoft Windows CE development team and to many others, both in and out of Microsoft, who told me their stories through 1997 and 1998. Many thanks to Anna Boyd, Anthony Lapadula, Arul Menezes, Bill Mitchell, Brad Silverberg, Bryan Trussel, Byron Bishop, Carlos Alayo, Cathy Linn, Charles Wu, Chris Stirrat, Dave Wecker, David Campbell, David Kanz, David Tuniman, Edward Jung, Frank Fite, Gilad Odinak, Greg Hullender, Harel Kodesh, Hon Keat Chan, James Stulz, Jason Fuller, Jay McLain, Jeff Parsons, Joe Quagliani, Keith Bentley, Keith Szot, Kenneth Macleod, Kieu Nguyen, Kimberly Gregory, Kirk Gremillion, Larry Morris, Mark Miller, Martin Shetter, Mauricio Lomelin, Mike Ginsberg, Mike Montague, Mike Thomson, Patrick Copeland, Patrick Halulpzok, Patrick Volk, Randy Kath, Raymond Manning, Robert O'Hara, Roberto Cazzaro, Roland Ayala, Sarah Zuberec, Scott Horn, Scott Shell, Sharad Mathur, Sridhar Mandyam, Steve Isaac, Steve Masters, Tandy Trower, Ted Kummert, Thomas Fenwick, TJ Forman, Tony Barbagallo, Tony Kitowicz, William Vong, and Yadhu Gopalan.

I apologize for the heavy editing and the omission of some interviews so that this version of the book could stay within its size constraints. The complete interviews are a fascinating chronicle of a major software development project.

This book hit its deadlines thanks primarily to the great people in the Microsoft Library and Word Processing Group. They are fun people who are also incredibly fast and accurate—true professionals. Thanks, Peggy and Denise.

I am also grateful for the help and support of many others, including Alicia Delserone, Ava Chen, Brad Joseph, Bruce Vanderpool, Callie Wilson, Cheri Christensen, Dan Thompson, David Pellerin, Doug and Peggi Goodwin, Guy Smith, Jason Black, Jill Stutzman, John Dohlen, Jon Christiansen, Laurell Haapanen, Lisa Matheson, Mike Pope, Nuan Wen, Peter Davis, Randy Ocheltree, Roberta Leibovitz, Shannon Rouse, Steve Kemper, Susan Klysa, Teresa Atkinson, and Tom Marchioro. One other person stands out for his many contributions to this book. In the ten years I've known him, Barry Potter has constantly been asked to do the impossible and has always delivered. His own writing has also received the ultimate compliment: two interview candidates who were asked to produce writing samples offered Barry's work as their own.

Eric Stroo was a steady hand at the helm guiding this project through two turbulent reorganizations—one at Microsoft Press and one in the table of contents. My new favorite editor, Victoria Thulman, and technical editor, Jim Fuchs, deserve all credit for the readability of the final manuscript. Travis Beaven and David Brunet converted my napkin sketches into professional artwork and spent hours preparing the photographs when my raw indie documentary footage proved to be just a tad below production standards. Barbara Remmele tweaked the design so that it accommodated the unique features of this book, and Paula Gorelick did a superb job flowing the text into the design. Roger LeBlanc proofread and convinced me to go out and conduct that one last interview.

Finally, all my love to Bim and my family (and many thanks to the extended family: Sue, Shellie, Lena, Mark, Salazar, Rich, and PeterP) for supporting this and many other projects over the years.

Redmond, WA
July 4, 1998

The Windows CE System Architecture

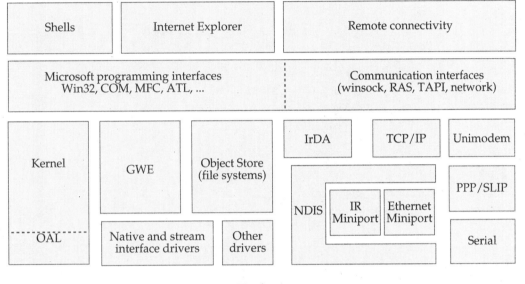

The Windows CE system architecture provides the roadmap for this book. The discussion of the system as a whole in Chapters 1 and 2 is followed by individual chapters on the kernel (Chapter 3), the object store (Chapter 4), GWE (Chapter 5), the OAL and device drivers (Chapter 6), communications (Chapter 7), user interface and shell services (Chapter 8), and other programming interfaces and tools (Chapter 10). Three chapters examine the system as a whole from different perspectives: quality assurance (Chapter 9), specific product configurations (Chapter 11), and possible directions for future development (Chapter 12).

1 Setting the Stage

I f the Microsoft Windows CE development team committed its mission statement to paper, it might read like this:

> Windows CE is a *new, portable, real-time, modular operating system* that features popular Microsoft *programming interfaces* and that is supported by *tools* that enable *rapid development* of *embedded and dedicated systems.*

Definitions of the italicized terms in the statement provide the structure for this chapter, setting the stage for a detailed look at the system architecture in later chapters. Throughout, the discussion notes those areas where embedded systems developers can extend or replace existing Windows CE code.

This book is aimed at three audiences—embedded systems developers, Microsoft Windows developers, and vertical market entrepreneurs—each of whom might be unfamiliar with the markets, interfaces, and development practices of the others. For example, many embedded systems developers might not be familiar with Microsoft Windows and the Microsoft Win32 API set. Likewise, many Windows programmers, already writing Win32 applications for the desktop PC, might not be familiar with the embedded systems market. And vertical market entrepreneurs, who package dedicated applications on existing Windows CE–based devices such as the Palm-size PC, and who offer marketing, sales, service, and training for a particular industry, might not fully understand the development process and the range of options available to them. This book establishes a common vocabulary for all three audiences by examining the highlighted terms of the proposed mission statement.

In the course of learning how Windows CE was developed and what it offers, you'll meet many of the individuals responsible for the creation of embedded systems and learn about their roles in the development process. Accordingly, this chapter also briefly explains the roles played by individuals on a typical software development team at Microsoft.

A Brand New System

The first italicized word in the Windows CE mission statement that introduced this chapter is *new*. Some people think Windows CE was ported from Microsoft Windows 95 because the first product to use the Windows CE operating system (OS) featured a graphical user interface similar to the interface of Windows 95. But Windows CE is unique. It has its own code base, written from scratch and specifically designed for embedded devices.

Windows CE is the third new major 32-bit operating system to be released by Microsoft this decade. But whereas Microsoft Windows 95 and Microsoft Windows NT were high-profile projects involving huge teams of people, Windows CE had the size and feel of a skunk-works project, with its development team operating anonymously and out of sight in one of the older buildings on the main Microsoft campus in Redmond, Washington.

Being a small team and keeping a low profile worked to the team's advantage, allowing them to try several different designs before getting it right. "We sometimes thought of ourselves as a covert group," said Cathy Linn, the lead program manager for what would be the first Windows CE device, Handheld PC 1.0. "We weren't on everybody's mind—the higher-ups' minds. We were an afterthought, in a sense, so we could try things without having somebody watching over our shoulders all the time."

Initially, the OS was to be used in two products: in the set-top boxes that were part of the end-to-end interactive television system and in "Pulsar." Pulsar was the internal code name for a small handheld personal digital assistant (PDA) that was based on a new object-oriented operating system. It relied on wireless communication networks to provide useful information to consumers. But the needs of the interactive TV and Pulsar groups quickly diverged.

Pulsar had tight memory constraints, but the ITV group began planning for large amounts of memory to handle the set-top box's multimedia features. And where ITV would ship a closed system sold as an end-to-end service, Pulsar would ship an open development platform that needed to attract independent software developers (ISVs). The OS was in the middle, and the two groups were pulling in different directions.

Tension grew within the Pulsar development team. The Pulsar team felt that the object-based OS team should be fixing bugs rather than researching isochronous data streams. They complained of being treated like second-class citizens.

The Pulsar team also had doubts about using brand new programming interfaces. Mike Montague, development lead for networking software, started pushing for the standard Win32 API set to attract programmers.

Knowing that the Pulsar team would face opposition from virtually all Microsoft vice presidents, who were promoting the new object interfaces in the new object-oriented OS, Bill Mitchell held a secret offsite meeting on his deck to start work on the Win32 approach. The team examined the entire Win32 API set, defining the smallest possible subset of functions that would support application developers. They first tried to port Windows NT and hack it down to the selected API subset, but despite its early promise, the Windows NT port was too big for the devices.

In the fall of 1994, the Pulsar team held one of its periodic review meetings with Bill Gates, which was known as the "BillG review." Within the same week or so, another team working on another handheld offering, the "WinPad," also held its BillG review. WinPad was a handheld device and office companion for business users. It was based on the 16-bit Microsoft Windows 3.1 system, which was an operating system different from the one used by Pulsar. Named Microsoft At Work and first launched in 1992, this embedded OS was designed for office equipment such as copiers and fax machines.

Neither of the reviews for Pulsar or WinPad went very well, recalled Robert O'Hara, a WinPad development lead. "Basically BillG said, 'I've got WinPad and Pulsar working on handheld computing, doing two completely different things. Why are we doing this?' " Gates reorganized both WinPad and Pulsar under Brad Silverberg.

"I looked at both of them," Silverberg recalled. "I had some fundamental questions about the viability of their visions as well as their execution. While there were some decent ideas, both were clearly destined for failure." WinPad, Silverberg explained, was already a few years behind schedule. Several original equipment manufacturer (OEM) partners had bailed out as the projected retail price had soared from $500 to about $1200. The device relied on an Intel microprocessor called Polar that did not appear to be competitive in the embedded market. At that time, Intel was having such enormous success with the Pentium that Silverberg suspected they "didn't really have their hearts in it." Finally, he said, the At Work OS, based on the 16-bit Windows 3.1, was already obsolete. It wasn't worth further investment.

Pulsar was just plain "goofy," Silverberg said. To him, the UI for the device seemed like a computer-science term project with a "space-age cutesy" design that reminded him of the children's cartoon *The Jetsons*. The team had not done the hard-core business research he thought was needed: talking with customers, studying the market to determine why products were successful or unsuccessful, talking to potential OEM partners and understanding their needs and, finally, demonstrating vision and leadership by specifying the product design.

"So Harel [Kodesh] and I basically decided to just push the plunger and blow up WinPad and Pulsar and then get serious about what we wanted to do," Silverberg said.

From WinPad, they took the notion of the Windows companion device. "As obvious as it seems today, it was a new idea then, and nobody else was doing it," Silverberg recalled. The $500 price point was also critical, he explained. Unit sales would drop for every dollar above that point and would increase for every dollar below that point.

Selecting OEM partners was another critical decision. They sought first-tier manufacturers who would commit exclusively to the Windows CE device rather than divide their resources by "throwing three different hand-held designs against the wall to see which one would stick." Silverberg said the new team also listened carefully to the OEM partners. For example, he pointed out that Hewlett Packard persuaded Microsoft to include a keyboard in the new companion devices.

The new device had the code name of Pegasus. Initially the group planned to continue to use the object-oriented OS, anointed by most of the upper management at Microsoft as the OS of the future. But with deadlines looming, the object-oriented OS team was not responding quickly to the team's requests for new design features and bug fixes. Another skunk-works project was launched.

Frank Fite's team, which had written the At Work OS for WinPad, and experienced Microsoft architect Thomas Fenwick started secretly writing a brand new OS from scratch.

"Thomas was getting very, very frustrated with the limitations and our inability to converge on a real product," Silverberg said. "So he started to write his own in the back room. It was one of these skunk-works projects that had some political risks." Unlike the developers of the anointed OS, the Windows CE developers weren't Ph.D. researchers but incredibly talented programmers. Mike Ginsberg and Thomas Fenwick, Silverberg added, cranked out high quality code at a level he had rarely seen in his career. "These guys instinctively made the right design decisions—one after the other after the other after the other—coded the design up really fast, and just did it. They didn't have to argue about it for three weeks. At 11 o'clock in the morning, you'd give them an idea and by 12:30, they'd say okay, Brad, come on back, it's running. The progress that they were able to make created an incredible amount of motivation and excitement and tremendous team spirit."

The most important goal was to reduce memory use, so the developers studied the cost of interprocess calls (IPC). The group hid its efforts from the ITV team until the new kernel was ready to compete in performance tests. The kernel executable was named Nk.exe, with Nk standing for "new kernel."

Battles over the Win32 API approach and the new kernel battered the program managers. Bill Mitchell recalled the time when he finally revealed the Win32 approach at the BillG review and disappeared quickly afterward to avoid the wrath of one of the vice presidents. Mitchell thought that this time he had gone too far, and that his Microsoft career was over. "That was the night before the Microsoft Christmas party, and I remember hiding at the Christmas party because the vice president was across the room," Mitchell said.

The current Windows CE OS is actually the team's third attempt to create a 32-bit OS for embedded devices. The advanced object-based operating system was not synergistic enough with the Win32 model, and the Windows NT port proved to be too big. Their third approach preserved the Win32 API using new, optimized code.

With the core OS design and the OEMs in place and the first product's clamshell and keyboard design in place, the team's efforts shifted to the user interface. Tony Kitowicz was the shell lead. Over a weekend, Kitowicz wrote a prototype UI that looked like the Windows 95 desktop. The prototype was a catalyst, speeding acceptance of the new UI design throughout the Handheld PC team.

The marketing team's research backed up the decision to make the interface resemble Windows 95.

The team then focused its creative energy on getting the most from the smaller display area and on adapting to the 1.0 product's limitations of four color values: black, white, light gray, and dark gray. One of the innovations, dubbed the command bar, combined menus and the toolbar into a single control.

After all the work involved in developing a brand new operating system, Tony Kitowicz considers it a compliment when users mistakenly think it is a port of Windows 95. "When we shipped V1 [version 1], a lot of people thought we just used the Win95 sources, and we didn't," he said. "It was all from scratch, brand new."

PORTABLE, REAL-TIME

The Windows CE system software is written almost entirely in C and, as such, is portable to many 32-bit microprocessors. Microsoft ports the processor-specific parts of the code and creates a complete set of system libraries for each supported processor. The list of supported processors is updated frequently as new processors are added in response to customer requests.

At the time this book was written, the supported processors included the following: ARM720T; DEC SA1100; Hitachi SH-3 and SH-4; Intel i486, Intel Pentium, and AMD Elan SC400 (x86 SX); Motorola MPC821; NEC VR4101, VR4102, and VR4300 (MIPS); Philips PR31500 (MIPS); and Toshiba TMPR3910U (MIPS). For the current list of supported processors, refer to the Microsoft Windows CE web site at *http://www.microsoft.com/windowsce*.

OEMs using Windows CE on their own new platforms must implement device drivers and a small layer of functions known as the OEM Adaptation Layer (OAL). These small layers effectively port the kernel to their specific hardware. Many systems integrators already provide this OAL and driver code or can arrange to develop it.

The OAL port includes mapping all the possible hardware interrupts on the device (IRQ lines) to interrupt service routines (ISRs), which are provided as part of the OAL. The interrupt-handling model is straightforward. When the interrupt occurs, it is routed to the appropriate ISR. The ISR returns a value indicating an event to be set by the kernel. The kernel sets the event so that the interrupt handler, which is the code in the interrupt service thread (IST) waiting for that event, can run.

The operating system is characterized as real-time because the delay between the hardware interrupt and the start of the ISR and the delay between the ISR and the start of the IST are all guaranteed to be bounded values. The OEMs and system integrators providing the ISR and IST as part of the port have complete control over the interrupt handling code and can ensure that it will run within the required bounded times.

MODULAR

Windows CE was designed to be a modular operating system. The system designer can select only the modules that are needed for a given platform, minimizing memory use. For embedded systems in which the complete operating system is in ROM, keeping the OS as small as possible can help to reduce the required memory size and manufacturing costs.

Although external support for a modular OS was planned for the first release, life at Microsoft means shipping products and establishing a presence in the market, and features are often postponed until a subsequent release to avoid jeopardizing ship dates. To ship the first Windows CE–based product on time, certain features had to be dropped, and complete external support for a modular OS was one of them.

Although it provided no external support for "componentization" (which is what the process of creating the modular OS was called in-house), the 1.0 code base established the infrastructure that would be needed in future releases.

As soon as H/PC 1.0 was out the door, the OS group immediately started to work on new OS features to support the next set of products, such as the Palm-size PC, the Auto PC, and several others (not yet announced at the time this book went to print). The design of the modular OS was driven by the very real needs of these internal product teams.

According to Sharad Mathur, the OS team development lead, the goal was to create "one set of bits that we would call the shipping OS." Embedded systems developers building an OS from the common bits should not have to absorb costs, in terms of memory and performance, that they would not incur with a custom-built OS.

The solution was to provide a complete set of system libraries and tools that could be used to build the ROMable executables. The final libraries that go in the executable are named modules. Some of the larger modules are built from many smaller intermediate libraries, called components. The process of creating an OS starts with specifying its list of modules and components.

Sharad Mathur developed the system generation (Sysgen) tool, which preprocesses the system files before the user invokes the Make utility. The Sysgen tool hides all of the complexity from developers. Developers need to edit only one small file to select the modules and components for the system.

Microsoft began shipping to embedded systems designers the same tools that were used in house. The first kits enabled the system to be built from the command line by using the tool Build.exe, which was used internally by the Windows NT development team and later offered in the Microsoft Windows NT Device Driver Kit (DDK). Current development efforts are focused on integrating the functionality of the OAK's command-line–based tools with the Microsoft Visual C++ environment and providing the tools to a much broader community of users. This new easier-to-use toolkit is called the Embedded Toolkit (ETK).

The initial hope that componentization would allow any combination of modules and components became unworkable as the numbers of components—and thus their possible combinations—continued to grow.

Potentially, the number of systems to be tested was equal to the number of platforms multiplied by the number of supported processors multiplied by the number of possible combinations of the modules and components. The Test team quickly pointed out that it would be unable to test every possible combination, and the group decided to focus on the most likely configurations to be used by embedded developers.

The team specified five common module and component configurations in the 2.0 release and seven in the 2.10 release. Embedded developers are not constrained from creating other systems, but Microsoft performs complete system testing on only the specified configurations, recommending that developers use these configurations or minor variations of them.

The library-based approach offered several unforeseen benefits, Mathur explained. Embedded developers could completely replace some libraries with their own. And new operating system features could be offered as modules and components, which gave developers the choice of adding them or not adding them. Because developers did not have to absorb additional features and their associated memory costs, the sizes of their systems did not grow automatically.

OPERATING SYSTEM

An operating system performs two main functions, according to the classic A.M. Lister text, *Fundamentals of Operating Systems*: it shares available physical resources among multiple users or multiple processes, and it provides a virtual machine that abstracts the hardware's capabilities. The OS exposes a common layer that offers access to memory, the file system, and other hardware resources so that application programs can be written to manipulate the virtual machine. The operating system thus serves as the application's intermediary to the hardware.

Windows CE has minimal hardware constraints, requiring only that the system use one of the supported 32-bit microprocessors and provide appropriate amounts of RAM and ROM for the selected system configuration. The amount of memory needed depends on the selected modules and components. A kernel-only 2.10 system requires about 300 KB, whereas a combination of all current modules and components requires slightly over 2 MB.

Many operating systems use a model for sharing the computer's resources that is defined in terms of processes. A process is an instance of a running application. Each process is divided into one or more threads of execution. Each thread is assigned a priority, which determines when it should be scheduled relative to other threads. This process/thread model is exposed by the Win32 API and is supported by all 32-bit Windows operating systems, including Windows CE.

Windows CE supports a maximum of 32 simultaneous processes but has no hard limit on the number of threads within those processes—the number of threads is subject to only the overall system resources of the device. Windows CE schedules threads in a round-robin based on the thread priority setting. Currently, eight discrete priorities exist. (Microsoft has announced support for more levels in future releases.)

Windows CE also supports Win32 memory-mapped files, in which multiple processes can share the same physical memory. This memory sharing results in very fast data transfers between cooperating processes.

Like the other Win32 operating systems, Windows CE implements a virtual memory system that provides a contiguous virtual address space of 2 GB, segmented so that each process can access its own 32 MB of virtual address space. The remaining memory is available for memory mapping. Developers obtain memory using the standard Win32 heap functions or C run-time library functions.

The demand paging system transfers applications into program memory in RAM as needed. The system does not perform swapping operations in the same manner as a desktop PC, where the state of a process is saved by writing it to the hard disk, because most Windows CE devices do not have this kind of backing store. When additional physical pages are needed, the Windows CE OS discards code and read-only memory because these pages can be reloaded from ROM as needed.

Windows CE systems place all persistent storage in system memory rather than on a drive. The file system, registry, and a structured storage system named the "Windows CE database" are built on a proprietary internal heap. The heap compresses all data and uses its own internal transactioning service to log all heap operations, ensuring data integrity in case of faults and power failure. To access the file system(s) or the registry, developers call the standard Win32 file system and registry API functions. To access the Windows CE database, developers call a new Windows CE–specific API set. Developers can add their own extensible file systems.

To handle interactive user input, Windows operating systems use a message-passing paradigm in which a small data structure (the Windows message) passes information between the system and the applications. Windows operating systems can associate threads with a message queue and with a window. The window is present as a logical window, even in embedded systems that do not have a physical display. Componentizing this part of the Windows CE code turned out to be one of the trickier parts of creating a modular system, because the code had to allow some internal calls to fail, recognize that the system did not require a window, and continue processing as if the call had succeeded.

Finally, the Windows CE operating system includes a number of features that enable the OS and applications to be localized, or modified, so that the product is appropriate for users in different countries. Messages and commands translated to other languages might employ different alphabets and require different character sets and fonts. Like Windows NT, Windows CE includes national language support (NLS), which addresses character order, sort order, date format, and currency format. Windows CE stores all strings in Unicode.

PROGRAMMING INTERFACES

The Win32 API set includes some redundancy of functions in the sense that multiple functions can accomplish the same goal. A small amount of redundant operating system code does not usually concern developers of desktop PC software, but small code size is crucial for embedded developers. The first release of Windows CE offered a carefully selected subset of the Win32 APIs.

The goal of the design process that started on Bill Mitchell's deck was to provide the most functionality with the least memory cost. Mike Ginsberg, who worked on the kernel, recalled, "We started at zero and said, 'What do we need' as opposed to 'What do we leave out.' " The first platform to use the Windows CE OS, the H/PC, would include versions of Microsoft Word,

Microsoft Excel, and Microsoft Internet Explorer. The set of API functions that could support these three development teams, the developers thought, would be enough for anybody.

When a developer asked for a Windows CE implementation of a particular Win32 API function, she was often advised to use alternative calls or sequences of API calls. Only when several developers requested an API was the API added. "We just added things as people screamed for them," Ginsberg said.

After the second release of Windows CE offered tools for building a modular OS, some of the constraints on developers could be relaxed slightly. As mentioned earlier in the chapter, embedded systems developers could select which libraries they wanted rather than simply accept the set chosen for the H/PC. The number of Win32 API functions available in Windows CE increased from about 500 to about 1500.

The initial platforms based on Windows CE—the Handheld PC and Palm-size PC—were intended to be mobile companion devices, so all communication services became very important. In addition to the API functions that manage core operating system functionality, such as processes and threads, memory, and persistent storage, many of the Win32 API sets implemented for Windows CE manage communications.

The key communication interface is Windows Sockets, or Winsock, which uses TCP/IP to communicate over a serial connection, Ethernet, or infrared port. Windows CE also supports several other communication-related Win32 API sets: the Serial API, the Telephony API (TAPI), Remote Access Services (RAS), the WinINet API, which provides FTP and HTTP services, and the Windows networking API, which enumerates network resources and manages connections.

In addition to Win32, Windows CE supports several popular Microsoft programming interfaces: COM, ActiveX, MFC, and ATL.

Microsoft's Component Object Model, or COM, offers a standard for creating robust components that can be reused and assembled into larger systems. COM defines binary objects that can be queried at run time. Each COM object exposes *interfaces*, or collections of logically related methods. The base interface *IUnknown* allows COM objects to query a particular object about its supported interfaces. The COM model is language-independent, allowing components to be updated independently without requiring any changes to its callers.

An ActiveX control is a specific type of COM object. It represents the latest in a line of specifications for extensible controls, a line that started with Visual Basic Extensions (VBX) and was followed by OLE controls (OCX). An ActiveX control usually presents a user interface and exposes properties, methods, and events. The control interacts with a *control container*, such as Visual Basic, through a specified set of COM interfaces. By exposing its properties, methods, and events, the ActiveX control can be driven by scripts.

The Microsoft Foundation Classes (MFC) is a class library for developing Windows applications in C++. It exposes much of the same functionality as the Win32 API set but within a complete object-oriented application framework. The Active Template Library (ATL) is a C++ template library specially designed to create ActiveX controls and other COM components. By using template classes, ATL produces more efficient software than MFC, which uses only inheritance.

In retrospect, the decision to support the existing Win32 programming interface turned out to be critical to winning "the platform game," as Mike Montague called it, and contributed to the rapid adoption of the Windows CE platform. With support for Win32 and COM, virtually any existing Win32 application can be ported to the Windows CE devices. In addition, other Microsoft programming interfaces can be quickly ported to Windows CE. As an example, a Microsoft team in Australia recently announced the port of the ActiveX Database Object (ADO) interface.

Microsoft has also announced that it will work on two other important programming interfaces for future Windows CE releases: Remote Procedure Call (RPC) and COM+.

TOOLS

Microsoft's flagship development tools allow source code editing, compiling, linking, and debugging from within an integrated development environment (IDE) on the desktop PC. Microsoft offers development tools for three languages: Microsoft Visual C++, Microsoft Visual Basic, and Microsoft Visual J++. For each IDE of these languages, the Windows CE team created add-on products that feature emulation environments on the desktop PC, the ability to download the program image, and the ability to debug the application remotely from the desktop PC while it is running on the connected target device. For Visual C++, the products also offer cross-compilers for the supported microprocessors.

Microsoft has traditionally provided three distinct development kits—the software development kit (SDK), the device driver kit (DDK), and the OEM adaptation kit (OAK)—for slightly different developer audiences. Each kit contains libraries, header files, sample program source code, and documentation. The SDK is produced for application developers who usually write in high-level languages. The DDK is produced for independent hardware vendors (IHVs) who write in high-level languages and assembly languages. The OAK is produced for OEMs who use both high-level and assembly languages to write code that ports the operating system to specific hardware.

These kits ship independently of any commercial tool products so that tools vendors can provide the libraries, header files, documentation, and samples within their software development environments.

As the product expanded to multiple platforms and as the componentization tools became available, the Windows CE tools group combined all three kits into one single kit for the embedded development community: the embedded toolkit, or ETK. Like the other development kits, the ETK is offered as a stand-alone kit to outside tools vendors. The tools team is currently integrating the embedded toolkit into the Visual Studio development environment to create a new development product, the Windows CE Embedded Toolkit for Visual C++.

RAPID DEVELOPMENT

During one of my first undergraduate courses, a top researcher in the computer science department visited. He spoke as one who was imparting secret wisdom. "Write this on your yogurt bowl and contemplate it," he said, drawing on the whiteboard a series of rectangular boxes that appeared to be floating, one above the other.

Each box, he explained, represented a model of reality, a distinct logical layer independent of all the other models. In between the boxes, he drew small, double-headed arrows that pointed to the boxes on either side of them. These arrows represented the interfaces between the logical layers. The arrows pointing off the top layer of boxes represented the human/computer interface. The lowest level of boxes represented the smallest known units of the physical universe: subatomic particles. Our domain as computer scientists, he said, was everything in between.

In a layered system model, you need to focus on only the immediate layer and its interfaces to adjacent layers. This allows a "divide and conquer" strategy: you can break up a large problem and allocate your resources to much smaller problems. The alternative to a layered system diagram is a monolithic model, where the system (and the developer working on the system) must understand everything about everything all at once, without the advantage of being able to break larger problems into smaller ones. The layered model is more manageable.

Developers draw block diagrams, similar to the one the researcher drew, with various levels of detail, all the time. In a very simple diagram, the bottom layer might be named "hardware," the center layer might be named "operating system," and the top layer might be named "applications." You can explode any block in the diagram so that you can zoom in to view another, more detailed block diagram. You can subdivide the hardware block to identify different logical levels of hardware: semiconductors, integrated circuits, microprocessors, circuit cards, and PCs.

By filling the system layer between the PC hardware layer and the application software layer, the Windows platform has been very successful at allowing innovation to continue independently in the adjacent layers. "Windows creates independence between the hardware changes and the software changes," Bill Gates said, "so you have total choice on the hardware side and total choice on the software side."

Harel Kodesh explained that the system layer filled by Windows CE is critical to the development of the new class of devices known as "information appliances" because Windows CE allows greater adaptability. A few years ago, he noted, our hardware rendered spreadsheets and documents, but today most information is rendered through HTML, and tomorrow will likely bring XML and other related standards. The system software is the buffer between innovation on information and innovation on the appliances. The system software allows users to adapt to changing data while preserving their investment in hardware.

The benefits of layering extend to other embedded platforms as well. Much of the past work involving embedded systems was related to the operating system. But by licensing Windows CE, embedded developers can acquire a robust, real-time operating system and concentrate their efforts in other areas. Many third parties offer assistance in porting Windows CE and writing device drivers, making acquisition of the entire operating systems layer possible with only a minimal commitment of internal software developer resources.

The widespread availability of Win32 software, tools, development experience, and training means that the entire embedded product development cycle can be reduced, compressing the amount of time between the initial product conception and the moment the end-product arrives in your customers' hands.

EMBEDDED AND DEDICATED SYSTEMS

An embedded system is usually a small computer system dedicated to a particular task as part of a larger system. It is not meant to be a stand-alone, general-purpose computer, and its functionality is related to other parts of the system. Embedded systems are available in a broad array of forms, with computing capacity ranging from 4-bit microcontrollers to 64-bit microprocessors. Storage space is typically not on a fixed disk but in RAM, and the system itself resides in nonvolatile ROM or flash memory. Embedded system software is not as accessible to the end user as desktop PC software and is typically updated less frequently.

The architectural and physical characteristics of embedded systems (as opposed to traditional general-purpose computers) often lead to the integration of operating system and application functionality. The end user of an embedded system might view the entire system through the interface of a single dedicated application.

Windows CE is positioned for embedded systems that use supported 32-bit processors and that use half a megabyte or more of RAM and ROM. Some of the first embedded markets to adopt Windows CE include the manufacturing and retail sectors. In applications such as factory floor automation subsystems, sensors transmit information from the factory floor back to the human/machine interface. Using multimedia kiosks, customers can order items using a Windows CE–driven system that communicates with a larger back-end system.

In embedded systems, and with Windows CE, the line between applications and the OS is often blurred. Some vendors package customized applications on commercial Windows CE platforms, such as the H/PC, where the end user is expected to interact exclusively with one application. Such a system is sometimes called a vertical market system or a dedicated system.

Vendors can also choose to provide their own shells that use the provided Windows CE shell services. A shell is the set of user-interface components and underlying support routines that translate user input into useful operating system actions. For such systems, the latest version of the Windows CE Embedded Toolkit for Visual C++ includes instructions on how to create a customized shell. The toolkit provides all the API support needed to establish a particular application as the front end for a dedicated system.

DEVELOPMENT PROJECTS AT MICROSOFT

The frontier hypothesis of the American historian Frederick Jackson Turner is a useful framework for considering a development project at Microsoft. Turner suggested that the long history of available land influenced the country's character and sense of identity, and his successors popularized the notion of successive waves of settlement in the American West: the first few early explorers were followed by outlaws and missionaries, entrepreneurs, farmers, and merchants, who gradually and in stages built an economically diverse society.

Although many historians dismiss Turner today, there are parallels between the waves of frontier settlers and the stages of a software project. The early explorers of a software project start with a blank map of the market, sketch in particular products and price points, and then map a proposed product plan and schedule. After a proposal gets the go-ahead, the team is built up, starting with those first few pioneers and ultimately including a wide assortment of disciplines.

The marketing team tracks the needs of the target audience as identified in the business plan. Program managers serve as an interface between the marketing team and the development team. Cathy Linn, lead program manager for the H/PC 1.0 product, said, "The marketing guys cannot talk to the development guys and have any sort of meaningful conversation. That just doesn't work. So you have to be able to understand what marketing says is needed, listen to what development says is possible, and come out with something that works." The program managers write detailed specifications for the product that serve as a blueprint for the developers and testers.

Kimberly Gregory, lead program manager for the OS, pointed out that her team balances requirements against existing resources to create a product specification and schedule. "We track the hell out of the project schedule," she said. "As the product development cycle passes through the milestones we've defined, we reassess how we're doing and make process improvements to do better next time." This last point, she emphasized, is one of the key strengths of Microsoft. "You don't wind up with projects that miss their deadlines by a year with no one able to figure out why. It doesn't mean we make our schedules every time, but we are able to recognize quickly when we're not going to make them and take appropriate measures."

As the project team grows, a separate Build team takes on the process of creating the daily versions of the software that are submitted for testing. The Test or QA team (which is composed of fully qualified software developers) creates suites of automated tests and plans manual tests to validate the software. The Test team monitors the bug database, keeping detailed metrics to determine when the software is fit to ship.

Usability testers design, conduct, and report the results of usability tests. These tests examine how users react to early prototypes of the product, especially the product's user interface. Cathy Linn recalled that the usability expert Sarah Zuberec encouraged the development team to attend the tests. "I found the tests very painful to watch," Linn said. "You just want to give them hints—'No! Just look there! Just push that button!' "

In the case of the H/PC project, the team also sought out expertise in industrial design. Steve Isaac, the initial UI lead on Pulsar, recalled that the idea of hiring an industrial designer was considered pretty radical at the time for a software company, but it turned out to be very important. The industrial designer, Will Vong, created foam mock-ups that showed the form factor of the devices and inspired the development team. Isaac explained, "Building them so that they were cool-looking made all the difference. The engineers could really get excited about them." Kodesh always carried Vong's foam models around with him, according to Isaac.

The User Assistance group, responsible for producing the online and printed documentation, also acts as a general advocate for end users. Their ultimate goal is to eliminate the need for documentation entirely by ensuring that the product interface is almost intuitive.

The interviews that follow in the remainder of this book include representatives from most of these disciplines. The interviews walk through the system architecture, focusing on the functionality available to embedded developers and exploring the tradeoffs involved in configuring different systems.

Although I wish that I could have included everyone, only a few of the people who played key roles in developing Windows CE and the Handheld PC, Palm-size PC, and Auto PC services and applications are represented in this book. The interviews that follow are predominantly from the developers of the core OS and from program managers in the other areas.

2
Overview of Windows CE

*T*his chapter describes Microsoft's strategy in the embedded systems market, the history of the Microsoft Windows–based embedded systems that preceded Windows CE, and the key pieces of the Windows CE system architecture. It also discusses the development tools that allow embedded systems engineers to build custom configurations of Windows CE from the complete set of modules and components.

This chapter features several top managers in the Windows CE group. Harel Kodesh is the general manager of Windows CE development. Bill Mitchell and Ted Kummert are the directors for Windows CE–based mobile products and multimedia products, respectively. Frank Fite is the director of the Windows CE Product Unit and Sharad Mathur is the development manager for the Windows CE Core OS team.

Kodesh discusses a specific class of embedded devices—named information appliances—which offer users the ability to render information. These devices are generally not designed to be stand-alone computers but are meant as mobile companion devices that supplement the desktop and synchronize information with the desktop PC.

In addition to making the OS available to embedded systems developers, Microsoft is focusing on information appliances in selected markets. Bill Mitchell explains that some devices are designed to be used where we spend most of our time—at work, at home, and in our cars—whereas other mobile devices are designed for all the places in between.

In this chapter, Frank Fite walks you through the system architecture. Sharad Mathur describes how the system generation tools that create custom configurations of Windows CE were driven by Microsoft's own internal product development teams. With these tools, embedded designers are able to build the smallest possible systems that meet their requirements. And the approach also offered unexpected benefits, he says, by allowing Microsoft-supplied, user-interface components and other modules to be replaced with custom versions.

Microsoft is also working on several multimedia devices. Ted Kummert describes Microsoft's interest in devices that connect to the hub of the home—the television set. Microsoft and Sony Corporation have announced plans to collaborate on digital television (DTV) formats for production, transmission, and reception. Sony will license Windows CE for devices that represent a convergence of the PC with consumer audiovisual electronics. Tele-Communications Inc. (TCI) has also announced that it will use Windows CE in a minimum of 5 million digital set-top boxes. Kummert describes other potential devices and applications that can be based on an advanced multimedia configuration of Windows CE.

INFORMATION APPLIANCES

Harel Kodesh

People ask, "Why does my consumer appliance need an operating system?" when the appliance is something like a toaster or a microwave. The answer is, it doesn't. A toaster doesn't need an operating system; it does only one thing. Or a microwave oven, you can just hardwire its functions. Toasters have been making toast the same way for 100 years; microwave ovens cook the same things the same way—that doesn't change.

But when you talk about *information appliances*, which is what we're building, the type of information and the way you render that information changes all the time. When you look at how information was rendered only three years ago, you see spreadsheets and documents and rich text formats. Now information is rendered through HTML. Tomorrow, information will be rendered in a mutation of HTML and, when you look back, you'll think that what we're doing today looks ancient.

So to build information appliances, we need to break this mold of a rigid consumer appliance and have a chameleon appliance that adapts to current information data types.

The operating system for an information appliance is the buffer between the rate of innovation on information and the rate of innovation on the appliance—which is not the same rate. Appliances change every five years, whereas the information probably changes every six months. The operating system allows us to add new functionality over time until a specific appliance is retired.

Harel Kodesh

In 1990 or 1991, Bill [Gates], Nathan Myhrvold, and others started thinking about intelligent devices that are not PCs, and it became pretty obvious that in terms of technology, one size *doesn't* fit all. We needed to cover different levels of functionality and different levels of resource economy—the processor, RAM, ROM—which are the resources that go into the machine.

We played with some strategies because Microsoft didn't really have a whole lot of experience with killing the sacred cow, the x86-only strategy. We tried an x86-only strategy in the past on WinPad, and that didn't go very well. Telling OEMs that we can't offer other processors is like telling them that we don't want to be in the embedded business. So we had to consciously decide to break away, and that put a mental, psychological, and technical burden on us because nobody was going to help us. So for the last few years, we've been developing everything from the applications to the tools to the system.

There were a couple of approaches, and unfortunately, we had to try all of them. We started with a pretty advanced object-based operating system, but when we started looking at what it took to build applications and system components, we realized it was an uphill battle. Our approach was not synergistic enough with the Win32 model, so we moved to Win32 and started porting components from Win32. We ended up with probably 80 to 90 percent of Windows, but it was big and didn't give us the flexibility we needed. Approach number three was to preserve the API model but not the code. We're using that approach today.

CREATING WINDOWS CE: THREE BETS

In terms of development methodology, we made three bets. Betting does not mean winning by sheer luck. It means making choices, sometimes without all the information. Think about a road to completion that has many forks and you have to decide which way to go. We made three bets, three key decisions.

First, we designed the system in such a way as to make it more componentized than what was warranted by the Handheld PC (H/PC). Fairly early in the process, we realized that the Handheld PC was going to be just the first product we would develop. Now, you cannot jump from one appliance to another before you finish because you'll never finish.

So we started modularizing because we knew that the components would have to be upgraded. For example, we knew that the graphical device interface (GDI) would have to be optimized for the available technology. Although at that time, in 1996, 2 bits per pixel was the most that you could put in a $500 device, we knew that color and reflective screens would come and that the module would have to be upgraded.

We created redundancy in the toolkit. In it, you have multiple modules and more than one way to do whatever it is you want to do. Once you've decided how you want to do it, you put one module in silicon. Although the toolkit is large, the system itself is extremely small.

Second, we never, ever wanted to be in a position where we depended on only one OEM for our technology, especially for new devices. So we decided to build a portable operating system, one that played the role of an OEM. Not compromising on a processor was a conscious decision, though while we were building the operating system we worked with the processor manufacturers to get things we needed, like the translation look-aside buffer (TLB) or memory management unit (MMU).

Third, we considered global truths about what a system needed to do, really thought about the end-user scenarios, and translated those into architecture. For instance, we said the operating system would run a limited number of applications, so we could limit ourselves to 32 processes—yeah, it's a limitation, and you know in the back of your mind that every limitation hurts, but it's not really a big limitation. We couldn't find a credible scenario that required more than 32 processes. And the truth is that because the operating system is multithreaded, the developer can just use threads instead of processes. There is no limit to the number of threads.

We agreed that the kernel can trash the application, but the application can't trash the kernel. Because the kernel can trash the application, the operating system is not super-secure; but then again, we wrote the kernel, so the burden was on us to make sure that it worked. Anyway, that decision allowed us to relax some level of code redundancy.

We changed some of our assumptions after we started. We added more file system support because we realized that this is one of the areas where technology had an impact on the design. In 1995, Flash Cards were about all that was available. Now there are disk drives in the PCMCIA slot, so you need a complete FAT file system. For TV appliances, you need CDFS and DVDFS.

We also had to be very compelling for embedded systems developers, and we believed that tools got you the best of both worlds: the PC tools world, which is rich in debuggers and source-code editors and compilers; and the embedded-systems design world, which is rich with cross-debuggers, ICEs, simulators, and design tools.

You can very easily write for our system; the market for our operating system is fairly big. Somebody who writes for it doesn't have to worry about Microsoft going under or abandoning Windows or its OS strategy.

Work, Home, Car—and Everything in Between

Bill Mitchell

Where do you spend all of your time? You probably spend the majority of it in one of three places—work, home, or car. And you go back and forth, transitioning between these spaces with whatever you have on your body and whatever you carry with you.

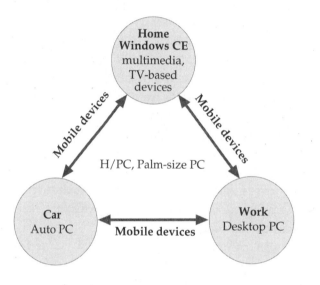

Some Windows CE devices are designed for the places where people spend most of their time, while other mobile Windows CE devices are designed for all the places in between. These devices enable users to access their personal information wherever they are.

Microsoft has the "Work" area pretty well covered with Microsoft Windows NT, Windows 95, Windows 98, and all of its desktop software. We pushed into this "Home" area a little bit with PCs and the Microsoft Home brand, but I think this market is really going to take off when we get Windows CE into the home in the form of entertainment devices (basically anything connected to your TV), because that's really the hub of the home. These entertainment devices would be WebTV and game players, and you'd have a host of other opportunities that Ted Kummert can tell you about.

The "Car" environment…think about it—you're trapped. I used to live down in the Bay Area. Seven miles to get to my job took an hour either way, and I just sat there. People read the paper, curled their hair, did all sorts of funny stuff.

Bill Mitchell

Think about what you could be doing during that time. By using some technology enablers like voice recognition and text-to-speech, you could receive your mail in the car, send mail in the car, and get news and information that's a little bit better than what you get on the radio, where the information is not very customized. If you could get the information that you really cared about, you would have a much better in-car experience.

When the AutoPC that runs Windows CE is a standard option in all cars, and when entertainment devices like game players, TVs, and set-top boxes that run Windows CE can run Microsoft software and communicate with the AutoPC in your car and with your desktop PC at work, it's going to be really cool. That represents a huge user base for Windows CE, creating new opportunities for developers, more than we even have at work right now.

Then think about the transition spaces. My group's charter is to pursue in-car opportunities and development of the devices that travel between places—the smart organizers, pagers, and phones—what I've been calling "digital personal effects." I hope we reach the point when we get computers into a bunch of these personal devices, like your watches, your eyeglasses, your wallet, and everything that already has body share.

That was our vision when we first started the group. We were working on organizers that you can carry with you, that you can put in your pocket or in your briefcase.

I credit Harel [Kodesh] with having incredible business savvy. He was cutting business plans for a Pulsar group from about the day he arrived at the company. Basically, Harel's goal was to build small personal appliances on a very small OS, an order of magnitude smaller than the desktop. He went around to anyone who would listen, trying to get a hearing for his biz plan on creating this type of device. And that's how he and I hooked up initially. When he got the mandate to do that, I was over here. I was about the third guy in the group.

We were fortunate enough to be a small group, not really considered strategic, and we escaped a lot of notice and attention. We were this tiny little group hanging off the side, working on Pulsar, which was a PDA. PDAs gradually drifted out of favor after the Newton failed. It was a rather spectacular flop, and everyone soured on it. And so we just kind of kept our heads down and continued working.

We actually had a false start in taking Windows NT and trying to hack it down. Initially we made huge amounts of progress, and it looked great, but in the back of our minds, we knew the system had to be an order of magnitude smaller. And that's when we decided to come up with a Win32 API subset that's complete enough for ISVs to write general purpose apps based on a larger OS.

We had this great offsite meeting on the back of my deck one day, and we pored through the entire Win32 API: "OK, let's look at all the line-drawing primitives—is there any single call that we can boil everything down to? Yeah, *Polyline*. We can make *Polyline* really fast and express everything else in terms of macros over *Polyline*, or just have ISVs rewrite their code using *Polyline*."

I'm exaggerating somewhat, but that was the basic approach we took. We started at zero and asked, "What API functions do we need?" as opposed to "What API functions do we leave out?" If we felt that only one person needed an API function, we tried to work around it by offering alternatives: If you use these three API functions together, you can accomplish what you're trying to do. If we felt that everyone was going to need that API function, we put it in. We did that across the board and then spent the next half year working toward that vision.

EMBEDDED SYSTEMS DEVICES

If you look at the whole expanding universe of devices, from white goods such as washing machines and dryers to home alarm systems, VCRs, and digital cameras, you notice that all of these devices are getting smarter. They also have to do more—perform more processing, communicate with other devices, and communicate with your PC. A lot of manufacturers are coming to Microsoft looking for an embedded solution.

These OEMs come to us and say, "The lack of standard software and third-party solutions is holding us back in this business. If we had Windows CE, we could focus on only our applications. We wouldn't need our huge software hordes working on the core OS; we could just use your OS." Independently, a lot of OEMs have arrived at that conclusion.

Today only a relatively tiny slice of this huge embedded space uses 32-bit processors with general-purpose register sets, memory management, and TLBs. Probably nine-tenths of the embedded space today is running 8-bit and 16-bit custom microcontrollers and microprocessors. But this huge embedded space will start expanding into the realm of 32-bit, general-purpose microprocessors. Pressure will come from the 32-bit RISC processors that keep going down in price and going up in performance. And as devices get smarter, they'll need more mips and high-horsepower, 32-bit microprocessors and microcontrollers.

Our long-term goal has always been to develop a general-purpose OS that could be used for all computing appliances. We never intended Handheld PCs to be the final product in this group; we envisioned a range of many other similar products. We identified the Palm-size PC and the Auto PC first, and we take on other devices opportunistically.

These devices get complete Microsoft support just as PCs do. We run developers' conferences, and we rally ISVs behind the platform. We run tool sets that are specific to those targets and that include emulators and special-purpose debuggers and sample code. We line up a large set of IHVs to provide peripherals. And finally, we align big-name OEMs behind them. We get all these guys lined up and producing the devices, and we come out and seed the whole software industry for those devices. In the case of the Handheld PC, for example, we kicked off the whole third-party shrinkwrap software market. We developed the Entertainment Pack, and we evangelized and helped Pocket Streets.

The Microsoft Windows CE Embedded Toolkit for Microsoft Visual C++ includes a kernel debugger and additional tools that are particular to embedded device development. You can get reference hardware to play with, and if needed we'll set you up with a system integrator. You'll have everything you need if you're building any of the millions of custom devices out there—you've got a huge opportunity.

We think the whole growing 32-bit embedded space is peppered with these kinds of opportunities. It's hard to predict which of these are going to be the ones that turn hundreds of millions of dollars for the company. So we're placing a lot of bets.

Ted Kummert

Windows CE will go in high-end multimedia entertainment consoles and in television set-top boxes. I think that over the next few years you'll see more connectivity into the set-top boxes and game consoles and less of a line dividing those types of products. You'll see more connectivity with digital cameras and other components in your home entertainment stack—for example, you might be able to hook up your set-top box to a DVD peripheral and play DVD videos. We will also build the operating system technology to allow set-top boxes to connect to different video sources, such as satellite and cable. And Windows CE is entering arcades, offering a game console

design and run time for public implementations such as arcade machines or multimedia kiosks.

There's the prospect of in-home networking, which enables the appliances in your home to talk to one another through RF technology, power line technology, or phone line technology. So if you have an intelligent phone and a WebTV set-top box, they could share the same PIM data—the same data associated with scheduling.

Ted Kummert

We're building the technology underlying all these products and making sure that we have the infrastructure supported in the operating system.

THE EMBEDDED SYSTEMS MARKET

Frank Fite

In early 1992, we started in earnest on Microsoft At Work, a general-purpose embedded operating system based on Win 3.1 for devices like fax machines, copiers, phones, and WinPad. WinPad was a handheld computer similar to the H/PC but without a keyboard. It was a cross between a Palm-size PC and the H/PC.

The first version shipped in some fax machines in Japan, and its spin-off products included the fax programs that are now in Windows 95 and Windows NT. But we never really got anywhere in terms of the business side.

We never really got a good version of an embedded 386, and this may sound like ancient history to a lot of people, but memory cost $20 a megabyte. We never could put a device down in the right price range.

In the summer of '94, we were looking at a Win32-based system for At Work 2.0. At the same time, Pulsar was working on a Win32 embedded OS specially designed for a pager, like the Palm-size PC but smaller. And at the end of '94, Brad Silverberg rectified the situation. He canceled the Microsoft At Work program, canceled the Pulsar program, and put all these people together to work on a new handheld device with an embedded operating system.

Frank Fite

So from day one of my arrival at Microsoft, my goal has always been to have a Windows-compatible embedded operating system. That's what I've been working on for six years, and with Windows CE, we finally have one. It took a while longer than I hoped, but one good thing about Microsoft is that we keep plugging away.

Right now the embedded market (the non-PC market) is pretty fragmented. Literally hundreds of operating systems are available. Most of that software is being developed internally by companies whose core competency probably isn't software. What OEMs need in the embedded marketplace is great development and debugging tools and a pool of software developers available to write specific applications for them.

We're going to provide a familiar underlying software platform, Windows CE, and deliver products that enable OEMs to use Windows CE. We're also going to build a team of companies that will revolve around Windows CE. We'll have semiconductor partners, and we'll have a set of partners called system integrators. System integrators are the people who provide reference platforms, do the device porting, write device drivers, and even handle support and training in some cases. These are the people who make the embedded market go. I hope to have thousands of OEMs building Windows CE devices over the next few years, providing business opportunities for system integrator companies to step in and fill. And of course the tens of thousands and someday hundreds of thousands of ISVs and IHVs, who are a very important part of the larger Windows CE team, will also participate.

What I have described sounds very fragmented, but it isn't. We actually have a very scalable system. A number of key features are unified to make Windows CE a single product:

- *Windows CE has a unified SDK.* Even though you might be building for a thermostat or an Auto PC, you use the same software development kit—you simply change your targets. All that expertise you developed with Microsoft Visual C++ for both Windows and Windows CE applies across the board.

- *Windows CE has a single development model.* Regardless of the API, a process is still a process, a thread is still a thread. You don't change the kernel in every system.

- *Windows CE has common communications protocols.* So any device that communicates will have these built-in protocols, and they'll be able to talk to each other.

The market for intelligent, networkable embedded devices will explode in the next couple of years, due to Moore's Law, the Internet, and the success of the PC. We've had inquiries about Windows CE in washing machines, golf carts, slot machines, refrigerators, point-of-sale terminals, automobiles, industrial controllers—you name it.

WINDOWS CE SYSTEM OVERVIEW

Windows CE is built on language-independent and Windows-compatible APIs and programming models. That's obviously why Microsoft is in this business—Windows CE is a small version of Windows, if you will. The big difference between our product and Windows 95, Windows 98, and Windows NT is that Windows CE is componentized and ROMable. We have built-in communications, meaning those components are available to talk to PCs, the Internet, and other Windows CE devices. And we offer easy adaptation to many kinds of devices.

Because the operating system is configurable, the only minimum hardware requirements are a processor, some memory, and a real-time clock. A system with only those features isn't a very interesting one, but it could be built and it could run Windows CE.

There's also no strict minimum on memory size. If you want to build an industrial controller that has the kernel, some communications, and a specialized app in it, you can probably create that device in half a megabyte of ROM and run it in half a megabyte of RAM. That number moves up or down, depending on what pieces are in the system.

I'm going to go on to talk about the Windows CE architecture and features.

THE KERNEL

Windows CE is a multithreaded Win32 system, with the same process and thread model as Windows NT and the same file formats as Windows NT. The kernel supports multitasking; it has preemptive, priority-based scheduling.

We use virtual memory for protection and sharing even though we don't have a backing store for most devices and we don't swap. We have demand paging, so if you want to run an application that's compressed on a ROM we can load it into RAM a page at a time—only what we need to run. We have shared memory and synchronization functions. Our ISR and thread latencies are plenty low for use in most real-time systems. And Windows CE is portable—almost all of the operating system is written in C and C++.

We execute in place in ROM; we can be paged into RAM. You can build a device that loads the OS off the network, or you can build a device that loads the OS off a disk, or you can build a device that puts the OS wherever you want it. It's all very flexible.

GWE

GWE stands for Graphics, Window Manager, Event Manager. It is the Windows CE implementation of the Windows GDI and User libraries. Our GDI supports a variety of displays from none up to 32-bit color SVGA. We also support bitmap printing so that a Windows CE device can generate a bitmap, wrap it with PCL, and send it to a printer. Windows CE doesn't do the sophisticated printing of Windows 95, Windows 98, and Windows NT, but it does enable printing from the OS. GWE also includes the event manager, so this is where we support the standard Windows message-based programming model.

FILESYS

We have file systems and a registry that uses the Win32 registry APIs. We also have an extra component that Windows doesn't have, a simple built-in property database, which is used for components such as address books in the Handheld PC.

We'll support multiple FAT volumes at the same time, so a Windows CE device that has more than one slot will be supported. We support installable CD-ROM file systems. You can support a disk drive in a Windows CE device; we have those APIs also.

THE OEM ADAPTATION LAYER (OAL)

This is the layer that the OEM implements to port the Windows CE OS to its device. We changed that name from Hardware Adaptation Layer (HAL) to OAL because Windows NT has a HAL and ours isn't the same.

The OAL is pretty easy to write. It includes small interrupt service routines and small interfaces for the hardware-specific functionality, such as the power management functions. We give you sample code for two different hardware platforms, the CE/PC and the reference development platform, and OEMs can adapt the code for use on their devices.

DEVICE DRIVERS

There are really two kinds of device drivers: built-in device drivers for the hardware; and installable device drivers for cards that you plug in, such as PCMCIA cards, mini cards, and Compact Flash.

COMMUNICATIONS STACKS AND COMMUNICATIONS APIS

The basic point of communication, of course, is to provide connectivity to Windows systems, the Internet, and other Windows CE devices.

TCP/IP is our main protocol stack; it's everybody's main protocol stack these days. We've improved our TCP/IP stack to take into account some of the specific issues with wireless communication.

We have a lot of the higher level APIs: sockets, serial, telephony, and WinINet, which provides HTTP and FTP. (We provide the smallest subsets of these APIs necessary for the Windows CE environment.) We allow installable telephony service providers so people can add more support.

We've added LAN support, so we have the NDIS driver, and we support a redirector so that a Windows CE device can sit on a network and find files and servers. We have our own remote access APIs that allow you to write a program on the PC that accesses the Windows CE device. We have both remote connectivity and remote networking. For corporate solutions, having this functionality is very important. A lot of corporate customers want to run apps that run on the server and talk to Windows CE devices, and we have the APIs available to do that. You can transfer files and synchronize databases, and you can execute and launch applications—whatever you want to do. We also have a dial-up connection, which allows people to dial in remotely. And our synchronization API is open, so people can plug in their own synchronization.

OTHER PROGRAMMING INTERFACES

The Microsoft ActiveX support today is for in-process COM functionality, and ActiveX will continually be enhanced. The goal is to enable Microsoft Internet Explorer on multimedia devices to access web sites and display that ActiveX content on the TV set. So you can bet that we're going to have a pretty robust ActiveX implementation.

We support Microsoft Visual Basic; we enable the scripting of forms and ActiveX controls. We have a componentized Java VM, just as we have a componentized operating system.

SHELLS AND INTERNET EXPLORER

Some people will have shells, some won't. A lot of vertical markets just want apps without an elaborate shell on their machines. We also have a minimum shell component that offers all the API functionality so that OEMs can write their own shells.

The H/PC shell, of course, matches the desktop look and feel. Right now we have a small version of Internet Explorer for Windows CE that's a good fit for a device like the H/PC. But as time goes on, Windows CE devices will be developed that let you spend hours and hours browsing the web, and we will have a larger, more capable Internet Explorer for those devices.

We know the market we're in. This market requires low memory usage, and that's what we are going to do. We're trying our best to keep our components small.

You know, the way our OS is componentized, vendors can compete in almost any area. You can replace our file systems with your own. You can write your own telephony service providers, your own synchronization, your own shell. We're enabling people to compete at a component level; we're enabling tools vendors to compete with our tools. We want to create a marketplace out there that's competitive even with things that we do.

Sharad Mathur

After we finished the Handheld PC, we shifted our focus back to the embedded market. Ted Kummert's group joined us and all these different product lines—the version 2.0 Handheld PC, the Palm-size PC, and the Auto PC—grew up, and at that point the project became a huge challenge for us. Suddenly we were in the position of having to support all of these different timelines, schedules, and requirements. And there was this big thrust to ship a general-purpose OS to the embedded world. A couple of challenges came out of these requirements.

Sharad Mathur

First, we tried to create an explicit OS group that had an independent identity. We treated each group within this OS group in exactly the same way we would treat external embedded customers. So as far as the OS group was concerned, we had an OS product, an OS product tree, and different groups of people working on all of it. That structure enabled us to ship code as a general-purpose OS. Some reorgs made this structure more obvious.

Second, we dealt with this big issue: how do we make the OS work for all these guys using the OS? We obviously didn't want to ship source code and have them compile it. We all had a strong feeling that the OS shouldn't have to be recompiled. We wanted to have only one build—one set of bits called the shipping OS—and all kinds of products built from that one set of shipping bits.

We wanted an across-the-board solution. We wanted customers who componentized the OS to end up with exactly the same system they would have had if someone had developed a custom OS for them. We didn't want them to pay extra overhead. We wanted to cut down the header files, cut down the import libraries, cut down the executables, and make everything consistent.

How Componentization Works

The natural design was to separate the compile and the link phases, so to speak: to compile all capabilities and features into component libraries and then allow a person to pick and choose component libraries to create the OS.

Every component has a stub version. When you leave out a library, you resolve references by linking to a stub version. So if one module has 10 component libraries, it also has stub libraries for all 10 different components.

We introduced the concept of a system generation (Sysgen) phase. You take a built version of the OS that has all libraries for all components, the master header files, module definition files, and a configuration file that defines the components you want. The Sysgen phase performs three tasks:

◆ It links together the appropriate parts of the OS.

◆ It filters all the master header files to take out the parts of the header files that aren't exposed by the components you selected.

◆ It filters the .DEF files so that you export only the functions you want.

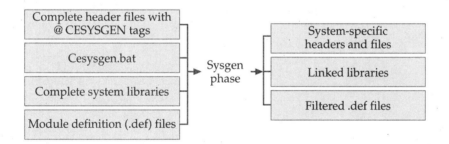

During system generation, the selected module and component libraries are linked while the header files and system-function export files are filtered to create custom versions for that system.

When you define components, you add a filter tag for each component in the master header file. These filter tags are in C++ comments so that they don't actually affect the C++ compiler. If you introduce a component named window manager (WINMGR) in the graphics subsystem GWES, you use the tag GWES_WINMGR. You can then tag different parts of the header file to filter definitions depending on whether the window manager is present.

The filter tools support conditionals. You can have "and" and "or" Boolean conditions so that you can say something like this: "If I have GWES_WINMGR *or* the base component GWES_WMBASE, then include the definition for a window; otherwise don't." Then the Sysgen tool is run and everything that isn't meant to be exposed is removed.

The .DEF files aren't as much of a nightmare as they might seem because modules don't directly export functions to the outside world. All exposed functions are thunked through a common library, Coredll.dll. Only one .DEF file, Coredll.def, controls everything exposed by the OS, and it has all the @CESYSGEN tags, just like the header files do. If you look at Coredll.def, you'll see all the OS APIs that can be exposed.

We ended up doing the entire procedure with makefiles, and while implementing componentization I learned more about makefiles than I had ever known before. When you look at this little Cesysgen makefile, you'll see that it's a pretty weird and complex beast.

The link phase started off being very simple—you just linked together the libraries you wanted. But there were stupid mechanical problems. If you specified a bunch of libraries on the link line, the functions got resolved in an undefined order. When someone used *CreateWindow*, the system was as likely to use *CreateWindow* from the stub library as it was to use *CreateWindow* from the actual window manager library.

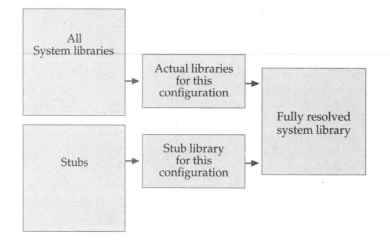

Because links are not resolved in a defined sequence, the Sysgen phase must link system libraries in two phases: first all selected modules and components, and then all stubs for modules and components that were not selected.

And so to resolve this problem, we developed a build process with two phases:

1.   You combine all the actual nonstub libraries into a single library.

2.   To link your final module (.EXE or .DLL), you resolve that single nonstub library with the stub library so that your module resolves calls to any components that weren't included in the configuration.

DEFINING WINDOWS CE COMPONENTS

Then we had to face the question, "What components do we create?" Our first approach was to get the easiest 90 percent of the components—the parts that aren't spaghetti—and build them as separate libraries. We took all the logical units that already had interfaces and made them into separate components. GDI is its own component, and User has window manager, clipboard support, caret support, accelerators, and dialog manager. It was very easy to make every individual control in the window manager (such as the edit control and the button control) its own component. Each was a relatively modular piece of code that we could build as a separate library.

But there were still a lot of dependencies. For example, you might want communications and not the window manager, but because the system used *PostMessage* and *PostMessage* used something else, you'd end up requiring the window manager.

During the first release, we were not actually able to create componentized configurations. But the first release helped us get the infrastructure in place so that we could componentize in 2.0.

One of the big problems with componentization is the difficulty with testing. I can create 10 different components that can be present or not present, but to QA the 2^{10} different configurations and make sure that all of them run is hard. So we had to scale back our concept to let OEMs choose some OS components from this column and other OS components from that column.

Our next step was to go to the market and say, "Okay, what configurations do people want?" We came up with a minimum kernel, a kernel with communication support for industrial controller applications, a minimum GDI configuration that has a graphical display but no window manager, a configuration with a window manager, and others. We continue to add configurations in each release.

Then we went back to User and recomponentized, working on the hard 10 percent to make these meaningful configurations work. We spent a lot of time on that in the 2.0 release. We rewrote the communications stack so that if you want to call a UI function such as *MessageBox*, the system first calls *LoadLibrary* and then calls *MessageBox* if it exists. If *MessageBox* doesn't exist, the system takes a default action and that allows us to use the communications stack without requiring the desired UI in the system.

We separated the UI into its own components and tried to isolate dependencies across modules. Within modules, we reorganized the code. User went through quite a significant reorganization so that now we offer messaging without a window manager. After this reorganization, you still have the concept of a window and of user input but no window manager infrastructure. As a result, you still get keyboard or touch panel input posted through to your *GetMessage* loop.

Our internal product departments, who were driven by their product requirements, also drove us toward these meaningful configurations. One group, for example, wanted to have DirectX and a minimal subsystem of User APIs but didn't want all of the GDI or all of the window manager.

We keep on finding new uses for componentization, but one of the other big uses is as a methodology that allows people to replace behavior. Because the OS gets linked in at Sysgen time, an OEM can have replacement components and thus change the way the nonclient area looks, change the way a particular message box comes up, or change the way the out-of-memory dialog looks. You can customize a lot by building your own versions of the components and plugging them into the component list at link time. You build your own library and just replace the existing one.

Whenever we add new features, we add them as components, which allows us to keep our minimal footprint down. If one product wants cascading menus, we don't have to add 10 KB of code to everyone's menu control. People can pick or choose whether they want the feature.

So what I just described comprises the four salient, high-level, important benefits of componentization:

◆   Scalability

◆   Allowing the OEMs to make trade-offs

◆   Allowing the OEMs to replace code

◆   Minimizing overhead as we add new features

RESOURCES

Topic	Resource
OEM opportunities for partnering with Microsoft	email: wceoem@microsoft.com
System integrator opportunities	email: wcesi@microsoft.com
Developing custom embedded devices	Microsoft Windows CE Embedded Development Toolkit for Visual C++ 5.0
Visual C++ programming	Microsoft Windows CE Toolkit for Visual C++ 5.0
Visual Basic programming	Microsoft Windows CE Toolkit for Visual Basic
Java programming	Microsoft Windows CE Toolkit for Microsoft Visual J++

The Kernel

*T*he kernel is the innermost core of the operating system, responsible for scheduling and synchronizing threads, processing exceptions and interrupts, loading applications, and managing virtual memory. The Microsoft Windows CE kernel supports execution in place (XIP) from ROM or demand paging into program memory in RAM. As explained in Chapter 1, the kernel is sometimes referred to as Nk.exe, which is the name of the file that contains its code.

The kernel was designed to be portable so that Microsoft could quickly port versions to different microprocessors. All of the supported microprocessors to date are 32-bit, little endian, and support a translation look-aside buffer (TLB), which is a fast cache that maps virtual addresses to physical addresses to improve memory access performance.

Windows CE supports the Win32 process and thread model using a round-robin, priority-based scheduler. Currently, eight discrete priorities exist, and Microsoft has announced support for more levels in future releases. Threads are defined as being in one of several states: running, suspended, sleeping, blocked, or terminated.

Within the Windows CE kernel, each priority level has its own circular run queue. The kernel's scheduler gives the CPU to the first thread in the highest-priority run queue, which in the simplest case runs until it yields. The kernel then moves that thread to the end of the queue and gives the CPU to the next thread. (The thread can also change priority or change from the running state to another state, which removes it from the run queue.)

By default, the Windows CE scheduler operates on a 25-millisecond quantum. Embedded developers can set this quantum to other values.

When multiple threads are allowed asynchronous access to the same resource, the threads can interfere with one another and cause incorrect results. The classic example involves two threads incrementing a value in memory. If both threads read from memory before either writes, the final result is incorrectly incremented by only one instead of two. To prevent errors, most operating systems provide ways for threads to request exclusive use of a resource until an operation is complete. A section of code that requires such exclusive use is known as a critical section. The threads use mutual exclusion to prevent one another from running while one is in a critical section.

The Win32 API provides a variety of objects for managing synchronization of threads. Windows CE supports wait functions that examine the state of critical section objects, mutex (mutual exclusion) objects, and event objects. The mutex and event objects can be assigned names so that they can be accessed easily by threads in different processes. Microsoft has announced that Windows CE will support another kind of synchronization object, semaphores, in a future release.

Unlike other Microsoft Windows operating systems, Windows CE has thread priorities that are fixed and do not change. Windows CE does not age priorities or mask interrupts based on these priority levels. Sometimes the kernel does temporarily modify thread priorities when the use of a resource by a low-priority thread delays the execution of a high-priority thread contending for the same resource. In this case, Windows CE lets the low-priority thread inherit the more critical thread's priority and run at the higher priority until the thread releases its use of the resource. This scenario is known as priority inversion.

Most operating systems distinguish between user-mode and kernel-mode processes. The mode indicates whether a process can access privileged microprocessor instructions and internal kernel functions, and it provides protection by ensuring that user-mode applications cannot corrupt the kernel.

In Microsoft Windows NT, device drivers are usually written as kernel-mode processes and can make privileged system calls that are not available to user-mode processes. In contrast, most of the device-driver work in Windows CE is performed by user-mode processes that call the common Win32 API functions. Windows CE uses a straightforward device-driver model in which one small part of the driver is linked with the kernel and the rest is implemented as a user-mode process.

This chapter discusses the kernel exclusively. The parts of the device driver that are linked with the kernel are examined in Chapter 6, "Porting to New Hardware." Because so many of the real-time features of the kernel are related to the implementation of the device drivers, the real-time characteristics are also discussed in Chapter 6.

The kernel design and development effort was a collaboration among many individuals. Michael Ginsberg, Thomas Fenwick, Gilad Odinak, and Mike Montague speak for all of the people whose brainstorming, experience, and hard work went into the kernel architecture.

Michael Ginsberg and Thomas Fenwick wrote the kernel code. Michael Ginsberg wrote the scheduler and, for Windows CE 2.0, modified the kernel to guarantee bounded latency times, enabling Windows CE to be used in real-time systems. Mike Montague was a development lead on Pulsar, a predecessor project to Windows CE, and on the Microsoft Remote Procedure Call (RPC) run-time project. Gilad Odinak worked on the original object-based OS for ITV and Pulsar, which used a similar design for the virtual page tables.

One of the important kernel design issues was the cost of interprocess communication (IPC). RPC, which Mike Montague discusses in some detail, is an IPC mechanism that Microsoft Windows NT uses internally for many of its services. Using RPC, a client calls a server using a straightforward programming model as if the client were calling a function provided in the server's library. With RPC, however, the server functions can reside not only in another process but also on another computer. The RPC tools create an extra layer of functions, the RPC stubs, whose role is to handle cross-process and network communication, copying all function arguments and referenced data between the client and server.

Gilad Odinak

Harel Kodesh knew me from the OLE days and asked me to join his operating system group for the new Pulsar product. Later there was a reorg, and the new world order was that Harel's group would create the Pulsar device, there would be an interactive TV group, and there would be a core technologies group handling the operating system. Harel asked me to work for that group. Shortly after that, yet another coup took place, and it was decided that all this work would be managed by Microsoft Research. So basically the Research group inherited me, and I was like a kind of a weirdo bird. They didn't know exactly what to make of me.

When all the dust had settled (this was October of '93), it became clear to me that no one was actually writing any code. So I decided to just go ahead and do the coding. In about two months, I had a core system that satisfied the original requirements: an embedded system, PDA-like, portable, using very little memory, consuming very little power, very object-oriented, and using COM interfaces and classes.

Gilad Odinak

I asked one of the hardware program managers from the Pulsar group to find a board for me, which I hacked so that we could download the code. This board was designed as an evaluation board for printers. It has a MIPS R3000, no coprocessor, a unidirectional parallel port, a few serial ports, a pretty slow speed, and proprietary ROMs. Basically, I built a bidirectional parallel printer port, and we changed the software in those EPROMS for bidirectional downloading/uploading. And this is how the PeRP started.

Two things happened after that. Technically, the ITV project started taking a very different route. There wasn't really an emphasis on being small. You needed a lot of memory, so the size of the kernel made no difference. Pulsar's goal was to be a platform. For a platform, you need documentation for developers and APIs, and to create that from scratch is really a big task.

Developers wanted the APIs to look like the Win32 APIs and didn't really care how they worked underneath. The ITV people wanted the inner workings to be like Windows NT, and they really didn't care what the APIs looked like. [laughing] ITV and Pulsar weren't a good match anymore.

Then the Pulsar group and the WinPad group were reorg'ed under Brad Silverberg. There was mistrust: "How are we going to depend on those external groups in Research? Those people in Research don't know exactly what they are doing," etc. So the Pulsar group went ahead and got themselves their own operating system group, and in secrecy they wrote a new kernel. For a while they did this camouflage work where they had two setups: they would work with our kernel on one side and with this new kernel on the other side and try to hide it from everybody.

It's interesting to know that their new OS group, to some extent, used some of the same ideas.

We didn't use page tables at all. We used what we called a virtual TLB, which was a cache of mappings between virtual and physical addresses for all processes. Nk.exe used a different structure but the same idea of using a software handler but not page tables for the MIPS. When they had to port their code back to the PC, they basically went through the same path. They ended up reinventing the same strategy that we had—to not use page tables on an x86 even though page tables are provided by the hardware.

The solution to the dilemma is to build page tables as needed and recycle them. So when you take your fault, you look in our virtual TLB (which is all software based), figure out the mapping between the virtual addresses and the physical addresses, create a page table with that entry, hook the page table up, and take the fault again. Now the x86 hardware performs the mapping correctly.

You have a small, fixed pool of those pages—say, 30 to 40 pages—and you don't let the number grow. Soon you use all of them. The next time you need a page, you take one that has already been used, disconnect it from the pointers that point to it, and use the page in another place. This approach works because on the next TLB fault, the page table will not be there, the x86 will give you a real fault, and again you will recycle one of the other pages.

By throwing the page tables out, we saved on average about one-half to one whole megabyte, which was a large portion, maybe 50 percent of the memory.

Mike Montague

I was hired on this cool project, Pulsar. I described Pulsar as every kid's dream: little, you put it in your pocket, you played games on it. It did everything. It was like the Dick Tracy two-way wrist radio. I remember we were looking at funky ideas for the UI, not in the traditional sense, but in the sense of the whole user experience: voice input, voice output. We had a character-based user interface for a while. Did a bunch of prototypes of it and some usability tests—we demo'ed it to Bill G.

Mike Montague

Parallel with this, a research effort for an object-based kernel was going on, and basically we were forced to use this object-based kernel. A bunch of us were from the production side of Microsoft, and we wanted to start cranking out products. I remember one guy, Wes Cherry—great guy, great programmer. Man, he just wanted to start cranking applications. He was ready to go. Even before the company had a system we could use, we started trying to build prototype software. And it was really hard because we didn't have anything to start with.

The problem was, we felt dual pressures. We had the pressure of shipping the product—at Microsoft you ship or die—and we had the pressure of "Let's do something new." And we couldn't add substantial value to the Win32 APIs. The APIs aren't perfect, but we couldn't do ten times better, and that's what we would have had to do. We were a new platform. It made sense to leverage existing stuff, take an incremental approach.

I don't want to sound like I'm against innovation, but you have to be smart about it. Windows CE is an innovative platform, and if you look under the hood, you'll see a whole lot of innovative stuff. But if Windows CE consumers have to learn a new API set, they're not going to pick it up. The first consumers of the platform are programmers. We've got to get programmers on board because that's how we get applications written. It's the platform game.

It was somewhere in this time frame that I really started pushing Win32: "We've *got* to do Win32." I distinctly remember being the sole drummer beating the Win32 drum. But the response was that new is better, that we would add value by defining new APIs, by defining new network protocols, by defining new user interfaces. They said to me, "We're the future. We have to be different." Being different in and of itself adds no value.

And it was this incredible struggle to get Research to deliver reliable drops and give us the schedule to be a real product team, because they tried to combine doing research with doing a production kernel, and the objectives conflicted. We had different sets of goals. It was really unfortunate because some really nice guys and some really smart guys were on that team. We struggled and struggled and got to the point where we had a little Windows-based system going. We were just beginning to be able to write Win32 apps.

Then Harel told me that Thomas Fenwick was coming on board. Thomas and my older brother, Jim, had worked together for six years, so I knew of Thomas, knew what he was capable of doing. Thomas had some amazing ideas for how to write a kernel.

I'd spent four years working on RPC, which is all about going process to process, so I had spent a lot of time thinking about RPC as a platform. I liked the RPC style of programming. It made writing servers really easy: you could just write the API on the server side as if the client had called the API directly. It helped the development team in terms of time to market. Less code written means fewer bugs. That style of programming was nice.

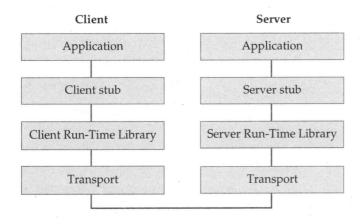

In the RPC programming model, computer-generated subroutines known as RPC stubs transfer function parameters and return values between processes. The data transfer is known as marshalling.

And I'd spent a lot of time thinking about where the costs are in RPC: the total amount of time it takes to make a procedure call, from the time you make the call, through the stubs, all the way until the call hits on the other side. We were tackling some interesting challenges in RPC, like trying to make stub interpreters to get the stub sizes down. I spent time profiling the code. I distinctly remember doing exact instruction counts of the cost of making a remote procedure call, and I'd seen that stubs are expensive. Generating efficient RPC stub code isn't easy. It usually makes for big code. You know, copying data is expensive. If you're not sharing address spaces, you have to allocate memory, and that's expensive. In thinking through the cost of RPCs, we decided that we wanted to drive the cost down as low as possible.

Thomas had some ideas about mapping address spaces together—the idea of just taking the thread, keeping the same stack, and bringing the thread into the other address space so that you could make procedure calls directly with basically no stub at all. The cost was driven way down in terms of taking the thread into the server process, in terms of memory mapping so that you minimize copying arguments. You just had to twiddle a few things on the stack, and for most cases that sufficed. By using the same stack in the server address space, you avoided having to copy arguments.

If you look at APIs, my guess is, about half the arguments are scalars and about half are pointers. You need to map only the pointers. By mapping only the pointer into the appropriate address space, you don't have to copy any memory. You can map the pointers directly on the stack. A very quick operation. It's simple. It's straightforward.

So the object-based kernel was running behind schedule and, in a great Microsoft tradition, two guys—Thomas Fenwick and Michael Ginsberg— went off and wrote their own kernel that was tailored to the needs of the small devices we were trying to build. Basically, they had a couple of months to come up with the proof of concept. We'd been struggling with the other kernel for at least a year before that, but those two guys produced the equivalent kernel in two months. It was up and running in such a way that the Win32 stuff could be ported over, and right off the bat the thing was three times as fast. That said a lot for the elegance of the design. So it was really a slick little kernel. I mean, some very clever ideas went on there. It all just came together, and we were back on schedule.

Thomas Fenwick

These were the design goals for the kernel:

◆ *Keep it small, in terms of both ROM usage and RAM usage.* We knew the kernel would be running on devices with limited storage capabilities.

◆ *Use a standard API rather than create a new API.* We kicked around thoughts of creating a new one, but the problems were tools and development and trying to evangelize a brand new API into the world.

◆ *Leverage existing tools.* So, for example, we used the exact same PE [executable and library file] format as Windows NT.

◆ *Run XIP right from the ROM, which none of the other Microsoft systems could do.*

◆ *Make it portable.* We knew from the beginning that we would have to run on at least two different processor families because the first two OEMs were using very different processors: SHx and MIPS.

◆ *Enable protection.* A bug in an app should not crash the system.

◆ *Keep the Windows NT client/server model and standalone subsystems independent of the kernel.*

Thomas Fenwick

We also had several *non*-goals for the system that affected our design. We were concerned about protection but not about security. We weren't trying to design an airtight system like Windows NT, a system that no application can damage maliciously. On a time-sharing computer, which has multiple users on the same computer, a hostile user can do damage to other users. But we knew that our target market was a single-use device owned by a single person. A single device is not open to the same kind of hostile environment. A vendor who downloads a hostile application in an H/PC may damage the data in the H/PC, but that vendor isn't going to get very far.

We never viewed Windows CE as a *big* operating system. We knew we weren't building a replacement for the desktop operating system. So we made very specific compromises, targeting smaller devices with less memory.

PROTECTION

I wanted to keep the Windows NT model, where we had the window management system, the graphics system, and file systems written as standalone subsystems, independent of the kernel. And they actually are. Our file system runs as a user-mode process. Our window manager runs as a user-mode process. We load device drivers as user-mode processes, running nonprivileged. That way a bug inside the window manager, for example, may crash the window manager and do damage to it, but the crash is isolated. And, if nothing else, when you're debugging the system you have a much better idea of where to look.

That same model allows us to keep a device driver in a separate process from the file system. A buggy device driver might end up crashing that driver and you'll have to reboot, but it's very unlikely the device driver will damage the object store. That's something we were concerned about, because the device driver is not on disk anymore. It's just part of RAM in the system, so if somebody goes scribbling all over it, it's gone.

MINIMIZING ROM USAGE WITH PSLs

We wanted to cut down the resources required in terms of processor horsepower and memory usage but still retain the client/server model.

The traditional client/server model normally has two threads. The client thread issues an API call to the server, then blocks. The server thread wakes up and runs, finishes, then wakes up the client thread while the server thread goes back to sleep. Each thread has its own stack and more storage in the kernel to track its state. And we're talking about virtual memory stacks, which are page-granular, so even if the server needs only 50 bytes of stack to process the API call, it uses the whole page. The pages are either 1 KB or 4 KB, depending on the processor, which means we need a minimum of 1 KB to 4 KB of RAM per thread.

Most operating systems also maintain two stacks per thread: a user-mode stack and a kernel-mode stack. And so with that model and a standard client/server arrangement, you actually need four stacks to process an API. We couldn't afford the memory to do that.

So what we do is *borrow the thread*. We borrow the client thread, pull it out of the client process, put it in the server process, and run it in the server until it finishes.

We designed a scheme that we called PSLs—protected server libraries—that behave as a kind of a hybrid between a DLL and a standalone process. PSLs are allowed to register what I call an "API set" with the kernel, which is a fixed set of entry points into that server. We register function signatures that tell the kernel the size of the arguments and whether they are pointers.

A client process makes a call to the PSL and ends up trapping in the kernel. The kernel cracks the address apart and decides which API in which server is being called. With that information, the kernel is able to adjust the argument list accordingly.

The kernel massages the state of the client thread a little bit and fixes up the argument list directly on the stack as it needs to. It maintains a linked list off the thread structure that records the return address and a few other things about the state of the thread at the time the call is made. The kernel then changes the return address to an address that will fault into the kernel so that the kernel can undo this process. So, when the API call to the server returns, it traps in the kernel again, the kernel pulls the first block off the linked list, restores the client thread state as it was before the call, and returns to the real return address.

We kept the basic client/server model, but the price of the interprocess call dropped enormously.

VIRTUAL MEMORY: THE SLOT MODEL

Very early on, we decided to limit the amount of virtual memory available with each process to 32 MB. This seemed to be enough, given that we were targeting smaller devices with 4 MB of ROM and 4 MB of RAM. Eight times the physical storage complement seemed to be a reasonable limit.

We took the lower 2 GB of the address space and sliced it up into 32-MB *slots*, reserving one slot for each process. Each of those slots is broken up into 512 64-KB blocks. The 64-KB blocks are broken up into pages that are either 1 KB or 4 KB, depending on the system.

The slot 0 virtual address space is special because it's always the currently running process. So the 32-MB slice of virtual memory for the running process is in two places: in its slot among the 32 available slots and in slot 0 for the active process.

The kernel, which is in slot 1, assigns the lowest available numbered slot to each new process. GWE (Graphics, Window Manager, Event Manager) is usually in slot 2. Filesys is usually in slot 3. So, if you've got the Shell in slot 4 and the Shell is running, the Shell's memory and data are in slot 4 *and* in slot 0.

The Shell calls a routine in GWE and passes a pointer that points to data in slot 0 because the Shell is the active process. The kernel will map the pointer up to slot 4 and then call GWE. Now slot 0 isn't the Shell anymore, it's GWE. GWE runs, completes, returns, and the pointers are swapped back. That's the reason the virtual memory structure is set up the way it is—it's simply a pointer swap for me.

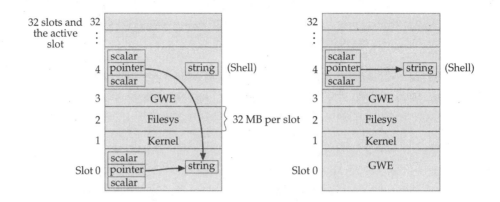

When the Shell calls GWE, the kernel modifies pointers on the stack to slot 0 to point into the Shell's slot (slot 4) and then makes GWE the active process in slot 0. Because the kernel manipulates the pointers, no data copies are required.

So when you make a PSL call, I walk across the argument list looking for arguments that are pointers. Any argument that is a pointer to an address in the first 32 MB gets moved up to the slot where the process actually lives. And then when you transition to leave the process, you can follow those pointers correctly because they're all pointing to addresses that don't change.

The end effect is that the kernel doesn't have to copy any data. If you call GWE to do something with a buffer, and GWE has to call the file system to fill that buffer, no data gets copied. The buffer is passed directly into the file system, and the file system fills it. You come back out and your data is sitting there.

HANDLE LOCKS AND ACCESS KEYS

I limited the number of processes to 32, primarily because 32 is the number of bits in a word. The virtual memory system and the handle management logic in the kernel use 32-bit bitmasks as access keys. Every 64-KB block has a lock on it, a bitmask that indicates who is allowed to access it. Every handle also has a similar lock. Every thread has a key that is a 32-bit bitmask. The simple test is a logical AND operation on the key and the lock. If you get a non-zero value, access is allowed.

As your thread hops from process to process making PSL calls, the keys on that thread gain access. Initially, your thread, just running by itself, has access to your process's address space and nothing else. After you call into GWE, that thread can now see all of GWE and all of the original process. If from within GWE that thread makes a file system call, the thread goes into the file system and picks up access to the file system. At that point, that thread can actually see all of the file system, all of GWE, and all of the client process.

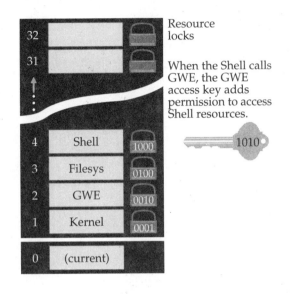

Resource locks

When the Shell calls GWE, the GWE access key adds permission to access Shell resources.

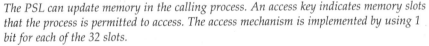

The PSL can update memory in the calling process. An access key indicates memory slots that the process is permitted to access. The access mechanism is implemented by using 1 bit for each of the 32 slots.

The system records the key before you go into each call. As the thread returns from calls, it loses permissions. The system restores the previous key as it comes out of each call.

An interesting side effect is that the kernel itself runs with that model. When you make certain calls in the kernel, the system just takes the thread into the kernel and allows it to be privileged for a short period of time while it's there. When you're in kernel mode, accesses to virtual memory are still limited by the same access key mechanism. So although the kernel can use back-door methods to get to physical addresses, it can't actually use a virtual address that the thread it's running with isn't supposed to access. If you called the kernel and told it to write to a buffer in another process, the kernel routine would fault. It doesn't have permission.

The kernel knows where the access keys are stored. It can edit a key if it wants to do that, but normally it doesn't. In a few special cases, we edit the key because we know we're about to go look at every process in the system, but those are special threads that live in the kernel and do housekeeping tasks.

The 32-MB size typically isn't a problem except in cases where we want to do mapped files on a CD-ROM. We actually have an escape hatch that allows us to have mapped files in a separate area. You can have over a gigabyte of mapped file data for the whole system.

PERFORMANCE GAINS USING THE PSL DESIGN

Our kernel enables critical sections to be very efficient. As you enter your PSL, which is your process, your critical sections are in your address space now, so they're a lot more efficient than named mutexes. If there's no contention, we don't have to enter the kernel.

A named mutex is nice and gets shared across a whole bunch of processes that don't know about one another, but you have to trap in the kernel. Because the mutex structure is contained entirely in the kernel so that multiple processes can share mutexes, taking ownership of and releasing a mutex requires two round-trips through the PSL dispatch in the kernel.

Critical sections are implemented using a user-space structure in which the take and release can be done without any kernel calls as long as there is no contention. So to implement a block of code that manipulates some shared data, a PSL uses an internal critical section. In such a case, one round-trip through the PSL dispatch in the kernel is needed to invoke an API in the PSL and, perhaps, no additional kernel calls would be needed if nothing was contending for the PSL's internal critical section. In the case of a more complex API involving multiple critical sections, you could end up saving quite a few kernel calls.

INTERRUPT HANDLING

We use a traditional microkernel model. It has very lightweight interrupt service routines that are responsible for doing extreme time-critical processing—dismissing the interrupt and scheduling a thread. One of the other systems we looked at had specialized APIs for interrupt threads and was hard to use. We were trying to avoid creating new object types different from Win32. We really wanted to build the system as Win32.

So the only real APIs I added to the system allowed the device driver to associate an event handle with an interrupt ID. When a driver wants to wait on its interrupt event, all it uses is *WaitForSingleObject* or *WaitForMultipleObjects*. These interrupts are all Win32 events. And if the event object is a kernel event, there's nothing special about the event.

STRUCTURED EXCEPTION HANDLING

The structured exception handling we use is pretty straightforward and very similar to Windows NT—we pretty much lifted it right out of the source base for Windows NT. The big modification was dealing with PSLs to allow the exception handling unwinders to unwind across process boundaries and undo all the appropriate things with access keys and slot 0.

I also provided an escape hatch. Any server that's registered as a PSL can also register an exception handler for itself. The purpose is to prevent a client process from calling the server, causing a fault, and leaving without that server having any knowledge of the fault, which leaves its critical sections dangling. So we let the server have a last shot at the fault before we go away. Typically, the server catches the fault at that point, cleans up its own state, and treats the fault as a failure return for the API call.

PORTABILITY

The bulk of the work in making the kernel portable was just writing it in C. There are only about three or four routines in which the assembly code actually calls into the kernel: the PSL dispatch, the interface into the scheduler to get the next thread to run, and the exception processing. As it turns out, most of the exception processing, although machine-specific, is still written in C.

So, when we port the kernel to a new CPU, we write the outer layer that wraps around and calls those three or four connection points. And we write all the hardware-specific code: how to service interrupts, how to save a thread's state (a thread's context), how to reload the thread, and how to handle the virtual memory code (how the memory management unit works).

From a virtual memory standpoint, the kernel uses nearly the same virtual memory structure across all CPUs we run on today. The kernel is designed as if it has a software-controlled TLB. Part of the reason for this is that the first two processors had the software-controlled TLB in the hardware. Typically, if a processor has real hardware page tables, you can simulate those page tables with a software TLB. We have a portability layer that adjusts all of the software TLB code into machine-specific stuff.

Michael and I sat down at the beginning and figured out the pieces we needed and divvied them up. I handled the virtual memory system and all the SEH (structured exception handling) stuff. And I also wrote all the assembly language bits. Michael did the loader and the scheduler.

Basically, in almost a month or less, we had a base OS with threads and processes and virtual memory, and it was running well enough to port a version of the graphics subsystem.

Michael Ginsberg

The scheduler is the guts that makes all the threads run. The basic premise was to do a very easy scheduler. We didn't want to have complex code because we had to get the code written very quickly. We also didn't want to have *researchy* code. We wanted code that we knew would do its job.

So we decided on a priority-based, round-robin scheduler with eight priorities. We use round-robin scheduling on each priority. The OEM can set the time slice—the default is 25 milliseconds. And we have unlimited numbers of threads per process and a fixed maximum of 32 processes at any point in time.

Michael Ginsberg

It's convenient to have the 32-process limit because a DWORD is 32 bits and you can represent each process by a bit in a DWORD. Comparing two DWORDs is very fast, whereas comparing multiple DWORDs is a little more complicated.

We schedule based on threads, not on processes. So if you have 10 threads in a single process and one thread in another, each thread gets one-eleventh of the time slice. They won't be weighted by process; they're weighted by thread.

Basically, the process and thread model are the same as Windows NT's, except we don't have priority classes like Windows NT, we just have priorities. But again, you can create up to 32 processes and as many threads as you want in a process. People have come at us with the one-thread-per-process, monolithic Win 3.1–type mentality. They tend to think they need lots of processes, when in reality more threads are actually more convenient because they can use shared variables. They don't have to send messages back and forth forever. They can just collect data in structures and do things intelligently that way. Pretty much everyone who has said they need more processes has been convinced to use more threads.

The scheduler handles priority inversion. If a thread blocks, waiting for another thread with lower priority, we bump that thread's priority and then keep going to see if any other threads are influenced. (Because, of course, influencing one priority may influence someone else's priority, and so on.) Any thread that is already running stays running; any thread that is already blocked stays blocked. Your thread just gets a higher or lower priority. And of course, when your thread finishes and releases an object, if it was inverted because of that object, its priority has to be lowered. A similar scenario occurs when your thread's priority is lowered. Your thread's priority is lowered, and the system checks to see what else gets lowered accordingly.

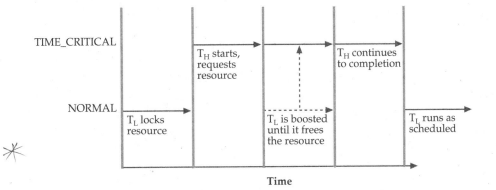

Time

When a higher priority thread needs a resource locked by a lower priority thread, Windows CE temporarily boosts the lower thread's priority until it completes and releases the resource. This process is called priority inversion.

In version 1.0, we had basic scheduling primitives: critical sections and events. We now allow you to block on processes and threads, and we allow named objects such as named mutexes and named events. And we allow *WaitForSingleObject* or *WaitForMultipleObjects*.

The queues got more complicated when we added *WaitForMultiple-Objects*. Because a thread used to be in exactly one queue, the queues were very simple linked lists. Now a thread can be on multiple queues, so you have to have a two-dimensional link. Or each thread can put itself on multiple queues, and each queue can link to multiple threads.

We also allow blocking on interrupts. Our interrupt model is such that an ISR can return to the kernel a request to wake up a particular event. And so a thread blocks an event and the interrupt signals the event. That's why a thread says *wake me when an interrupt goes off*—the thread waits on an event.

In version 1.0, there were places in the kernel where an interrupt couldn't come in, and there were places in the kernel where you couldn't preempt. If either of those is unbounded, you have the potential for unbounded latencies.

In version 2.0, we made all the places we turn interrupts off very short—of fixed size, constant, without any loops—and we made all the non-preemptible parts of the kernel bounded pieces. We used to loop and turn off preemption until an operation completed. We now turn off preemption, do a bit of work, turn on preemption, and try again. The code is slightly less efficient, but now the nonpreemptive periods are bounded.

start of ISR = $value1 + dISR\_Current + \textbf{sum}(dISR\_Higher)$
value1 = Latency value due to processing within the kernel.
dISR_Current = The duration of an ISR in progress at the time the interrupt arrives. This value can range from 0 to the duration of longest ISR in the system.
sum(*dISR_Higher*) = The sum of the durations of all higher-priority ISRs that arrive before this ISR starts; that is, interrupts that arrive during the time *value1* + *dISR_Current*.
start of IST = $value2 + \textbf{sum}(dIST) + \textbf{sum}(dISR)$
value2 = Latency value due to processing within the kernel.
sum(*dIST*) = The sum of the durations of all higher priority ISTs and thread context switch times that occur between this ISR and its start of IST.
sum(*dISR*) = The sum of the durations of all other ISRs that run between this interrupt's ISR and its IST.

Windows CE guarantees upper bounds on the latency between an interrupt and the start of its associated real-time priority thread. This guaranteed performance makes the OS suitable for some real-time applications.

So the interrupt comes in, and you might have to wait until one of those little nonpreemptible parts finishes before waking up a thread, but it will finish in a bounded amount of time. And that's where we get our real-time behavior. We guarantee that ISRs will run within a fixed time of the interrupt and that interrupt threads will run within a fixed time of the ISR returning.

THE LOADER

One of our goals was to keep tools changes to a minimum in the early days because we were a shoestring project back then. We didn't want to have to go to the compiler group and say, "Start from scratch; make us a compiler." The loader's goal was to load the same file format as Windows NT, so we didn't have to change the linker. The loader was pretty much a workhorse. It was basically like this: "Here's the spec; go code it up."

The interesting part, of course, was the multiple address space slices for DLLs.

We reserve space for DLLs in the same place in every slot in virtual memory. The first time the DLL is loaded, the loader allocates the memory for the read-only pages and actually pages them in as needed. If another process loads the same DLL, we map the read-only data—the code—so that the slots of both processes point to the same physical page. You want to have only one copy of the code, so both of the copies are really pointing to the same physical page. If the DLL has any variables, the loader makes a copy of them in a new physical page.

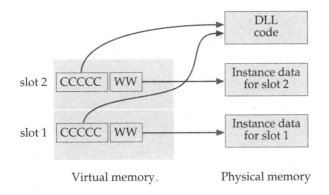

Virtual memory.   Physical memory

DLL code always appears in the same place in the slot, and the DLL always looks for its instance data in the slot for the active process, slot 0.

Then we fix up the DLL code so that it is always pointing to slot 0 for any variables. In that way, the DLL always points to the data for the current active process. As you switch processes, slot 0 always tracks the current process. The code always knows to look in slot 0 to find the variables. That's why we have the 0 slot.

Basically, the code is shared and the data is instanced. Other than that, the loader is incredibly straightforward. It is basically coded to the Win32 executable file format spec.

RESOURCES

Topic	Resource
Current list of all microprocessor families supported by the kernel	*www.microsoft.com/windowsce*
Win32 process and thread model, and thread synchronization	*Advanced Windows, Third Edition,* by Jeffrey Richter (Microsoft Press, 1997)
Windows NT internals and RPC	*Inside Microsoft Windows NT, Second Edition,* by David A. Solomon (Microsoft Press, 1998)
Viewing virtual memory	"Windows CE Process Viewer" tool documentation, in the Microsoft Windows CE Toolkit for Visual C++ 5.0

4 Data Storage

*T*he generic term "object store" refers to the three types of persistent storage supported by Windows CE: file systems, the registry, and property databases. Standard Win32 API functions provide access to the files and the registry, while new Windows CE–specific API functions provide access to the property databases. Embedded systems developers building custom configurations of Windows CE can add the object store to their systems by selecting the components that go into the Filesys module.

Because many embedded devices do not include a hard drive, the object store is built on an internal heap that resides in RAM, ROM, or both. The internal heap provides a transaction model that uses logging to ensure the integrity of the object store data.

For file systems, Windows CE supports its own proprietary file system, which is built on the internal heap, and installable file systems that can be mounted on PC Cards, such as Flash RAM. Future platforms will add support for CD-ROM and DVD drives and for ATA hard disks.

A proprietary design was chosen for the file system to minimize overhead and to squeeze the most use out of the available storage memory. Embedded developers can configure the Filesys module so that the proprietary file system supports either RAM, ROM, or both.

To simplify the process of developing new file systems, Windows CE 2.10 offers the File System Driver (FSD) Manager. Microsoft also provides an implementation of one important installable file system: the FAT file system. In keeping with the modular design of Windows CE, two FAT file system components are provided: the base file system module and the UI module. Embedded developers can replace the UI element with their own versions, or, when building systems without a display, can use a stub in place of the UI element.

Unlike the PC model, the file system does not use drive letters such as "M:" to indicate different logical or physical storage devices. Local drives instead use a string to identify the drive, such as "Storage Card", and network drives exclusively use the universal naming convention (UNC). The UNC is a string that indicates the computer name and shared directory followed by the relative path to the filename, such as "\\Johnmur\Public\Object Store Description".

The registry was designed to replace the clutter of proliferating application initialization (.INI) files. Historically, each Microsoft Windows–based application provided its own .INI file of configuration information, which the application's setup program was free to put anywhere on the computer. The PC user's hard drive over time became littered with configuration files in a variety of formats. To prevent that *situation, the registry provided a hierarchy of registry keys and values to hold the system configuration data. The Win32 API includes functions to manage these registry entries.*

Windows CE itself makes extensive use of the registry to expose configurable system settings. When embedded systems developers have an option to replace behavior or specify configuration parameters, they can use a specific registry entry to provide that custom configuration information.

The Windows CE property databases store application-specific data. For example, a sales contact application can store name, address, phone, and relevant sales information; a scheduling application can store appointments. Windows CE property databases can either be built on top of the internal heap or can be placed on mounted volumes.

The property stored in the database is loosely based on the definition used in the Microsoft Messaging API (MAPI): a property consists of a unique identifier, the property type, and the data item of that type. Related properties are organized into groups called records; the database consists of a set of these records.

The Windows CE property database is not to be confused with a relational database. Windows CE features a high-level interface to standard Microsoft relational databases—the Active Data Objects (ADO) interface offers C++ and Microsoft Visual Basic developers access to Microsoft SQL Server and Microsoft Access relational databases on the desktop. However, this is a completely different technology than the property database in the object store. The property database is simply a small, fast, and efficient structured storage. Windows CE version 2.10 requires only 4 bytes of overhead for each property and only 20 bytes of overhead for each record.

Application developers access the property records using a seek function that reads records in one of four user-defined sort orders. The object store maintains the sort sequence based on the value of the specified property.

The object store resides in "storage memory," which the system differentiates from "program memory." Windows CE gives embedded systems developers the ability to modify the relative sizes of these two areas of memory. The maximum size for the object store overall is 16 MB.

Sharad Mathur and Michael Ginsberg worked together to design the Windows CE internal heap. During the interview in which they discussed its design, they frequently finished each other's sentences. Ginsberg implemented the heap and later wrote the heap-based registry, while Mathur wrote the database. Jeff Parsons wrote the FSD Manager library that provides support services to developers installing new file systems.

DESIGN GOALS FOR THE INTERNAL HEAP

Michael Ginsberg and Sharad Mathur

Our biggest goals were to

- *Be very small—and there are two kinds of small.* The actual code needed to be small because we had space restrictions. But more importantly, we wanted the representation of the data to be as compact as possible.

- *Be robust against power and/or crashing such that you would never lose your entire file system because of a glitch.* The big goal was *transactioning*: to be able to essentially take a fault or have the power go off anywhere and be able to roll back appropriately and leave the object store in a consistent state.

- *Have a small working set in terms of memory requirements.*

- *Be fast.*

Michael Ginsberg

In terms of overall design, because we wanted to optimize for being built on top of RAM, we decided that proprietary was definitely best. We were going to store the file system in RAM as opposed to on a big disk, so we couldn't afford the drawbacks of clusters and the FAT file system, which rounds up to the nearest 512 or nearest 1024 bytes.

The key decision was to have a common heap and a heap manager that managed the RAM for the object store. We'd build the file system, the database, and the registry on top of this common heap. This internal heap is the heart and soul of the file system.

File system	Registry	Property database

Heap	
Compression	Transactioning

All elements of the object store—the built-in proprietary file system, the registry, and the property database—are built on a common underlying heap. Windows CE 2.10 sets their combined maximum size, which is the overall size of the object store, at 16 MB.

TRANSACTION SUPPORT

The goals for the heap were to provide enough functionality to support a file system and a database while incurring very low overhead, and to provide transactioning so that even if you were in the middle of allocating a block, you would not lose the entire heap.

Sharad Mathur

We achieved that by logging our changes. Every time a byte is changed in the heap, if that byte needs to be recovered to undo an operation, we log the previous value of that byte, then perform the operation. When we finish enough operations and reach an atomic stage, we flush the log, committing those changes. If we don't make it, we reboot and look at the log and see the three or four changes that were made. We can then undo them, because we stored the previous values.

We don't necessarily have to log every single byte. For instance, if we're copying a buffer, we take a free block, mark it as allocated, and fill in the bytes. If we die, we unmark the block. We don't have to restore the bytes because the block had been free.

We restrict the amount of space reserved for this log, so we can't do unbounded logging requirement operations. And so for tasks like deleting a file or deleting a database, since we have an unlimited number of operations, we roll *forward* instead of rolling backward. We leave a note saying, "I am deleting file Foo," then shorten the file bit by bit. We blow away the first block, commit that, blow away the second block, commit that. The log says, "My goal is to delete the file." So if we reboot, we see that the goal is to delete the file and we keep hacking away at it. But we hack away at it piece by piece, telling the heap, "I've killed this block, reset; I've killed this block, reset." Otherwise we have to *free* potentially thousands of blocks, remembering each *free* as we go, which would require infinite storage space for the logging.

The log is basically a chunk of uncached memory. That's why we wouldn't want to log every single byte, because writing to uncached memory is very slow—the log's bytes have to be written out to the actual RAM. You want to log only a few bytes for every operation. The log grows a little bit and then just bounces back and forth. Its maximum size is 4 KB, with 16 bytes for each entry—an opcode and three DWORDs. The DWORDs often represent an address, a value, and a length.

```
LOG_STARTBLOCK
LOG_RESTORE          Addr1, PreviousValue1, Size1
LOG_RESTORE          Addr2, PreviousValue2, Size2
      .
      .
      .
LOG_RESTORE          AddrN, PreviousValueN, SizeN
```

The log allows the object store heap to recover from a shutdown or fault. This example shows a memory operation; the log also supports file deletion and memory compaction. If the atomic operation does not complete, the heap can restore the previous values. When an operation successfully completes, a LOG_ENDBLOCK is issued, and the log entries are discarded.

The file system and database also need logging, so they use the same logging structure. "Delete a file" goes in the log in the same way that a block marked as free goes in the log, even though the blocks are at different logical levels. Big notes and small notes all fit in the log.

The log is single-threaded: only one thread at a time can manipulate the log. The log is for our internal use only. If we were to allow apps to get to the log and the apps were slow, everyone else would be locked out of the file system.

If we were to expose transactioning at the user level, we would severely restrict the possibility of concurrency, and one person would be able to block everyone else out indefinitely. So we don't support it. Even if we wanted to have two logs or multithreading, we couldn't really do it because we would violate the ability to transaction the heap operations. In terms of allowing concurrency, you can't have two logs within a single heap. You can have only one transaction at any one time.

TESTING THE HEAP

One of the biggest issues was how to test the heap. We had to make sure that we could reset at all points in time. We can't just say, "The Handheld PC has been off and running for three months and hasn't had any problems," because faults won't occur at every possible place during the heap operations. We actually have to target the heap operations for testing by putting debug breaks in the code.

We wrote a test where every time you wrote to the log, you pretended to roll back the whole log to make sure you could walk the entire heap, and then you rolled it forward again. In the test you say, "If we crashed right now, could we walk the heap?" That's a pretty good test of whether the heap is intact. It doesn't prove you have all your data, but it does prove that both the file system and the database are still reachable, that no large nodes are chopped off.

We were forcing single-threadedness and that was a good enough test. We wrote the critical sections without interthread race conditions, so it was good enough to stop, look around, say everything looks good, and then go forward again.

The Master and Secondary Handle Tables

The heap is organized as a series of movable blocks with handles. Everything outside the context of the heap is referenced by a 16-bit handle. These handles point to the actual memory locations, so we're free to move blocks around when you're not in a transaction.

Movable blocks are also important because when you reboot, the file system might not be at the same place it was the last time you booted. When you reboot, the app goes away, it's re-created, and you have no guarantee that the virtual mapping is the same. Everything must be relative—basically, an offset—and the handles provide that. We keep pointers that are valid only in the sense of a virtual memory context, in terms of your app.

When you either perform lots of *free* operations relative to the number of *alloc* operations, or when you have very little free space in the largest single free block compared to the overall number of free bytes, a compaction thread starts sliding the blocks and trying to create bigger holes.

We had to figure out how often to compact. We observed the heap in action and came up with empirical numbers. The heap tries to compact on the fly, but if it gets desperate it locks down memory and then performs the compacting. If the heap's really in trouble, it will loop until it has created big pieces. Otherwise, it yields as it goes; people can't perform operations while it's compacting.

When we were designing the handle table, we said, the problem with a fixed table size is that it's pre-allocated. If you allocate a small amount of memory for the table, you can't have many handles; but if you allocate a big amount, you're wasting a lot of memory up front.

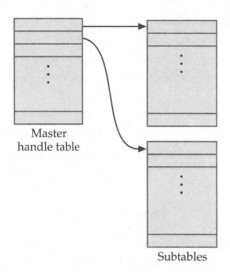

Master
handle table

Subtables

The heap design is a good example of general Windows CE design goals: use memory efficiently and be flexible. The two-level handle table structure minimizes overhead while allowing the number of entries to grow as needed.

So we created a two-level handle table. We have a small master table with 64 entries. Each entry in the master table points to a subtable containing 1024 handles. With this scheme we can have up to 64,000 handles. To prevent reuse of the same handle, we store the current ID of the handle in the secondary handle table. Versioning bits make the IDs unique. So if you free a handle and allocate a handle and you get the same handle, you'll see a unique handle ID. The handle is in the same place but has a different number, which prevents bugs in apps. If an app has a stale handle lying around, its ID will be invalid.

Our design turned out to be very nice when we decided to add databases on external volumes such as Flash cards. The solution is to create a similar looking heap on that external volume. Because the addresses are free to change and everything is just an offset into a handle table, we can create a database volume on a card—all different memory out in the middle of nowhere—and the database code doesn't know the difference. It just says, "I've got a handle table, I've got a pointer, I can go party." We made some code changes to recognize multiple tables, but deep down, bytes are manipulated the same way.

THE WINDOWS CE DATABASE

Sharad Mathur

Our requirements were to provide small, really efficient storage and to make the storage simple and easy. We needed to be compatible with the property design in MAPI because we knew that synching with the desktop was going to be a big requirement. We had a PIM, we had an address book and a calendar, and we knew Microsoft Outlook and Microsoft Schedule Plus stored properties and PROPIDs.

But we didn't have the option of just saying, "We'll be compatible with Win32," because Win32 didn't have a database API. And the MAPI interface was COM-based, and we wanted to minimize the amount of data copying and other overhead. In MAPI, when you read a bunch of properties, you get back a structure that points to one memory block per property, and when you're done you have to free each individual memory block. We found that this process was very error prone—applications were leaking memory.

So we said, "Let's just take the minimalist approach. We have property sets, and we have a database that consists of property sets." (We call a property set a record.) We stayed away from a fixed schema. We said the developers can define their own properties. They can also have multiple databases, but we won't make a huge namespace of databases—we'll just keep all databases flat, in one common area.

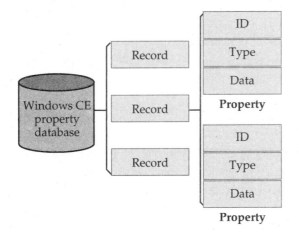

The Windows CE property database consists of records, which are sets of properties. Like the MAPI property on which its design was based, the Windows CE property consists of an ID, a data type, and a data item.

When you read a bunch of Windows CE properties, they are marshaled into a single structure so that you have to free only one piece of memory. We allow developers to pass in the memory and have us fill it so that they can reuse the same block of memory. If they don't know the size, they can just pass a NULL and we allocate the block of memory in their address space. To minimize overhead, we store one PROPID per property. That's just 4 bytes.

The transactioning was a very important requirement. We wanted people to be able to read or write an entire property set in a single transaction. We didn't want every property to be an individual heap block because that fragments the heap a lot more. So we decided that every property set—every record—is a heap block in a single contiguous piece of memory. And because we wanted to be really efficient on space, we wanted to have sizable pieces of memory at the heap level. So we move these blocks while compacting, and to keep the time bounded per iteration of the compactor, we limit the size of a heap block to 4 KB. If the record is within 4 KB, it's a single memory block, and if it's over 4 KB, it's a linked set of memory blocks.

We have restrictions on the maximum size of the property set. Those restrictions come directly from the fact that we have a limit on how much we can log in the heap because we need to transaction the write operation of the property set. For a single record, we limit the number of heap blocks that we need to allocate. And so that's where the limit for the size of the record comes from.

We didn't want a fancy structure for each property set. We didn't expect to have millions of records in a particular database, but we knew that developers needed to be able to read sorted property sets. In your address book, you sort by last name, first name, things like that. We knew we needed to have some way of keeping sorts in the database. And so we decided not to have any sort of fancy hashing or indexing schemes—we don't keep B-trees of all the property sets. Instead, we did the really simple thing. From the design, it turned out that it was cheap for us to keep four sort orders. We have four linked lists threading through the entire set of property sets, one for each sort order. And that's where we got our four sort orders: because these handles are 16 bits (one word), with just four words, you have access to the entire sorting scheme.

To be able to do things a little more efficiently, when you seek to a particular record, we don't start from the beginning and walk the entire list. Instead, we keep pointers that divide the set into 64 different spaces, we walk down that pointer list to find the section of the database your seek value is in, then we search for the record within that section. So we basically cut the seek operation down by a factor of 64, which helps a lot considering the numbers of records we're optimized for.

To speed things up, we cache a DWORD worth of data from properties that we sort on. For instance, if you're sorting on the last name, we cache the first two Unicode characters. So most of the time you don't actually have to unmarshal the property and extract the data.

Again, because space was such a huge issue, we wanted to compress everything in the database, especially because we expected that a lot of the data would be Unicode text. Getting good compression ratios is really hard unless you have a reasonable amount of data. What helps us is that all the properties are globbed together in one marshaled memory block, and we compress that entire memory block. We also keep the PROPIDs separate from the properties themselves so that when you're looking for a specific property, you can just walk the PROPIDs and find the property. This process allows us to keep like data together without breaking it up with the PROPIDs in the middle.

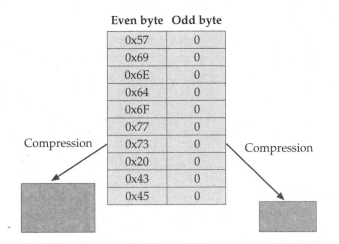

Even byte	Odd byte
0x57	0
0x69	0
0x6E	0
0x64	0
0x6F	0
0x77	0
0x73	0
0x20	0
0x43	0
0x45	0

Windows CE tries several compression schemes and uses the winner. One that is often very efficient for Unicode strings involves separate compression for its odd bytes and its even bytes.

We try compressing the data in two ways. We do a normal LZ pass on the data, and we also do a pass where we split the data into two streams: the odd bytes and the even bytes. Because a lot of the data is Unicode, more commonality exists among the high bytes than across the whole stream. If you have a Unicode string and most of the high bytes are zeroes, then one stream ends up being compressed into a really small number of bytes. We compress it both ways, see which way is better, and then perform the compression the better way. The compression itself doesn't actually cost that much because most of the cost is in writing out the compressed bits.

THE REGISTRY

Michael Ginsberg

In Windows CE 1.0, the registry was based on a file, so it lived on top of the file system. The drawback was that the registry was a layer on top of a layer on top of a layer—the *ReadFile/WriteFile* API. In 1.0, the registry didn't know anything about the heap. The file system and the database shared common decompress buffers and common cache buffers, but the registry was its own world and needed its own buffers. And it was a little bit slow.

In version 1.01, we decided that implementation wasn't good enough. So I rewrote the registry from scratch, on top of our heap layer, similar to the way the file system and database are on top of our heap layer. Therefore the registry uses all the native logging and transacting. Basically the registry is Win32-compatible. It's currently designed for small devices, but it can hold hundreds of thousands of keys—whatever you want to throw at it—quite happily.

THE FILE SYSTEM

The file system is pretty straightforward. The hard part was designing the heap. Both the file system and registry are, pretty much, very lightweight layers on top of the heap. The database is a somewhat more complicated layer, with sorting and seeking. The file system just lays out the data and provides simple functions to walk the data.

An interesting feature of our file system is that it also supports files stored in ROM. These show up in the Windows directory in the same way that files in the RAM file system do, but they don't take up any RAM.

If you create a file with the same name as a ROM file, it *shadows* the ROM file—you see only the new one. So if you have a ROM file that the file system exposes as \Windows\Foo, and a user opens an editor and saves \Windows\Foo, any user who looks for Foo now sees the RAM version instead of the ROM version. You're in essence modifying the ROM file without actually modifying the ROM. This has an interesting side effect in that if you delete the RAM version of the file, you'll again see the ROM version with the old size and the old time. The user can hide a ROM file by putting something else in front of it, but he can't delete it. He can hide the bytes but not the filename.

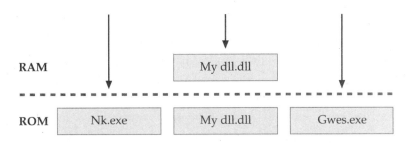

The file system searches for the specified filename in RAM before searching in ROM. This feature offers a way to "update" ROM files: supply a file in RAM with the same name as the ROM file. This is known as "file shadowing."

Initially, we provided ways to add new file systems. We had PCMCIA, FAT file system cards, and SRAM cards. The Auto PC guys were supporting a CD player. We had a DVD player, an ATA hard disk. Previously only we at Microsoft could write installable file systems because the design was cobbled together and you had to have internal header files. With Windows CE 2.10, we started exposing a layer to ISVs so that they could write their own file systems. Now we have a very nice layer. Jeff Parsons wrote a library so that you don't have to actually understand it all; you just have to hook in. You say, "Here's my read function, here's my write function, here's my seek, go," and it hooks you into our layers very nicely—all the behind-the-scenes stuff is taken care of for you. It's a brand new, very light layer, designed to isolate you from the OS.

INSTALLABLE FILE SYSTEMS

Jeff Parsons

Windows CE 1.0 offered some services for registering your own alternate file system: *RegisterAFS* and *DeregisterAFS*. In version 1.01, we added *RegisterAFSName* and *DeregisterAFSName* so that if you used the AFS services, you could control how your file system was registered. But the work involved in creating and installing a file system driver was still pretty substantial. You had to understand how to create API sets and vtables. The FSD also had to be hardwired to a particular release.

We wanted to abstract that process of creating and installing a file system driver a little bit and make it easier. So I went ahead and created the FSD Manager component. The way you should think of the whole system architecturally is that applications make file system calls which go to the built-in file system first, then to the FSD Manager (if the request specifies a volume it registered), and finally on to the appropriate FSD. The FSD Manager has complete control over what the FSD sees. The FSD shouldn't see any calls across power cycles, for example.

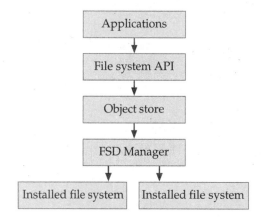

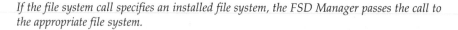

If the file system call specifies an installed file system, the FSD Manager passes the call to the appropriate file system.

Let's say you want to create the Foo file system. You create Foo.dll, which exports all desired functionality. By convention, all of its exported function names start with "FOO_". If that DLL is appropriately registered in the registry, when a new device is detected, the Device Manager (Device.exe) loads Foo.dll, notices that Foo.dll has the *FOO_MountDisk* and *FOO_UnmountDisk* exports, and in turn, loads the FSD Manager (Fsdmgr.dll) to talk to this new Foo file system.

All Foo.dll has to do is export the interfaces it wants to support. There are 30 different interfaces: the path-based interfaces such as *CreateDirectoryW* and *RemoveDirectoryW*; the handle-based interfaces such as *CreateFileW*, *ReadFile*, and *WriteFile*; and the find interfaces such as *FindFirstFileW* and *FindNextFileW*.

The FSD Manager looks up all these required export names, such as *FOO_CreateDirectoryW*, fills in the appropriate vtable, creates an API set, and registers the file system. The FSD Manager automatically supplies stub functions for any missing exports, so if an FSD doesn't want to support a folder hierarchy, for example, it simply doesn't export any path-based functions. The stubs return ERROR_NOT_SUPPORTED.

FSD MANAGER INTERFACE CATEGORIES IMPLEMENTED BY THE FILE SYSTEM

API Category	API Functions
Path-based functions	*CreateDirectoryW, RemoveDirectoryW, GetFile-Attributes, SetFileAttributes, DeleteFile, MoveFile, DeleteAndRenameFile, GetDiskFreeSpace*
Handle-based functions	*CreateFileW, ReadFile, ReadFileWithSeek, WriteFile, WriteFileWithSeek, SetFilePointer, GetFileSize, GetFile-InformationByHandle, FlushFileBuffers, GetFileTime, SetFileTime, SetEndOfFile, DeviceIoControl, CloseFile*
Find functions	*FindFirstFileW, FindNextFileW, FindClose*
System event functions	*CloseVolume, Notify, RegisterFileSystemFunction*
Device event functions	*MountDisk, UnmountDisk*

Once Foo.dll is loaded, it calls back into FSD Manager, which provides a variety of services. *FSDMGR_RegisterVolume* records the volume name and a DWORD of FSD volume-specific data that the FSD must keep associated with that volume. That data is passed in turn to the various entry points. So when *FOO_CreateDirectoryW* or one of the other path-based file system interfaces is called, that volume-specific data is passed as the first parameter. The rest of the parameters are identical to the standard API prototypes for those functions.

If Foo.dll registers a volume as Foo Disk and an application wants to create a folder on that disk, it calls

```
CreateDirectoryW("\\\\Foo Disk\\\\NewFolder", NULL);
```

which would ultimately result in a call to

```
FOO_CreateDirectoryW(dwVolumeSpecificData, "\\\\New Folder",
    NULL);
```

When an FSD's *CreateFileW* interface is called, it must call the *FSDMGR_CreateFileHandle* service to create the file handle object. The same goes for the find services—when *FindFirstFileW* is called, it must call *FSDMGR_CreateSearchHandle* to create the actual search handle. No special service is required to close those handles; they're all closed with *CloseHandle*.

Like *FSDMGR_RegisterVolume*, both of the handle-creation services also record a DWORD of FSD handle-specific data that the FSD needs to keep associated with that handle. So if an application wants to create and write to a file on the Foo Disk volume, it would call

```
hFile = CreateFileW("\\\\Foo Disk\\\\New File",
    GENERIC_WRITE...);
WriteFile(hFile, buffer, sizeof(buffer), ...);
```

which would ultimately result in calls to

```
FOO_CreateFileW(dwVolumeSpecificData, hProcess, "\\\\New File",
    GENERIC_WRITE, ...);
FOO_WriteFile(dwHandleSpecificData, buffer, sizeof(buffer),
    ...);
```

FSD Manager also sends device-independent interfaces (*FSDMGR_GetDiskInfo*, *FSDMGR_ReadDisk*, and *FSDMGR_WriteDisk*) back to the underlying device driver. FSD Manager provides these services to avoid forcing the FSD to have specific knowledge about how a particular device driver works. Drivers shipped with Windows CE 1.0 support one set of IOCTLs for reading and writing sectors on a disk, and the WDM drivers support a different set. FSD Manager figures out what kind of driver you're talking to and uses the right IOCTLs.

Another issue is power cycling. Every time you turn the system off, the PCMCIA hardware loses its power too. When you turn the system back on, we have to simulate a device removal and reinsertion which, to a file system, would look as if the user pulled the card out and put the card back in. If we didn't do anything special, every time you turned your device back on, the folder would disappear for a moment and then reappear.

So we have some logic that detects the power transitions. This logic gets called right before the device is turned off and sets a mark on the wall: a flag. When the device comes back on, if that flag is set, the FSD Manager doesn't let any more API requests go to the FSD. It knows the requests are just going to fail because the driver is being unloaded and reloaded. It holds off all API requests until it gets a special broadcast from the device subsystem that says, "Okay, all the devices have been reinitialized," and then it allows requests to come in again. An FSD shouldn't have to be aware of this goofy case. The card wasn't really removed—the device just lost power and got it back later.

Before the power goes off, all the FSD should see is a flurry of *Flush-FileBuffer* requests as the FSD Manager tries to ensure that all the files on the media are as up-to-date as possible.

One of the reasons we implemented FSD Manager as a DLL is that if our requirements change over time and we have to support device driver types other than the two basic kinds we have now, we can provide this new DLL to developers distributing their own file systems. When developers install Foo.dll, they can install the new FSD Manager as well. The alternative was to build the DLL as a static library that third-party file system writers could statically link to. That alternative would give them the benefit of abstraction, but it wouldn't give them the benefit of being able to work with any device. The writers would have to build new versions of the binaries for different devices.

Let me briefly summarize the benefits of FSD Manager:

◆   It registers a volume with a file system.

◆   It creates file handles and find handles.

◆   It installs the necessary API handlers, meaning that the FSD just provides a bunch of exports and FSD Manager takes care of registering those addresses.

◆   It masks arbitrary differences between drivers such as the IOCTLs.

◆   It takes care of blocking API requests to ensure file system consistency across power cycles.

This model incurs a small amount of overhead. For example, FSD Manager has to keep track of all the handles being allocated to ensure that all handle-based requests come to it first. Then it has to decide that it's okay to go ahead and pass the call on to the FSD. FSD Manager allocates a small amount of additional memory for every registered volume and every open handle. But that shouldn't be a big deal.

RESOURCES

Topic	Resource
Configuring the Filesys module	Microsoft Windows CE Embedded Toolkit for Visual C++
Windows CE database API functions	*Programming Windows CE,* by Doug Boling (Microsoft Press, 1998)
Registry and file system API functions	Microsoft Platform SDK documentation MSDN
Creating your own installable file system	Microsoft Windows CE Embedded Toolkit for Visual C++

5

*The GWE
Subsystem*

T *he Microsoft Windows NT and Microsoft Windows 95 libraries that contain the core Windows functionality are named Kernel32, User32, and GDI32. The Microsoft Windows CE libraries have different names. The kernel functionality appears in Nk, while the GDI32 and User32 functionality is combined into one library called GWE, which stands for graphics, window manager, and event manager.*

Windows CE developers still use the shorthand term "User" to refer to the GWE functionality that comes from User32: the user input system, the event manager, and the window manager. The user input system handles input from the keyboard, the mouse, or the stylus; the event manager handles messages and message queues. Both of these subsystems work with the window manager to route Windows messages to the appropriate application window.

"GDI," which stands for graphics device interface, refers to the 2-D raster graphics API package, which supports drawing operations using the GDI primitives: lines and curves, filled areas, bitmaps, and text. Windows CE supports either raster fonts or TrueType fonts.

In this chapter, the Windows CE developers offer a brief overview of each area of GWE and then discuss how Windows CE differs from other Windows implementations.

Sharad Mathur introduces the overall design goals. Mathur, the core OS development manager, wrote the dialog manager. Jason Fuller explains the challenges involved in the componentization of GWE and describes the window manager code.

Keith Bentley describes message queues in detail. A message loop is a while *loop in a Windows application that gets and dispatches messages from the system until the system indicates that no more messages will be sent. Every Windows application must have the entry point* WinMain, *which contains the message loop. Every window must also provide a window procedure, or* WndProc, *which processes that window's messages. For example, most implementations of* WndProc *handle the paint message, WM_PAINT, and the shutdown message, WM_DESTROY. The window procedure is usually implemented as a large switch statement. It explicitly checks for the messages it wants to process and performs the processing for those messages. The window procedure can also choose to let Windows handle messages by dropping through the switch statement and calling the default window procedure,* DefWindowProc. *The Windows CE SDK contains full documentation for all Windows messages and associated data. The best single introduction to the Windows message–based architecture is the book by Charles Petzold,* Programming Windows 95 *(Microsoft Press, 1996).*

Note that the term "event" has two distinct meanings. It refers to events such as user input or timer signals that can be represented by Windows messages and placed on a message queue. It also refers to the general-purpose Win32 thread synchronization objects managed by the kernel. To distinguish between the two meanings of the term event, the Win32 thread synchronization objects are called "Win32 event objects" throughout this chapter. (GWE implements the synchronization offered by the SendMessage *call by creating its own internal Win32 event objects.)*

Anthony Lapadula and Martin Shetter worked on the team that wrote the multiple bit-depth implementation of GDI. They introduce the Windows graphics model, explaining the key concepts of device contexts, realization, and raster operations. They then list the graphics objects defined by GDI and describe how Windows CE differs from other Windows implementations. One of the most significant differences involves the Windows CE palette model.

———◆———

DESIGN GOALS

Sharad Mathur

When we moved to the new kernel and to the Win32 APIs, one of the first things we did was to redo GDI and User. User has several different levels: the window manager, user input, and the message queue. The design goals were to be really fast, small, and efficient.

Sharad Mathur

We decided to optimize the window manager for small devices. We expected most of the apps to be full-screen all the time, so we optimized the paint algorithms to work well when you had full-screen apps coming and going. We eliminated the minimize/maximize states.

We also tried to minimize the number of process transitions. We didn't see the need to allow people to customize the non-client area: all these non-client messages are sent to the process space and come back to *DefWindowProc* in the server space. *DefWindowProc* usually just handles default processing for non-client messages and then returns. It's a lot of back and forth for no real reason, so we don't send the non-client messages.

The user input at the message queue level is where we discovered that the focus activation and capture semantics of the Windows API are really weird. Windows 95 and Windows NT do completely different things, so we had to pick and choose which one to be compatible with. Keith Bentley can tell you the gory details. Because the semantics are so complicated, we didn't really want to invent our own. We just bit the bullet and did all the work so that we were compatible with Win32.

In terms of user input, again our goals were to eliminate extra threads, eliminate extra layers. And so we just integrated the keyboard driver and touch driver directly into GWE, and we made the drivers deliver events directly into the global event queue.

Apart from that, the basic design and concepts of Windows CE are very much the same as Win32. We really don't innovate any new APIs or designs, but we do have a much cleaner implementation of the Windows semantics. Once you know everything you have to do, you can design the code to be fairly small.

Jason Fuller

Before we actually started writing any of this code, there was the idea that maybe these three components—the graphics, the window manager, and the event manager—should be different processes living totally independently: you'd pass all data across processes. We decided not to do that, which was the right decision. Because the window manager and the event manager can share data, the event manager can look into the window structure.

I was mainly working on the window manager, although I touched on the other areas. We originally looked at supporting the Windows NT window manager but found that it wouldn't meet our size and performance goals. And so basically, we decided to start from scratch. In some cases, we had small utility functions that were relatively independent of the operating system, and so we could just take the code from [Windows] NT. In other cases, we read the Windows NT code, understood what it was doing, and copied the basic algorithms.

So these were our original design goals and reasoning:

◆ *Small ROM footprint.* To get this, we wrote the code from scratch and componentized it.

◆ *Small RAM footprint.* Writing the code from scratch kept this small. We didn't want all this extra legacy code that was in the operating system only for historic reasons.

◆ *Good functionality on devices with small screens.* We tried to conserve screen real estate and provide enough functionality so that you could write apps that work well on small screens.

◆ *Win32-compatibility.* We take that compatibility for granted, but that's one of the most important features of GWE. We're Win32-compatible so that if you know how to program to Windows, you know how to program to Windows CE.

◆ *Support for multiple bit depths and small bit depths, such as 2 bits per pixel.* Windows NT and Windows 95 never had to support multiple and small bit depths.

◆ *A design that accommodated low-powered, battery-powered devices.* This kind of design includes functionality like time management and knowing when to shut the device off, knowing when the user hasn't used it.

GWE FUNCTIONALITY OVERVIEW

Currently the window manager is very componentized. You can pick and choose which features you want. You can have a non-client area or not. You can pick and choose any combination of the individual controls such as the edit control, list box, and so on.

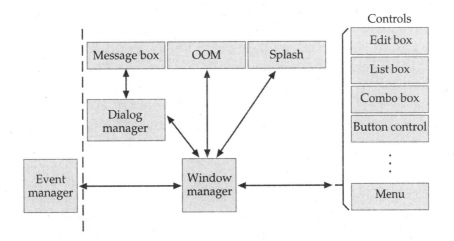

All the controls are provided as individual components. The Windows CE implementation of menus differs slightly from other versions of Windows: menus are implemented as controls.

The non-client area in Windows CE is quite a bit different from the non-client area in Windows NT or Windows 95. It is tightly integrated with the window manager. For some products, having a separate menu bar and a separate toolbar takes up too much screen real estate, so we combined the menu bar and the toolbar and invented a new control called the *command bar*.

Originally menus were built into the non-client area. When developers added toolbars, the toolbars ended up in the client area. When we went to do it all over again, we decided that menus should just be a control like any other control. So we actually have a menu control, although it's not publicly exposed as such. To put a menu inside the command bar, the command bar uses the menu control.

The menus are very componentized. You can have or not have cascading menus. You can have or not have scrolling menus. The menu UI can work in two different ways: you drag a stylus over the menu, or you tap on the item you want to select. The cascading menus can overlap or be next to each other. Some products with very small screens need overlapping menus so that the menus don't hit the screen edge quickly.

The dialog manager sits on top of the window manager. If you have a dialog manager, you can implement a message box on top of that: a message box is really just a dialog. All of the controls (edit box, list box, combo box, button, etc.) also sit on top of the window manager. A menu historically has been thought of as something different, but it's implemented as a control.

The graphics are totally componentized. You can have either TrueType or raster fonts. You can have or not have message boxes. You can have a dialog manager or not. Some utility functions in GWE are also pretty independent, functions like *LoadBitmap, LoadIcon, LoadImage, LoadString, DrawIcon.*

GWE is responsible for keeping track of the amount of time the system has been running. It keeps track of the idle timeout, so if you don't type anything for three minutes, GWE shuts off the device.

GWE also contains the out-of-memory dialog and the out-of-memory handler. Technically, this dialog and handler don't have to be part of GWE. But it was the most obvious place to put them because they have UI associated with them. The out-of-memory dialog pops up a window when you're low on memory, gives you a list of all the running applications, and gives you the opportunity to close them. The out-of-memory handler is something new that we added because we work on devices that don't have a hard disk and don't have a lot of RAM. Once you run out of memory, you can't just swap to the disk because there is no disk. So you have to explicitly deal with the case where you might run out of memory or come close to running out of memory, which is not something that normally happens on a Windows NT device.

GWE contains the startup screen that appears when you first turn on the device and that asks for your password or tells you your name or splash screen. The screen is optional. GWE also contains the calibration screen, so if your device has a touch screen, you've got support for calibrating the touch screen to the LCD. The UI to do this is in GWE, too.

The event manager is pretty tightly coupled to the window manager, although we have factored this out to the point where you can combine the event manager with a minimal window manager. The minimal version gives you a GWE that has only nongraphical windows as event handlers. That configuration of GWE still manages window creation, window destruction, window lifetime, event passing, extra window data, and window styles but nothing graphical. You still have classes, *WndProcs*, and message pumps, but they just pass messages.

And obviously there are some dependencies between the modules. The standard window manager depends on GDI to do the actual drawing and to manage regions and device contexts. Both the 1.0 and 2.0 versions of GDI implement a subset of the Win32 interface. GDI doesn't call anything in the window manager. It's entirely one-way. The window manager just calls GDI. Taking the existing window manager and plugging in a new GDI wasn't that hard. I mean, the GDI group did it practically without even telling us.

The whole point of componentization is that products don't have to pay a price for features they don't want. If the code doesn't exist on a system, it doesn't take up ROM space. We try not to make products absorb features they're not using. But there are always trade-offs. When you design something to be componentized, you've always got at least a little bit of overhead that you wouldn't have if you just combined the code monolithically. The advantage is, however, that if you're not using a component, you can just get rid of all its code. And so it's a big win.

USER

Keith Bentley

When we first sat down to look at User, we realized right away that we weren't going to be able to take existing Windows code and pound on it and get it small enough for what we wanted for Windows CE. So we wrote the major portion of GWE from scratch. We looked at the original Windows code to guide us or, in other cases, we just coded completely from scratch.

The message queue, event passing, and input system—those are the core parts of User. Built on top of the event management system is the input system, which handles mouse and touch and keyboard input. Basically, the input system takes information passed up by the keyboard driver and the touch/mouse driver and then uses the message passing mechanism to pass the input messages to the foreground window. User employs both the windowing system and the message passing system to implement the input system.

Keith Bentley

These are the main components of User:

- *Msgque.* Message queue is needed for anything that passes messages, which tends to be just about everything, right? Because you generally need message passing if you're going to have any kind of input.

- *Wmbase.* This is the component required to create a window, give the window a *WndProc*, and send messages to it.

- *Winmgr.* Window manager is the component responsible for drawing on the screen—all the real graphics parts.

THE MESSAGE QUEUE

The message queue performs two functions. It handles all aspects of sending and receiving messages, and it acts as a repository for input state information—for example, the cursor size and caret blink rates—everything associated with an input context.

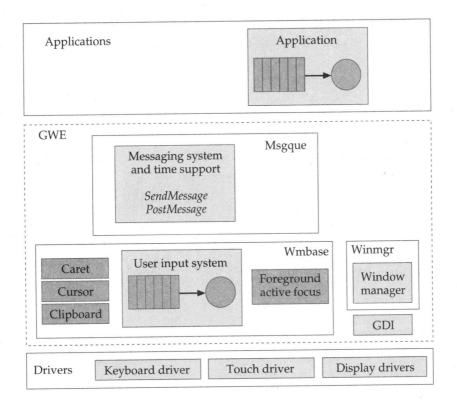

The main components of the "User" part of GWE include the window manager, the message queue, and the base window functionality components.

In terms of message passing, the two basic flavors are *SendMessage* and *PostMessage*. *SendMessage* is a synchronous message-sending mechanism: a sender sends a message, the receiver picks up the message, and then the sender waits for the message processing to complete. A one-to-one relationship exists between threads and message queues; if you look at the actual API call, you see that you send messages to windows, and each window is owned by a particular thread. The *SendMessage* call specifies the window that the message is supposed to go to. Behind the scenes, we look up which thread is associated with a particular window and synchronize the message passing. If the window is in the same thread that is calling *SendMessage*, the call just degenerates into a subroutine call into the *WndProc*, the window procedure specified for that window.

PostMessage works a little bit differently. The message just gets packaged up and put into the message queue. The sender continues running, regardless of where the message is being passed. At some later point in time, the posted message is removed from the queue and dispatched.

So as you can see, each window is associated with a particular message queue by virtue of being associated with a thread. The windows act as targets of sent messages. So we've got threads, associated message queues, windows, and window procedures. The relationships are set up: a window knows its owner thread, its message queue, and its window procedure.

And then there's the infamous message loop in the application's *WinMain*:

```
while (GetMessage(&msg...)) {
    TranslateMessage(&msg);
    DispatchMessage(&msg);
}
```

When a thread calls *GetMessage*, we go out and look on the actual message queue for that thread.

The simplest part of this process is posted messages. In our implementation, part of the internal message queue structure points off to all the messages that have been posted to it. When *GetMessage* is called, it looks at this posted message queue. Assuming a message is out there, *GetMessage* plops the message into your *msg* argument, where you want the message information to go. *GetMessage* then returns, and the main loop calls *DispatchMessage. DispatchMessage* looks at the message information, finds the window that goes along with it, finds its particular window procedure, and then calls that procedure with the message and the *wParam* and *lParam* parameters. This result is exactly what you'd expect. There are no tricks to it. Pull the message off the queue, stuff it into the argument. When it comes time to dispatch the message, find the window, find the procedure, call that procedure.

From the sender's perspective, all that happens in the call to *PostMessage* is that arguments are packaged up and put into the appropriate message queue. Posting to a window in your thread or in a different thread is handled the same way. The message gets packaged up and goes into the appropriate queue. At some point, assuming that thread is running correctly, the thread pulls messages off its queue and eventually gets to that message and dispatches it. There's no explicit form of synchronization for posted messages.

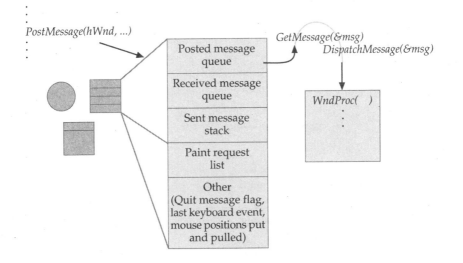

Whether posted by the thread that owns the window or by another thread, posted messages are handled the same way. The message is simply put into the "posted message queue" portion of the message queue structure and processed asynchronously. The calling thread continues.

SendMessage is a little bit trickier: it is synchronous so you know that when it returns, the message has been processed by whomever you sent it to. It can go through two paths, depending on whether you're sending a message to a window in your own thread or in another thread.

The simplest case is sending a message to your own thread. *Send-Message* realizes that the window is in your thread, directly calls the window procedure, and then unwinds. If the message is going to your own thread, it just turns into a subroutine call.

The more complicated case is sending a message to a window in another thread. The message queue has a subqueue that deals with the messages that are sent to a particular window and thread. *SendMessage* realizes that it's sending a message to a different message queue, packages up the message, puts it into the other message queue, and then waits. So now we have this calling thread waiting for a response, waiting on an internal Win32 event object. This wait allows the receiver thread to pick up the message and process it.

The key point here is that when the message is going to a window in another thread, the owner thread *of that window* actually executes the code. Your thread calls *SendMessage*, but the *WndProc* of the other thread gets the message.

SendMessage(hWnd, ...);

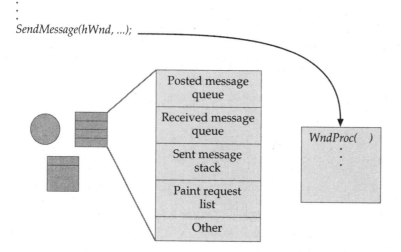

When the thread that owns the window sends a message to that window, the message is not actually placed in the message queue. SendMessage directly calls its WndProc.

And just to get into all the details—while the sending thread is hanging out waiting for a response, it also has to look for messages that may have been sent back to it. The window that the sending thread sent a message to can in turn sends a message back. And so while hanging out waiting for a response, that thread is also waiting for incoming sends.

The other difference between sent and posted messages is that sent messages are handled by *GetMessage* completely internally. When a thread is in its message loop, the sent message comes into the loop and gets completed within that call to *GetMessage*:

```
while (GetMessage(&msg...);) {
    TranslateMessage(&msg...);
    DispatchMessage(&msg...);
}
```

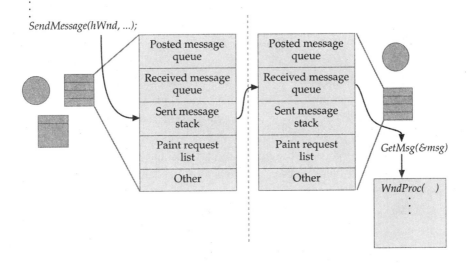

When a thread sends a message to another thread's window, the message is placed in the "received message queue" and GetMessage *makes the call to the* WndProc. *The caller waits on a Win32 event (managed by GWE) until the* WndProc *is complete.*

The main loop of the application never sees the *GetMessage* call return. *GetMessage* looks and says, "Okay, have any messages been sent? Have any messages been posted?" *GetMessage* just works its way down the hierarchy of messages. Sent messages are handled and dispatched right then and there.

There's a behind-the-scenes priority for messages that you don't actually see spelled out in the documentation. You see hints of the priority in the documentation, but it's never actually spelled out.

Priority	Message Type
1	Sent messages—Messages sent to a thread are processed with the highest priority.
2	Posted messages—Messages posted by calling *PostMessage* are processed with the next highest priority.
3	WM_QUIT messages.
4	WM_PAINT messages.
5	WM_TIMER messages.

So if you've got a window or a thread that's hung for some reason, the most common reason is that some thread is waiting on a Win32 event object instead of being in its main message loop. And if this thread is hung, the sender will also get hung waiting for a response to come back. That led to development of *MsgWaitForMultipleObject*, an API that says, "Wait for a Win32 event object, but if a message comes in, go ahead and process it." That's the best that you can do if you want to use the mixed model, which uses both Win32 event objects and sent messages.

If you don't go with the mixed model, you have to decide that either a thread waits on Win32 events and does its own event handling or a thread works strictly with messages.

These are the key issues to remember:

◆ Sending is synchronous.

◆ Posting is asynchronous.

◆ All messages, from dispatched messages to behind-the-scenes messages in *GetMessage*, work their way to the window procedure.

◆ When you're using the message passing mechanism, the thread that created the window always has the window procedure that is executing the code. You won't have one thread calling *Send-Message* and then that same thread executing another window procedure. You don't have to use critical sections or anything like that in your window procedures, because you know that as long as you get the messages via *SendMessage*, they've been serialized by the message queue mechanism.

MANAGING INPUT

In terms of managing the input context, there's a whole subsystem that deals with, in the Windows parlance, the foreground window, the active window, and the focus window. All this tends to confuse a lot of folks, so it's worth describing.

Each thread has one particular window called the *active window*. This is a top-level window that is owned by that particular thread and picked out to be active. The active window or one of its children can be the *focus window*.

The focus is generally set up to receive keyboard messages. One particular thread/message queue in the system is picked to be the foreground thread, and the active window of that thread becomes the *foreground window*.

These three windows interrelate. Setting the focus can change the active window. Setting the active window can change the focus. Setting the foreground window or the active window can change the Z-positions of windows, and changing window positions can change the foreground window. So all three form a sort of "rock, paper, scissors" arrangement, where if one of them changes, the others are affected.

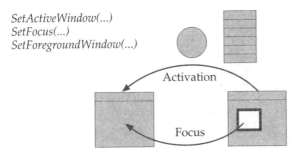

SetActiveWindow(...)
SetFocus(...)
SetForegroundWindow(...)

Activation

Focus

The active, focus, and foreground windows are interrelated, and changes to any one setting can affect the other two. Each thread has an active window and a focus window. One thread in the system is the foreground thread; its active window is the foreground window. The SetForegroundWindow *function sets the window that receives keyboard input.*

The active window and focus window information is kept in the message queue structure, so the active window and focus window are on a per-thread basis. By calling *SetActiveWindow*, a thread can move the activation around to windows that are in the same thread. *SetFocus* changes the focus to any window in your thread—to either a top-level window or a child window. When the focus and activation change, the WM_SETFOCUS, WM_KILLFOCUS, and notification messages are sent.

This works on a systemwide basis because a thread in the input system is responsible for sending out input events. This thread keeps track of the foreground thread and by implication its message queue. It picks one thread out of the entire system to be the foreground thread, and when the user presses a key, keyboard input is sent to that foreground thread's focus.

What tends to confuse folks is, in the older Windows versions, you called *SetActiveWindow* to change the activation. But calling it doesn't work in this model. Windows CE is the same as Windows NT and Windows 95 in that the input information is on a per-thread basis. You've really got a third function call now—*SetForegroundWindow*—that's responsible for changing this information in the input system so that keyboard input is routed properly.

A user can get confused because his app might not be the foreground thread. Internally, his app calls *SetActiveWindow* and *SetFocus*, and he doesn't see his window come to the top. Everything looks consistent. *GetActive-Window* says that his window is the active window. *GetFocus* says that the app's window has the focus, but it doesn't. It hasn't been chosen as the foreground because its thread is not the chosen foreground thread.

And so that's why this call for setting the foreground window was added. It tells the system, "This is the window you want in the foreground to handle user input." This call causes a whole series of interactions so that the desired window will be repositioned on the top. It can potentially change the activation from one thread to another and possibly trigger focus changes so that the proper window gets keyboard input.

Similarly, if you are the foreground thread and you bring some other top-level window to the top (by using *SetWindowPos* to position it, for example), that top-level window will become the foreground window. And if you decide to change the focus from one window to another, the activation can change.

The one invariant in the midst of all of this change is that the focus window is always the active window or a child of the active window. It can also be null.

So the big picture is, you've got your entire memory structure, with one slot per process. GWE exists as one of these processes. Internal to GWE is a thread waiting for input events. The keyboard driver or the touch driver puts an event into this main input queue, which corresponds to the system input queue but is not quite as elaborate as the Windows NT and Windows 95 system queues. A thread in there pulls off an event.

If an event is a touch event, the event manager calls into the window manager to find out which window was hit. It then uses the *PostMessage* mechanism to package that message up and put the input message into the appropriate queue for that window.

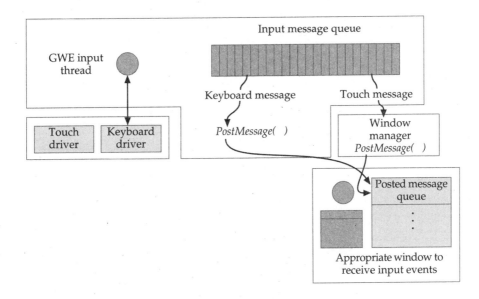

The system input queue posts touch events into the message queue of the appropriate window and posts keyboard events into the message queue of the foreground thread.

If the event is a keyboard event, the event manager goes back and posts the information it has about the foreground window and foreground message queue to the foreground thread. The information would show up as a posted message. So this posting mechanism is running asynchronously, just taking all this input and routing it to whichever thread it needs to go to. When the other threads get a chance to run, they will pull these messages off their message queues and process them.

COMPONENTIZATION IN GWE

During our first pass at componentization, we actually tried to do some of the sample configurations, which exposed a few problems in terms of dependencies between components, problems that we weren't aware of. Envisioning some of these configurations let us see where the dividing lines between components actually were.

Our first sample configurations didn't have any graphics. The app writers just wanted to pass messages between windows, to use the windows as abstract objects that could send and receive messages. So when we pulled out the GDI component, even though there were dependencies in terms of creating regions for the window on the screen, we realized that these calls could fail *and* we could still allow the system to continue running. The window manager was calling into GDI. Because the windows are still useful for passing messages, we put checks in there to say, "If this call comes back and says that it's not implemented, it's okay to keep running."

What we're trying to do is split out what we're calling *hard dependencies* from *soft dependencies*. Currently, most of the dependencies in the system are hard dependencies, meaning one component needs the other component to function correctly. For soft dependencies, the caller can continue even though another component returns "not implemented." Soft dependencies are resolved by using stubs, which are essentially do-nothing functions.

We've done a pretty good job in terms of coming up with at least two flavors of the window manager: just enough of the window manager to be able to send and receive messages to and from windows, and the more full-blown window manager that actually draws on the screen.

To guide this whole componentization process, we're trying to come up with realistic scenarios. So for example, in the case of the message queues, we couldn't really imagine somebody saying, "I want *SendMessage* but not *PostMessage*." That really sums up our overall guiding principle—not to componentize just for the sake of componentizing but to try to come up with realistic scenarios.

THE GDI

Anthony Lapadula and Martin Shetter

In other graphics packages, you pass all the pens, brushes, and fonts—everything you want for every drawing operation. In the Win32 GDI, the device context (DC) is the drawing surface. You select into the DC the objects that you want to use, and the objects stay in that device context. The DC is the collection of everything. The draw operation uses all the objects currently selected in the DC.

The API is designed this way for a reason. When you pass a pen or a brush to each API call, the pen or brush has to be converted to a format that's compatible with that target surface. So if you had an API that took a surface and a pen, for every call, you might have to *realize* that pen against that surface. In Windows, you select the pen into the DC, and a target surface–compatible representation of that pen gets cached inside the DC. The pen is realized only once, but you can make a million lines or rectangles.

Realization is a nebulous concept that applies to nearly all GDI graphics objects and means different things for different objects. You ask for pens and brushes in an ideal color—maybe a color that doesn't exist on the system—and then the system finds a real color as close to that one you wanted as possible. That's realization. Fonts get realized: you specify an idealized version of what you want for a font and select it into a DC, where it is matched to an available physical font. Palettes get realized, too; *RealizePalette* sends the idealized palette to the physical device. When you select a pattern brush into a DC (it can be a bitmap of any bit depth), you create a brush that matches the destination bitmap. This concept of realization applies to all graphics objects that you can select.

Most of the time when you're blitting or drawing, you just take the source and copy it to the destination. But other logical operations also let you combine the source and destination. The raster operation, or ROP, is your way of specifying what logical operation to use.

Anthony Lapadula

When you're using a pen to write on a surface, one possible raster operation (ROP) you can use is to copy the pen pixels onto the destination surface. You can also use other operations like XORing pixels or ANDing them or ORing them. There are 16 possible combinations of source and destination, and those combinations are known as ROP2. For all the BitBlt APIs, there's a ROP3, which combines three pixels to produce one destination pixel: the brush currently selected in the DC is combined with the source and the destination. The ROP4 is even more obscure and really comes into play only with *MaskBlt*. With a ROP4, a mask says whether pixels are foreground or background.

BASE GDI OBJECTS

Inside the Windows CE GDI, everything is a C++ object. The base class is called *GDIOBJ*, and it has only a few methods on it: *Increment*, *Decrement*, *DeleteObject*, *GetObject*, *GetObjectType*, and *SelectObject*.

All GDI objects are reference counted, but they're not strong ref-counts like they are with COM objects, where when the COM object's ref-count hits zero, the object can basically destroy itself. For a GDI object, if the ref-count hits zero, a *DeleteObject* call is allowed to succeed. The programmer is still responsible for deleting the resources.

The base GDI object has some virtual functions for tasks all the other actual GDI objects do: deleting themselves, getting a description of themselves, and selecting themselves into a DC.

Our handle table is just an array of handles to objects: it takes the handles that we give to the user process and maps them to the actual objects in our code. For us, the mapping is fairly direct. The handles we give to developers have a 2-bit reuse count that says how many times a slot in the handle table has been reused, and a 16-bit index into our handle table (which is just an array). The reuse count just wraps around.

Apps have a lot of problems with stale handles. Let's say an app calls *CreatePen* and gets an *HPEN*. It deletes the pen and creates a brush, but it still has this *HPEN* floating around. So it calls *SelectObject* to select it into a DC and, goodness, the *HPEN* is no longer an *HPEN* but an *HBRUSH*. And the call is going to succeed anyway! You thought you selected a pen, but you actually selected a brush! The app is going to get very, very confused. That's just the problem with the Win32 API. It's very polymorphic. You pass a handle and something inside has to figure out what kind of handle it is. It's very type-unsafe.

By putting those two reuse bits in the handle, we have a 75 percent chance that a scenario like that won't happen. Our debug builds print error messages warning people about stale handles. These bugs are really difficult to track down without help from the operating system.

The operating system is responsible for not leaking objects when apps don't clean up after themselves. Suppose an app creates an *HPEN* and forgets to delete it before the app goes away. Gwes.exe gets notified when that application terminates. Then, because of some sleazy bit-packing tricks and our handle table, we're able to know which process created which GDI object. So basically we just sweep the handle table and look for any objects that were owned by the dying process and delete them. The app misbehaved, but the OS has to make sure that nothing bad happens.

We actually sweep the handle table a couple of times. We sweep through once and delete all DCs, and then we sweep through again and delete everything else. If you have a pen selected into a DC, when the DC goes away, the DC releases one ref-count on the pen. After we delete all the container DCs, we can delete the objects safely.

Of course, the right way for apps to behave is not to leave stuff around when they go away. In debug builds, we print out an error message telling the app which object handle it should have freed. In Win 3.1, if you didn't delete things, they just leaked out; whereas in Windows CE, as in Windows 95 and Windows NT, the system cleans up after you.

GRAPHICS PRIMITIVES

A fairly significant architectural feature is that the Windows CE GDI never touches pixels. Everything goes through the driver; the driver does the actual pixel pushing.

The driver is a subset of the Windows NT DDI. It looks a lot like a Windows NT DDI, but without a lot of handshaking capability. A lot of the functions are eliminated.

On the desktop (Windows NT, Windows 95, and Windows 98), the driver always has the option to say, "I don't know how to do that operation," and then punt back to GDI; the desktop GDI has the ability to write the pixels. We don't have that capability. To keep our memory footprint small, we just decided the driver has to support everything that actually touches pixels.

The GDI primitives are: rectangle, polyline, polygon, ellipse, and roundrect. The driver really only knows how to do lines and blits. So how do you get from all of the GDI drawing primitives to lines and blits?

SetPixel and *GetPixel* are blits that treat a pixel as a 1-pixel-by-1-pixel rectangle.

Rectangle is fairly easy because all you have is a series of blits, and you call into the driver with a brush for the interior and 4 blits for the edges of the rectangle. You take the brush currently selected in the DC and paint the interior, and then you take the pen currently selected in the DC and draw around the exterior. If you want to paint a rectangle, one way is to select the null pen into the DC and call *Rectangle*. That will paint the interior of the rectangle.

Polyline draws a line through the points. If the pen is wide—more than one pixel wide—we turn it into a region to fill; GDI makes every line segment an area to fill and passes the areas to the driver.

Polygon assumes the series of points is closed. If it isn't, we close it for you. We paint the interior and then go around the outside. The driver sees one polygon fill followed by either a polyline or, if the pen is more than one pixel wide, another polygon fill for the wide band on the outside.

Ellipse and *RoundRect* are the only objects that actually have curves in them. You pass the bounding rectangle of the ellipse. You can fairly easily figure out the appropriate Bézier spline for each quadrant of that ellipse: we have a Bézier flattener that turns each Bézier spline into a series of straight-line segments that the driver can handle.

RoundRect, if you think about it, is nothing more than an ellipse with a couple of straight-line segments stuck between the curves on the corners. So it turns out that *RoundRect* is a pretty trivial addition to an ellipse.

The Microsoft Windows 3.1 default had cosmetic pens. Windows 95 and Windows NT have geometric pens, and you can ask for beveled ends and square ends. Windows CE doesn't support geometric pens. We support the simpler pen implementation, closer to cosmetic pens.

The way we handle drawing these shapes is a good example of the trade-offs we make—we trade memory footprint for execution speed of uncommon operations. We could have wide pens, wide-pen ellipses, or any number of things special-cased in the driver, but it's just not worth the extra bytes.

PALETTES

One of the questions we get asked a lot is, "What is the Windows CE palette?" The answer is that we don't have a Windows CE palette. The device driver provides its preferred palette on startup and says whether the palette is changeable. Some devices have a hard-coded palette; the Windows CE palette on those devices is that hardware's palette.

Although you don't have a universal system palette, you do have a palette for the device driver that you happen to be talking to. We do recommend strongly that OEMs build into their devices the halftone palette that we ship as source code. That halftone palette is called different names, such as the Windows 95 palette or the halftone palette. Windows 95 uses it; Windows NT uses it; Internet Explorer uses it. So you can author your resources to that palette and, we hope, have no color conversion at run time.

If you ask developers about the most confusing part of GDI on the desktop, I think, hands down, they're going to say the palette model. There's a famous paper on MSDN called "The Palette Manager—How and Why It Does What It Does." It's a 20-page document. You read this thing; you scratch your head; and you read it again, and then you scratch your head some more. I've probably read it ten times. Every time I glean a little bit more from it.

On the desktop, the palette manager merges requests from multiple applications to make everybody as happy as possible. When you create a palette on the desktop, you can put in these little flags, the *peFlags* element of each PALETTEENTRY, that tell the palette manager what you're intending to do with the palette entry. These flags can say, "Don't map this. Don't let anybody else use this palette entry, or I'm going to change this palette entry a lot." The desktop makes it very hard to change the upper 10 and bottom 10 colors, the so-called Windows colors. Even though a call can tell Windows, "Look, I know what I'm doing," the desktop won't let you set the first and last entry, which are black and white, respectively.

In Windows CE, we ignore all of that. You just select a palette into the DC, and the colors have a one-to-one mapping between the logical palette and the physical palette on the device. All Windows CE palettes are identity palettes. Windows CE has no palette manager. We refer to the Windows CE palette design as "the civil libertarian model of palettes." You can do what you want to with the system palette. We trust that you'll be a good palette citizen.

We have no restrictions. You want to select a 256-entry palette that's all shades of red? Go for it. Your screen will turn red. The task bar, the system dialogues…everything will be red.

We really simplified what it means to support palettes in Windows CE. We're hopeful we have a model that people can actually understand and fit into their heads. I think we did a good job of simplifying, minimizing the footprint, and maintaining reasonable functionality.

Our palette allows us also to do a few things that I think the desktop doesn't do. For example, sometimes on the desktop, if you blit from one DC to another DC, you simply won't get the right colors. Some weird artifacts on the desktop cause you to get the wrong colors unless you use *StretchBlt*, which is smarter about performing color conversions than *BitBlt*. No such restriction applies in Windows CE. You can blit from one DC to any other DC and get the best color conversion possible.

If color must be converted from one source to one destination, we actually cache that color conversion object in the display driver. Color conversion is a very complex problem. Think about blitting from one 8-bit palettized surface to a different 8-bit palettized surface. In the places where the palettes don't match, you basically have to take the first entry in the source, find the nearest entry in the destination, and then repeat. It's a 256-by-256 problem. It's a very expensive operation. So caching the result of the operation is a really big performance win.

But developers don't use lots of different kinds of palettes in your application. The more palettes you use, the more combinations of sources and destinations you use, and the more likely you are to blow that cache. Your performance will suffer miserably. Even if the color conversion is cached, if you're really serious about performance, you should perform blit operations to the same format and palette as your destination. Do the work up front to handle the conversion—whether it's cached or not—so that the blit you really want to be fast can proceed without conversion.

People accustomed to the desktop palette model can get into trouble if they assume that the palette manager is going to bail them out. If you have a window on top of other windows and you want to change the palette, you call *RealizePalette*. On the desktop, the palette manager runs around and tries to make everything in the background look good. But on Windows CE, items in the background look terrible because they are mapped to a different palette and there is no palette manager. So we tell everybody, don't muck with the palette. If you must change the system palette, make sure your window is full-screen exclusive and you cover everything else on the screen or it will all look bad. Of course, developers can do whatever they want, but if they have to change the palette, we ask them not to change the so-called Windows colors, the first 10 and last 10 colors. For games and for some applications, owning the palette completely makes sense, but those developers will have to work harder to be good neighbors.

We have some strange corners in our palette model as well. If you call *CreateDIBSection* to create a bitmap, you have to pass in a color table—basically a palette that's attached to the bitmap—which defines how you interpret the pixels in that bitmap. Other APIs that create bitmaps don't accept a color table, and in these cases the color process gets a little bit confusing.

If you call *CreateBitmap* for any bit depth other than 8 bits, that bitmap gets associated with the default color table for that bit depth. For 1-bit bitmaps, the default we used was (of course) black and white. For 2-bit bitmaps, the H/PC set the precedent that the default was to be black, dark gray, light gray, and white. For 4-bit images, we selected the desktop 16-bit EGA palette, a really hideous neon palette. For higher bit depths than 8—that is, for 16, 24, and 32—we used the default RGB mask specifications that the desktop uses. So we had compelling defaults for all those cases except for an 8-bit image.

To allow palette animation to work, we do something different for 8-bit bitmaps. For 8-bit bitmaps, *CreateBitmap* returns a bitmap that has no color table associated with it: how do you interpret the colors? What does a pixel value of 17 mean? Well, that's where the palette in the DC comes into play. If you have an 8-bit bitmap with no color table, you interpret the bitmap's colors relative to the palette that is selected into the DC. That enables things like palette animation. You can create a bitmap, select in a palette, blit the bitmap to the screen, then change the palette in the DC and blit it again, change the palette, blit it again. In retrospect, that's probably one of the more confusing things about the palette model. When you run on a 2-bit device, create an 8-bit bitmap without a color table, and then try to blit off of that surface, we try to interpret that 8-bit image relative to the four-entry palette in your DC, and bad things happen. So when people complain that they're blitting from what they think is an 8-bit color bitmap and all they get are shades of gray, there's a good chance they forgot to select a color palette into the DC.

BITMAPS

There are different kinds of bitmaps. You can get a handle to a bitmap by calling *CreateDIBSection*, *CreateBitmap*, or *CreateCompatibleBitmap*. The first two are allocated in system memory. *CreateCompatibleBitmap* asks the driver to allocate the memory and, depending on the driver and the hardware, the driver might be able to allocate video memory. Video memory is a prized resource because blit operations to it and from it can be much faster. If you're really concerned about speed, and you really want your bitmaps to be fast, call *CreateCompatibleBitmap*.

On some platforms, hardware acceleration is available only when both the source and the destination are in video memory. So having both the source and the destination in video memory boosts video performance a great deal.

FONTS

Windows CE has a fairly complete implementation of TrueType fonts. Rasterizing a glyph takes a long time—when you ask for a letter in a brand new font, we have to get that glyph out of the font file, scale it to the right size, and rasterize it. To keep the time down, we have a glyph cache. Once you've created a glyph at a particular size, it makes sense to cache it and leave it sitting around. So there are some big performance vs. memory trade-offs involved here with respect to how big you make that cache and when you flush it.

As a developer, you have control over that in two ways: you can set the global size of the glyph cache via the registry at the time you build the Windows CE system, or the individual app running on the Windows CE system can control when the font gets thrown away. The glyph cache is tied to the *HFONT*, which is the handle of the font, so when you call *DeleteObject* on that font, the glyph cache goes away. If you want fast text performance, it behooves you to keep that *HFONT* sitting around: the glyph cache will live for that duration. If you're bringing up some line of text over and over again, and every time you bring up the text you create the font, write the text, and then delete the *HFONT*, your system is going to be really slow.

The cache defaults to 4 KB, which is a good cache size for accommodating the typical point size for the English alphabet. Most of the letters in the English alphabet will fit in a 4-KB cache. Really huge letters that fill up the screen will exceed that cache size. And if you're running a Far East device, which instead of 52 uppercase and lowercase letters has 10,000 characters, you have little hope of caching all the glyphs. If you're really serious about this, try running your app and timing it. You'll see a fairly sharp knee bend in the timing curve as you increase the size of your cache: because your fonts stay in the cache, your performance will suddenly get much better.

We support anti-aliased fonts, but only with the cooperation of the driver, because anti-aliasing is platform-specific. If the driver doesn't report that it supports this capability, we just turn off the anti-aliased font support. We don't emulate the capability in GDI.

GDI COMPONENTS

The GDI in Windows CE 2.0 has 17 components. You must include the core GDI component Mgbase, but other than that, most components are optional. There are a few dependencies, but for most of the components, you have the choice to add them or not add them. The common configuration consists of all the components using either raster fonts or TrueType fonts. That's basically what ships in the H/PC.

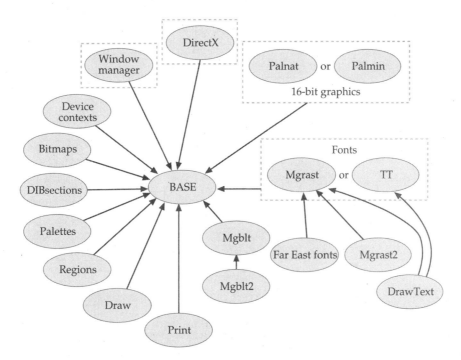

Although the GDI is componentized, not all possible combinations have been tested. For a current list of tested configurations, see the Embedded Toolkit for Windows CE.

We also have a game platform under development that handles most of its graphical output through DirectX. It needs only a very small subset of GDI. Basically all you can do with that system is to load the bitmaps as resources and blit them to the screen, create off-screen bitmaps and draw to them, and load raster fonts and use them to draw text on the screen. All the other drawing in that system is done through DirectX.

RESOURCES

Topic	Resource
Microsoft Windows message-driven programming	*Programming Windows 95*, by Charles Petzold (Microsoft Press, 1996)
Componentizing GWE	Microsoft Windows CE Embedded Toolkit for Visual C++
Specific Microsoft Windows API functions and Windows messages	Microsoft Windows CE Toolkit for Visual C++

6 Porting to New Hardware

*T*his chapter is about porting Microsoft Windows CE to a new device. Using the Microsoft-provided kernel for the targeted microprocessor, the OEM or embedded developer implements the boot loader, the OEM Adaptation Layer (OAL), and device drivers. Drivers are usually organized into four categories: Windows CE native drivers, Windows CE stream interface drivers, NDIS network drivers, and Universal Serial Bus (USB) drivers. Other driver models may also be supported in future releases of Windows CE. Several third-party companies provide porting development services and can assist with OAL and driver development. In this chapter, "OEM" is used to refer to whoever is doing the port.

Note that although Windows CE supports a variety of different microprocessors, it is not processor-independent. The Microsoft Windows CE OS team ports the kernel to a specific processor and then makes that processor-specific kernel library available to OEMs.

The OAL functions communicate between the kernel and device hardware such as timers, serial ports, parallel ports, and Ethernet hardware. The OAL porting effort also includes power management interfaces and hardware interrupt handling. The OAL is designed to be very easy to implement, enabling a wide variety of Windows CE devices. The routines used to implement the boot loader represent a subset of the OAL and can be reused in the OAL implementation.

Native device drivers are linked with the OS, whereas stream-interface device drivers can be installed at any time. These differences correspond to the distinctions in the hardware that the drivers operate. The Windows CE native drivers operate hardware built into the device, such as the keyboard and touch-sensitive LCD display. The Windows CE stream-interface drivers operate peripherals that can be connected to the device via its serial port or PC Card slot, such as modems and digital cameras.

Microsoft provides sample native device drivers that are split into two parts to make driver implementation fast and efficient: the Model Device Driver (MDD) and the Physical Device Driver (PDD). The OEM can choose to make device-specific changes to the thin PDD and simply link with the MDD. Although their use is strongly recommended, the MDD and PDD libraries are provided for convenience only and are not required.

This chapter discusses the new driver models that are unique to Windows CE. Frank Fite, Thomas Fenwick, and Larry Morris discuss the native drivers, offering a high-level description of the interrupt service routine (ISR) and interrupt service thread (IST) model and several examples of implementations. David Kanz discusses *the stream interface drivers as implemented using the PC Card Services interface. Kanz wrote the Plug and Play system and describes its use of the Windows CE registry for configuration.*

Complete procedural documentation and sample native and stream interface drivers appear in the Windows CE Embedded Toolkit for Visual C++ and the Windows CE Device Driver Kit.

Display drivers and printer drivers are considered to be native drivers but differ slightly from other native drivers. They are not linked to GWE like the other drivers, and users can load them on demand. The display driver uses a subset of the Microsoft Windows NT DDI but is most commonly implemented by using the Microsoft-provided Graphics Primitive Engine (GPE). The printer driver works with the display driver. Anthony Lapadula and Martin Shetter continue their discussion of the GDI that started in Chapter 5, "The GWE Subsystem," to explain the internal workings of the display driver and printer driver.

Developers can use several tools to debug device drivers. These tools include debug messages embedded in the code that can be conditionally activated by using "debug zones," the remote Windows CE debugging shell with commands to examine the state of the software on the device, and the remote kernel debugger WinDbg. The debuggers are transport-independent and allow connection to the device using a serial port, a parallel port, or Ethernet.

By allowing the OEMs to control the lowest levels of the operating system, Windows CE is suitable for real-time applications. Although Windows CE is a general-purpose operating system, it was written so that the OS turns off preemption for bounded amounts of time, guaranteeing that interrupts are processed within specific latencies. And although the OS supports paging, the OS assigns lower priority values to the paging threads so that they will not interfere with real-time threads. The OEM can lock real-time threads into memory so that paging is not required.

Because the OEM implements the native device drivers that process the real-time threads and controls the thread priorities of these device drivers, the OEM can ensure that the overall system meets its specified performance requirements.

Several options are available to OEMs when profiling the operating system port to guarantee that it meets requirements. These include kernel timing and Monte Carlo profiling. Monte Carlo profiling interrupts the OS rapidly to record the instruction pointer, providing statistical information about where most OS processing occurs. In addition, Windows CE supports hardware-assisted profiling, with hooks for OEM-supplied routines to track thread creation, termination, and scheduling.

PORTING FOR EASY ADAPTABILITY

Frank Fite

Easy adaptation is critical. My group doesn't want to get swamped with a thousand phone calls. We have to make sure the OS is easy to adapt.

Porting Windows CE involves three steps:

1. *Porting to a particular processor.* Right now, this is done only by Microsoft, not because we're trying to keep it secret but because to make a really small, fast kernel, we have to abstract every single aspect of the processor, which is hard. And so the processor is bundled into our system; you get a version of the kernel for your processor.

2. *Porting to a particular bus/memory/interrupt architecture.* Windows CE doesn't require any particular architecture: it doesn't require a particular bus, it doesn't require memory to be in a certain place, it doesn't require interrupts to be in a certain place. All those aspects of the architecture are adaptable by the OEM.

Frank Fite

The OEM just has to implement the OEM Adaptation Layer to communicate this hardware-specific information to the kernel. This layer is really a collection of small interrupt service routines and a small number of interfaces, pretty easy to write. We provide sample code for different hardware platforms, and the OEM can adapt it to their specific hardware.

The OAL includes, for example, the power management functions. Not every single Windows CE device is going to need power management—a lot of them are going to be plugged into walls. But devices that need it may have different ways of handling power management, so the hardware people write this layer.

This step also includes writing the built-in and installable device drivers.

3. *Selecting specific components.* After you adapt the sample code to the hardware, you pick the software components: which APIs you want in the system, which communications protocols you want in the system. And that completes the adaptation.

OAL FUNCTIONS FOR IMPLEMENTATION

OAL Function Categories	Functions to Implement
Initialization	*OEMInit, OEMGetExtensionDRAM*
Ethernet	*OEMEthDisableInts, OEMEthEnableInts, OEMEthGetFrame, OEMEthGetSecs, OEMEthInit, OEMEthISR, OEMEthQueryClientInfo, OEMEthSendFrame,* (and debugging-related *IOCTLs*)
High-performance counter (optional)	*QueryPerformanceCounter, QueryPerformanceFrequency*
Interval timer	*GetTickCount*
LED	*OEMWriteDebugLED*
Parallel port	*OEMParallelPortGetByte, OEMParallelPortSendByte*
Power management	*OEMIdle, OEMPowerOff*
Profiling ("instrumented kernel")	*KCP_ScaleDown, KCP_GetStartTime, KCP_GetElapsedTime, OEMProfileTimerEnable, OEMProfileTimerDisable, OEMProfileTimerInit, OEMProfilerISR*
Real-time clock functions	*OEMGetRealTime, OEMSetRealTime, OEMSetAlarmTime*
Object store (registry and database)	*CeChangeDatabaseLCID, ReadRegistryFromOEM, RegCopyFile, RegRestoreFile, WriteRegistryToOEM*
Serial port	*OEMClearDebugCommError, OEMInitDebugSerial, OEMReadDebugByte, OEMWriteDebugByte, OEMWriteDebugString*
System information	*OEMIoControl*
Task tracking	*LogProcessCreate, LogProcessDelete, LogThreadCreate, LogThreadDelete, LogThreadSwitch*

Many of our semiconductor partners and system integrators already provide the appropriate device drivers and adaptation layers. So really, many OEMs will never have to go through this porting process. They'll just get the adaptation code from a system integrator or from the providers of their hardware. That's important, because some of the OEMs we work with really aren't software people at all. They're hardware people, and they would rather get the code they need from someone else than write it themselves.

Thomas Fenwick

The OEM Adaptation Layer is linked with the kernel, Nk.exe. On top of the kernel and the OAL are GWE, the window manager/User subsystem, and Device.exe, the device-driver services. The drivers appear in parallel because they talk to the hardware directly, but they also talk to the kernel and the OAL, and they can talk to GWE. There's no good way to draw the picture—they can all talk to one another.

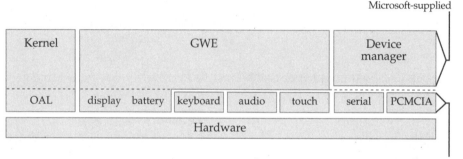

Microsoft-supplied

OEM-supplied

The native drivers—display, battery, keyboard, audio, and touch screen—are linked in to GWE. Device.exe provides higher-level device driver services to make writing drivers for serial and PC Card devices easier.

The Windows CE kernel startup code can't run until the OEMs initialize their hardware. During initialization, a CPU boot vector runs OEM startup code, which has to set up ROM and DRAM access—anything to do with turning off refresh and getting the minimum CPU running. So the OEM startup code runs for a bit, then jumps to *KernelStart* (a symbol that the kernel exports) in unmapped, uncached space.

Thomas Fenwick

The kernel performs some initialization, then calls *OEMInit*. *OEMInit*, which is one of the OAL functions implemented by the OEM, performs any additional hardware setup needed to actually run the system. If as an OEM, you want to perform minimal hardware diagnostics or anything like that, you can do it either in that little bit of OEM startup code or in *OEMInit.*

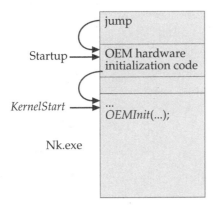

The CPU boot vector jumps to OEM hardware initialization code, which upon completion jumps to the start of the kernel. Early in its startup sequence, the kernel calls the OEM-implemented function OEMInit, which typically installs timers, sets up interrupts, and initializes variables that OEMs can set up.

If the platform—for example, the MIPS or Intel platform—doesn't have a well understood timer channel for generating periodic interrupts, the OEM needs to install that timer in *OEMInit* so that the kernel can conceptualize the passage of time. Some of the device drivers and other processes need to be able to count time, and they can't do that unless the interval timer is running. We expect the timer to have millisecond resolution, so we can get millisecond accuracy for *GetTickCount*. In fact, *GetTickCount* is one of the OAL interfaces that the OEM has to implement.

OEMInit can also set several variables, such as the variable that indicates the end of DRAM. We initialize *OEMInit* to the value we believe it to be so that the OEM can move the function up, if desired. Shortly after *OEMInit*, we call *OEMGetExtensionDRAM* to find out whether an additional noncontiguous bank of DRAM exists. Interrupts are enabled right after *OEMInit*, and then shortly after that, the kernel starts up.

Depending on the configuration, we then load Filesys, GWE, and Device—whatever files are specified in the registry—and then we're running. GWE and Device start loading drivers. For the Handheld PC, for example, GWE loads the keyboard and touch drivers, and Device loads Serial and PCMCIA.

As part of our device driver model, during this initialization, the kernel tables are set up to associate the interrupt IDs with the interrupt threads. Probably the easiest way to explain this is to walk through the initialization for the serial driver. Device.exe is going to call *LoadLibrary("Serial.dll"...)*, and then Serial's initialization routine will set up the hardware:

```
// Serial Initialization routine
// Setup hardware.
hEvent = CreateEvent(...)  // Create an event.
// Set the event, then an ID.
InterruptInitialize(hEvent, SYSINTR_SERIAL);
CreateThread(...)
```

The *InterruptInitialize* call goes down into the kernel and associates an event, specified by the event handle, *hEvent*, with an interrupt ID called SYSINTR_SERIAL. The ID identifies what kind of interrupt was received. And that's actually all the kernel really understands. The kernel knows about the ID, and it knows about that handle. And then, typically, the initialization routine calls *CreateThread* to create the interrupt service thread, which is a standard Win32 user-space thread. So the kernel doesn't really have any understanding of a particular thread associated with an interrupt; the kernel just sets an event whenever the interrupt occurs.

The driver calls *InterruptInitialize*, passing an ID and an event handle, and says, "Anytime an ISR returns this interrupt ID, set this event." The kernel takes that interrupt ID and interrupt event, records them in its tables, and then calls *OEMInterruptEnable.* The kernel is really just a messenger for most of this interrupt handling. Let me go over what that interrupt service thread does. The normal service model is this:

```
while (...) {
    WaitForSingleObject(hEvent, timeout);
    // Process interrupt
    InterruptDone(id);
    // Additional processing
} // Loop and wait for next interrupt to process.
```

The IST calls *WaitForSingleObject* to wait on the event. You do all the work associated with processing the interrupt, then call *InterruptDone*. That tells the OEM adaptation layer that the driver has satisfied the need for this interrupt; the interrupt can be enabled again when the driver is ready to take the next ISR.

The ISR is typically very short:

```
// ISR
// Interrupts are disabled.
identify the interrupt;
mask or dismiss the interrupt;
return the interrupt ID;
// Interrupts are on again.
```

The ISR masks the interrupt and returns the ID to the kernel; the kernel calls *SetEvent*. The IST waiting for that event sees that it has been set and starts running.

The hardware holds off all interrupts while the ISR is running. That's actually an automatic process that the chip performs when it generates the interrupt exception—another reason not to spend a lot of time in an ISR. The more time spent in the ISR, the longer the ISR latency is going to be.

THE DRIVER MODEL

Larry Morris

The Windows CE driver model is probably not as familiar as other models to some of the Win32 people, but it is a pretty traditional driver model in which the interrupt service routine does as little work as possible. It's more like the UNIX model.

Larry Morris

The reason you don't want to do a whole lot of work in the ISR is that this version, Windows CE 2.10, doesn't support nestable interrupts. While you're servicing one interrupt, all other interrupts are masked. And as a result, the longest code path through an ISR ends up affecting the ISR latency for the entire system. You should do the smallest amount of work to service the interrupt and get out of there and do most of the work up in the thread, which is just a normal Win32 process.

When a driver is initialized, it creates a standard Win32 event and calls *InterruptInitialize* to associate that event with a DWORD representing a system interrupt SYSINTR value. When a hardware interrupt comes in through the kernel and gets routed to the ISR, the ISR does its work and returns the SYSINTR value to the kernel. The kernel looks at that SYSINTR value and signals the Win32 event that is associated with the SYSINTR.

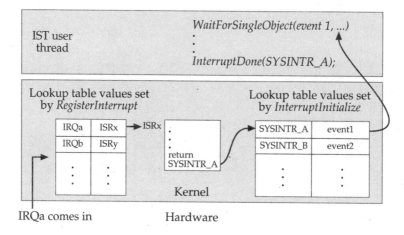

The OEM implements the ISR and IST and makes calls to set up the mappings in the kernel's lookup tables. The kernel sets an event, which is a very fast thread synchronization object, to signal the interrupt service thread.

The other important functions associated with interrupts are *Interrupt-Done* and *InterruptDisable*. The IST calls *InterruptDone* when the function has finished servicing the interrupt and is ready for the kernel to unmask it. *InterruptDisable* is the opposite of *InterruptInitialize* and cancels the Win32 event/SYSINTR pairing that was established in *InterruptInitialize*.

Most ISRs decide only whether the interrupt is a spurious interrupt, handle that, and then immediately return the SYSINTR. The IST does all the work and calls *InterruptDone*. At that point, we can unmask that interrupt. All other interrupts could have occurred during that time, but that particular one is masked until we call *InterruptDone*.

InterruptDisable is not usually called. Most drivers are not loaded dynamically; they load up once at boot time and stay there forever, so the interrupt is never disabled.

This is how all the native, or built-in, drivers work. To a large extent "built-in" means that the driver has an ISR. Drivers can be layered on top of built-in drivers that typically won't do any of this handling. (For Example, the PCMCIA and serial drivers commonly have other drivers layered on them.) An upper level driver written to open and communicate through the serial driver isn't going to actually handle any of the interrupts. It won't have a specific ISR associated with it but will use the serial driver's ISR.

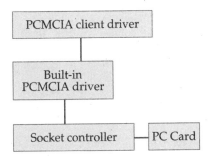

Rather than deal directly with the ISR and IST, PC Card client drivers use a different, higher-level stream interface. A native PC Card driver handles the direct hardware interaction with the card and passes the appropriate information to the higher-level client driver.

Or if the driver is layered on PCMCIA, the PCMCIA driver deals with all of the actual interrupts. It has the ISR for the PCMCIA card and provides socket services. You can write a driver that layers above PCMCIA, but that driver won't deal with interrupts at the bus level. Of course, the driver will deal with acknowledging the interrupt at the peripheral. If you need to clear the interrupt condition on the modem and the modem is a 16550, you might have to read the LSR or the MSR to clear the interrupt condition at the peripheral. But that situation is separate from the OAL functions *InterruptDone* and *InterruptEnable*, which operate on the interrupt at the system's interrupt controller.

THE MDD AND PDD

The Module Device Driver (MDD) and Platform Device Driver (PDD) libraries confuse people a lot. Architecturally, the MDD and PDD don't have anything to do with how the driver works. It's really more an issue of how the driver code is organized into libraries.

The theory behind the MDD and PDD is that two big tasks are involved when an OEM writes a driver: talking to Win32 and controlling the peripheral. Of those, the task that the OEM understands is how to control the peripheral. If I have an SH3 built-in serial port and one of the OEM's SCIs, how do I enable it? How do I set the baud rate? How do I perform a variety of functions? The OEMs know how to answer those questions. What we try to do is split up the responsibility for the tasks and let the OEMs write the platform device driver that accesses the hardware.

117

The MDD contains the Win32 part: the model of the API set and all the structures and functions. In theory, the MDD works on any similar device. For example, as long as your hardware more or less looks like a typical serial peripheral, the serial MDD will work with it.

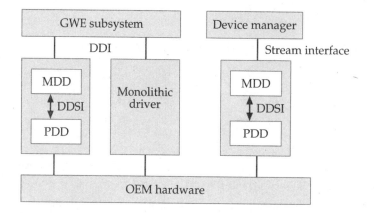

OEMs can write the entire device driver themselves (shown here as a monolithic driver) or can provide a smaller piece called the Platform Device Driver that interacts with the Microsoft-provided Model Device Driver. The MDD and PDD are simply libraries that can help OEMs develop drivers quickly.

But remember that MDD/PDD is not the actual driver model: MDD/PDD refers to the files. The question that often comes up is "What if I don't like the MDD code or don't want to use it?" That's fine. We provide the code for your use if you want it. Again, using it is not required. If you wanted to implement all the Win32 work yourself, you could definitely cut down some of the overhead. I sure wouldn't say that you'd *significantly* cut it down, but I would say that you could *mildly* improve the performance of your driver by writing a monolithic driver. However, the trade-off is being unable to take advantage of our fixes. We keep the MDDs consistent across releases, so if I find a bug in the upper layers, you can pick up my fix in a subsequent release. Once you've gone to a monolithic driver, you're responsible for fixing all bugs.

There have been rare cases of people writing a monolithic driver but not for performance reasons: they wanted to tweak our MDD to do something that it wasn't currently doing. They copied the MDD into their directory, made a few modifications to it, and then linked to the private version rather than to the one we supplied. Most people use our MDDs.

We try to define the DDSI layer—the layer between the MDD and the PDD—so that it looks like one of the generic peripherals for that class. The audio driver was generically patterned after some DMA-based audio transfers. For the PCMCIA controller, we figure out the generic functions of most any PCMCIA controller. For the serial driver, the interface looks like a 16550 and assumes that four general classes of interrupts exist. For example, whenever the serial MDD sees a line status interrupt, the MDD calls your line status handler. If it sees a transmit interrupt return, the MDD calls your transmit handler.

If you had some really esoteric peripheral that didn't look anything like a generic serial device, you could just override the interrupt. You could decide that the receive interrupt is the only interrupt you'll ever return from your interrupt status function. The MDD would see that and call your receive routine: you could just write a receive routine that did all the work by using that one function. As you can see, you can override our definition.

GETTING TO PERIPHERALS

One question people ask quite often is, "Since the ISTs are running as just a standard user-mode thread, how do I get to a peripheral?" Because the ISR is running in kernel mode, it has access to all the physical memory. However, once a driver gets up into the interrupt service thread, it's running in the process space, and it has to map that.

You use the *VirtualAlloc* and *VirtualCopy* functions to map physical memory into your virtual address space and then access it via the pointer. If you look at all of our sample drivers, you'll see that they call *VirtualAlloc* and *VirtualCopy* to get at that memory space.

We also added support for a number of the Windows NT HAL functions: *HalGetBusData, HalSetBusData, MmMapIoSpace, MmUnmapIoSpace, READ_PORT_UCHAR, WRITE_PORT_UCHAR READ_REGISTER_UCHAR,* and *WRITE_REGISTER_UCHAR.* These functions abstract the way memory is accessed and, in theory, allow you to write a driver that's basically CPU- and platform-independent.

ISR AND IST DESIGN: LATENCIES

ISRs are relatively fast—a few microseconds maximum latency into the ISR—but the speed depends, of course, on who wrote the ISR and what it's doing. The exact value is platform-dependent. But I would hope that the value is fairly small, on the order of tens of microseconds maximum, because the latency in your ISR defines the maximum latency for the entire system. Most ISRs that I've timed have been significantly under that.

The latency to get up to the interrupt service thread can vary substantially, depending on the processor and the clock rate of the processor. It's on the order of 100 or 200 microseconds.

We support priority inheritance, which is a method for handling priority inversion. Priority inheritance is not a driver issue, per se, but if you're an OEM and you're writing a driver, you want to think about it. The system currently has eight priority levels, and drivers normally run at one of the upper two levels, either THREAD_PRIORITY_TIME_CRITICAL or THREAD_PRIORITY_HIGHEST (which is actually the second highest level).

THREAD PRIORITY LEVELS, FROM HIGHEST TO LOWEST PRIORITY

Value	Priority
0	THREAD_PRIORITY_TIME_CRITICAL
1	THREAD_PRIORITY_HIGHEST
2	THREAD_PRIORITY_ABOVE_NORMAL
3	THREAD_PRIORITY_NORMAL
4	THREAD_PRIORITY_BELOW_NORMAL
5	THREAD_PRIORITY_LOWEST
6	THREAD_PRIORITY_ABOVE_IDLE
7	THREAD_PRIORITY_IDLE

Windows CE is fully preemptive, and we round-robin within a priority level except in the case of THREAD_PRIORITY_TIME_CRITICAL. Once a time-critical thread loads, it's going to run to completion. To eliminate unnecessary scheduling time, we do not round-robin among the time-critical threads.

So if you have a serial driver and a PCMCIA driver that are both time-critical, and a PCMCIA interrupt comes in while the serial IST is running, that PCMCIA interrupt is going to be held off until the serial IST is finished.

The interrupt itself is dealt with, but the IST, the handling of the event resulting from the interrupt, is held off. You should not design many time-critical threads into the system. And you should have a clear understanding of the impact that one time-critical driver will have on another. THREAD_PRIORITY_TIME_CRITICAL is powerful, but it's to be used with caution because of the scheduling characteristics.

We've seen cases of a shared resource between an IST and its lower-priority worker threads. The problem, of course, is that if the worker thread owns that resource at the time the interrupt fires, then we have to do a priority inversion—we have to raise the priority of that worker thread and let it run as long as it takes to free up the shared resource. Then we have to go through a context switch to schedule the highest priority thread, which costs time.

And so even though we can say, "Yes, we have deterministic scheduling to get to a thread," and "Yes, we have very good latencies into the IST," if priority inversion occurs, it becomes nondeterministic by the time it's all said and done. If some unknown number of priority inversions occurs based on resource contention, it's a driver issue.

Ideally, the OEM sets up a producer/consumer model that doesn't require critical sections. You can design the data structures so that the critical thread doesn't ever block on the other thread, as with a properly constructed ring buffer. Then you don't need to protect that resource. You can figure out how to make the really time-critical part be their IST and move all the rest of the work out into worker threads.

The main goal is to get rid of resource contention between a high priority thread and a lower priority thread, or even between two threads with the same priority level. You don't want someone else to own the resource that prevents your interrupt service thread from running.

WRITING NATIVE DRIVERS: CASE STUDIES

We've done a lot of work with the OEMs on drivers; in Windows CE 1.0, the people on my team were the primary contacts for all the OEMs.

TOUCH DEVICE DRIVERS

The best case scenario is when the ISR does nothing. Let's say you're an OEM, and your touch hardware takes care of all the work so that when your get an interrupt, the hardware says, "Here are the time-correlated, closely clustered touch samples." It sends a group of three x and three y positions, and 12 milliseconds later sends another group of three x, y values. We go right up to the IST, the IST reads out of the DMA buffer, and we continue. That's the beautiful scenario.

But with some touch hardware, you won't find an application-specific integrated circuit (ASIC) or any hardware assist. You need to go out and enable some circuit on the left edge of the panel, then wait for a settle time so that the panel can charge up. Then you kick off the ADC to measure the x value. You wait another very small amount of time, typically a few microseconds, and then enable some other circuit. You delay for a period of time, and then set up again and grab the y sample. You need to go through that routine multiple times because normally a single sample isn't sufficient; you want some type of voting or filtering, so you take three time-correlated samples. And in order to take three samples, you need about 8 or 10 microseconds, far faster than the IST's scheduling time. So you need to take care of that in a little state machine in the ISR.

But, then again, we want to keep the latency small. A 12-microsecond delay is kind of on the hairy edge. I wouldn't recommend doing a spin loop in there, but on the other hand, I think you need to look at how fast the processor is. If the overhead to get out of the current ISR and into the next ISR is 20 microseconds, then one way or another you're going to eat up the CPU, so you can do a spin loop. It just comes down to doing the math and figuring out the maximum blocked interrupt latency time.

SERIAL DRIVER TIMING ISSUES

Another example scenario involves a 16450-type device. At 115-KB baud, a character arrives about every 86 microseconds. Even if we run a fairly fast processor, another character will arrive by the time the IST finishes executing. And as soon as we do the *InterruptDone*, the IST immediately fires again with the next character, and we have just eaten 100 percent of the CPU by bouncing back and forth between the ISR and the IST.

So we actually put a small ring buffer in the ISR that stores not only the characters but also some of the line status information, because we wanted that information correlated with the characters that arrived. The ISR gobbles characters and stuffs them into the software ring buffer.

We implemented different designs. When we had a hardware timer available and could implement a character-timeout interrupt, we stuffed characters into the software buffer until a certain amount of time had gone by without any new characters arriving, then we signaled the IST that we had the data. Or sometimes we'd signal the IST all the time and just assume we're going to eat most of the CPU because the IST is continually getting interrupts saying data is available. But at least we don't ever have to worry about overrunning the FIFO and actually dropping a byte. If you don't have some type of character timeout, you have no way of knowing when to signal the IST. You can't say, "Oh, I'm going to signal at eight characters," because the device on the other side might only send seven and the ISR will never generate the interrupt. So you're going to use most of the CPU.

I can't think of any other interesting ISRs we've handled. But you can pretty much tweak the driver model however you want within certain constraints—if you consume time in the ISR, you're going to change the latency of the system.

Porting Development Tools

We offer a number of development tools to bring up Windows CE on a new platform. Let me describe them.

Boot Loaders

Once the basic kernel is running, typically you install a boot loader. The boot loader is a very small Windows CE image, usually modified from the sample supplied in the embedded toolkit. The boot loader communicates with the debug shell and downloads .bin files to either RAM or Flash. RAM images are preferred since they let you set breakpoints in the debugger.

Remote Debug Shells

We just added a new shell called Cesh.exe, which supports the parallel port and two more transports: serial and Ethernet. Ethernet is the preferred transport because it allows the boot loader, the debug shell, the debugger, and the debug console to communicate over a single physical transport.

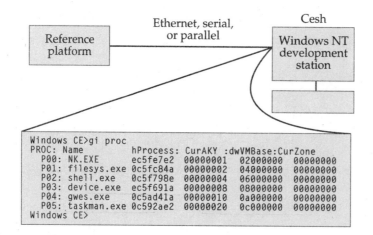

```
Windows CE>gi proc
PROC: Name        hProcess: CurAKY :dwVMBase:CurZone
  P00: NK.EXE      ec5fe7e2 00000001 02000000 00000000
  P01: filesys.exe 0c5fc84a 00000002 04000000 00000000
  P02: shell.exe   0c5f798e 00000004 06000000 00000000
  P03: device.exe  ec5f691a 00000008 08000000 00000000
  P04: gwes.exe    0c5ad41a 00000010 0a000000 00000000
  P05: taskman.exe 0c592ae2 00000020 0c000000 00000000
Windows CE>
```

To examine the state of the device, the Cesh remote debug shell can communicate with the device over Ethernet, serial, and parallel connections. This illustration shows the GI, or Get Information command for processes, including the process name, its access key, and the start address for its slot in virtual memory.

The debug shell lets the developer launch executables and examine the state of the system. If a file and/or an executable is requested but not found in the target's local file system, the debug shell acts as a remote file system, loading the file into the device as if it were part of the root file system. Other debug shell commands list all threads, modules, or processes; examine the state of all threads in the system; and turn on and off various debug zones.

DEBUG PORTS

The debug port is an output-only port where RETAILMSG and DEBUGMSG send their output. In version 1 and version 2, this port was always a serial port, and the developer typically used a null cable and ran a terminal program on the desktop to display the messages while debugging. In Windows 2.1, the debug console can be routed through the debug Ethernet connection and displayed in a window on the desktop. Eshell is the controlling program for all of the Ethernet debug utilities and the Ethernet boot loader.

KERNEL-LEVEL DEBUGGERS

The kernel-level debugger is typically used for debugging kernel, OAL, and device-driver modules. The kernel-level debugger requires a special kernel stub to run. When a break occurs in the kernel-level debugger, all processing on the target stops. With the application-level debugger, a breakpoint stops scheduling for only the process containing the break. The app-level debugger does not use a dedicated transport but instead communicates over the standard IP stack. This is why the app-level debugger can't be used to debug device drivers—as soon as a breakpoint is encountered in a device driver, the debug link is dropped because the process containing all of the device drivers is no longer scheduled.

In Windows CE 1.0 and 2.0, the kernel debugger communicated over the debug serial port by calling the *OEMWriteDebugString* and *OEMReadDebugString* functions. This functionality has now been extended to enable either the serial interface or the Ethernet interface. Again, the Ethernet interface is preferred if available, since it is easier to configure and significantly faster than the serial-based debugger.

We also added another API to support debugging, *OEMWriteDebugLED*. This routine provides a standard way for drivers and applications to write values to diagnostic LEDs.

PC Card Services

David Kanz

On Windows NT and Windows 95, drivers are .SYS or .VXD files, but on Windows CE, the native drivers are Win32 DLLs. And so instead of using port I/O, the peripheral is mapped to a range of memory, and you use regular read and write operations instead of port in and out operations.

Because the drivers are user-mode Win32 DLLs, they can't access the physical address directly and have to use a virtual address. You know your device's physical address range and its length in memory, so you call *VirtualAlloc* to get the virtual address, and then call *VirtualCopy* to map the virtual address to the physical range. The driver can then use that virtual address to access the device. You call *VirtualFree* to clean up when you're done.

David Kanz

The PCMCIA specification defines a card-services interface that shields the PC Card driver from system-specific PCMCIA hardware. On WinCE, Pcmcia.dll abstracts the hardware specifics so that a PC Card driver can run unchanged on systems with wildly different PCMCIA socket controllers.

Typically in the CPU's memory map, a physical range is mapped to PCMCIA. The PCMCIA driver itself then maps regions of PCMCIA to the card. The PCMCIA driver is platform-specific, but the card-specific drivers are not. All they know about is the particular PC Card that they're going to drive, such as the modem or the flash disk. The client driver knows the registers it wants to control, and the PCMCIA driver knows where the registers are in system memory and can provide the virtual mapping. So the card-services interface calls set up this virtual mapping, and then the client-specific driver can use that virtual address to directly access the PC Card.

The PC Card driver calls *CardRequestWindow* and *CardMapWindow* and, if the card is an I/O card, *CardRequestConfiguration.* Our implementation of *CardMapWindow* in the native PCMCIA driver makes the calls to *VirtualAlloc* and *VirtualCopy*.

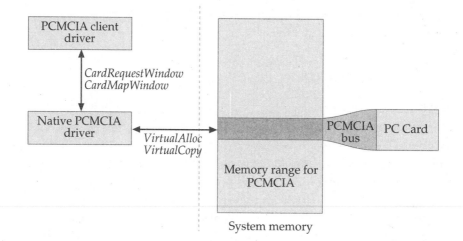

System memory

PC Card device-driver developers can write one driver that will operate on all platforms. Their client drivers use the card services interface to interact with the native PCMCIA driver, and the native PCMCIA driver makes the VirtualAlloc *and* VirtualCopy *calls on their behalf.*

The PCMCIA driver handles the actual interrupts, such as the card detect interrupt and the one that is usually the most interesting, the data interrupt. The PCMCIA IST associates the interrupt with the correct client driver and directly calls that client driver within that IST context. All the demultiplexing is handled by the PCMCIA driver. To the client driver, no number is associated with the interrupt—all it knows is that the interrupt is attached to its card.

PLUG AND PLAY

When we designed the Plug and Play system, we decided to keep track of active devices in a way that any other process could access: by using the registry. We also added two APIs that make it convenient to access these registry entries: *EnumDevices* and *GetDeviceKeys.*

With PCMCIA, you can load a PC Card driver in two ways. The first way is to detect the driver based on the card's Plug and Play ID. The Plug and Play system reads the appropriate tuples in the card's attribute space, generates the Plug and Play ID, then looks for the ID in the registry under HKEY_LOCAL_MACHINE\Drivers\PCMCIA\PNPID, where PNPID is the Plug and Play ID. The system tries to open that key and look for the DLL name and the device prefix. If it finds those values, it loads that driver.

```
\HKEY_LOCAL_MACHINE\Drivers\PCMCIA\PNPID
    DLL=...
    Prefix=...
```

If the system doesn't find an entry for the generated ID, its second approach is to run through its list of detect functions, listed in the registry under \HKEY_LOCAL_MACHINE\Drivers\PCMCIA\Detect. This list is numbered, with detect functions ranging from 00 through 99.

```
\HKEY_LOCAL_MACHINE\Drivers\PCMCIA\Detect
    [10]
        Dll=SERIAL.DLL
        Entry=DetectModem
    [50]
        Dll=ATADISK.DLL
        Entry=DetectATADisk
    [60]
        Dll=NE2000.DLL
        Entry=DetectNE2000
    [99]
        Dll=SRAMDISK.DLL
        Entry=DetectSRAMDisk
```

If the independent hardware vendor (IHV) knows that the Plug and Play ID won't be constant but that a range of devices can use the same driver, the IHV can choose to create the registry entries under a detect number.

The IHV should decide the sequence of its detect function based on how intrusive it is. The least intrusive detect method should run first, and the most intrusive should run last. With Serial.dll, and even with Atadisk.dll, all the IHV has to do is read the card's information structure to figure out what's going on. The Sramdisk.dll detect function is the most intrusive, so I put it last, at detect function No. 99.

Most SRAM cards don't have a card information structure. So OEMs have to write a test pattern, read the pattern back and compare it with what they originally wrote, and then restore the original data. They have to do the testing in chunks because they're not only detecting whether it is an SRAM card but also how big the SRAM card is.

When the detect function detects the card, it returns a string value that is used as a key under HKEY\Drivers\PCMCIA. Device.exe opens this key and uses it. For Serial.dll, the string value is "Modem". And for ATADisk, it's "ATADisk".

There is also a third way to load the driver—you can ask the user for the DLL name. Let's say a user sticks in a new PC Card, but because you haven't registered the device driver's detect function yet, the registry doesn't have a Plug and Play ID entry and the detect functions in the registry do not detect that card. When all the detect functions fail, Device.exe displays a dialog that says, "Enter the DLL name." To enable users to just stick in the card and enter the DLL name, driver writers should implement a function called *InstallDriver*. If the user enters a valid DLL name, Device.exe calls *LoadLibrary* to load the DLL, then calls its *InstallDriver* function.

The *InstallDriver* call also provides an opportunity for the driver to install its registry keys for the next time the card is inserted. Driver writers can implement the *InstallDriver* entry point so that it sets up the registry keys.

One other interesting fact about the Plug and Play system that I designed for Windows CE is that I originally did it for PCMCIA—you know, the PC Cards. But when we added USB support, USB also used the Plug and Play support routines.

DISPLAY DRIVERS

Anthony Lapadula and Martin Shetter

In Windows CE version 2.0 and later, GDI talks to a display driver and the display driver talks to the physical device. The display driver exports an interface called the DDI—the same DDI interface as Windows NT.

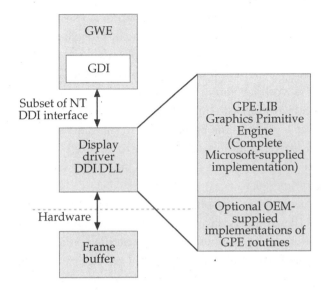

Although the display driver uses the standard Windows NT DDI interface, most embedded developers will not implement the DDI routines. They will instead use the Microsoft-supplied implementation called GP and supply their own optimized implementations of selected GPE routines. Full documentation for the GPE classes appears in the Windows CE DDK.

You can replace the display driver with your own. But the default version that we ship has all kinds of functionality—such as any bit depth to any bit depth conversion blits—so we don't expect you to rewrite the display driver from scratch. What people usually do is add extensions to the display driver. For instance, if special hardware capabilities can give accelerated blits, your display driver can enable that hardware. This is a pretty common thing for OEMs to do. The main component in the display driver is just a library named graphics primitives engine (GPE) that does all the actual pixel twiddling. All you do is add hardware capabilities and build them into your own DDI.DLL.

I've talked about how we map GDI drawing operations to the display driver and how Windows NT DDI is the interface layer. GDI talks to the driver through this Windows NT DDI layer, but nobody ever writes a display driver to that layer and you really shouldn't. We have the GPE library, which handles all the communication with that DDI layer. It's a huge helper for display driver writers.

The first thing any prospective display driver writer says is, "Well, I write to the DDI layer." In most cases, that's the wrong approach. The right approach is to start with the GPE. You can write a display driver to that DDI layer, but you'd be a whole lot better off taking advantage of the GPE class. It'll do a whole lot of the work for you.

By sitting down and working with this GPE class, you can make a driver pretty quick. If you have a video frame buffer that's in standard Windows bitmap format, which is pretty common, all you have to do is tell GPE how big the memory is and give it a pointer to its pixels, and GPE will pretty much take care of everything else.

It can be pretty easy to write a display driver that way, but the driver might be slow. To speed up your display driver, you need to hook out specific operations. Every time there's a blit call, you get notified, and you can look at all the parameters for that blit and say, "Oh, I have hardware that can do that faster." Then you can replace the slow blit operation with your fast hardware blit operation. Illustrations of how to do this are in the DDK sample code.

You can also write code that runs faster than the generic implementation in GPE. For example, GPE has one function that handles all blits, all color conversions, and all ROPs. This one monster function literally does everything, but it's pretty slow. So if you profile your system and learn that you spend 50 percent of your time setting the background of windows to white—well, you can create a solid white color fill in software. You can target the fill operation to the bit depth of your device and get a significant increase in speed from tiny pieces of code.

We ship sample source code for a function library with GPE, and you can hook out and decide which of those functions to use. If your hardware doesn't support an operation that you really want to be as fast as possible, you can examine the source code to see how it's done and then pick the fastest software version of the operation.

For example, the library supports certain ROPs that show up frequently, like *DSTINVERT*. This is what Microsoft Pocket Excel uses to display inverted colors when you select a range of cells. We provide sample source code for source copy blits where there's no color conversion: we have sample source code that shows how to do 2-bit to 2-bit copies or 8-bit to 8-bit copies or 16-bit to 16-bit copies. You can take these functions and extend them pretty easily.

PRINTER DRIVERS

In Windows CE version 2.0, we added printing support. We shipped one sample printer driver for PCL3 printers called PCL.DLL. You would expect the printer driver to be analogous to the display side, but it's not. We do all the page imaging on the client.

Suppose a program needs to print a page. The page has some text, some graphics. The program creates a printer DC and makes all of its calls: it calls *StartDoc*, then *StartPage*, then everything else to fill up the page of output. These calls are actually stored away in an internal data structure in GDI. And then it calls *EndPage*, and it has now accumulated all the commands necessary to draw the entire page.

To create the page, we allocate an in-memory bitmap that's as wide as the page but not as tall as the page. The in-memory bitmap represents a *band*, which is a bitmap strip, a piece of the final page. This band can be incredibly big because it's at printer resolution—say, 8 1/2 inches across at 300 dpi and as tall as we can allocate. We take this page data and play it against this band, clipping it so that only the appropriate piece of the page is drawn. The display driver does all of this drawing. It has no idea that it's doing a print job: all it knows is that it's rendering the image at a particular height.

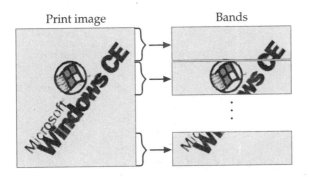

Each page of output is sent to the printer driver in sections called bands, which are rendered by the display driver. The size of each band depends on the amount of available memory.

Once this band is complete, we give it to the printer driver. The printer driver is very simple—it knows how to initialize itself, how to start a new page, and how to receive a band. It's really pretty incredibly stupid. The printer driver takes this print band, which is just a normal bitmap like anything else, and compresses it into whatever format the physical printer supports. Run-length encoding (RLE) and five or six different kinds of compression can go on here. The driver just picks the compression type that works best for the printer.

So the first band gets compressed, shipped over the wire, and rendered on the page. Then GDI shifts down to the next band and does the same thing: it sends the bitmap to the printer driver, the printer driver compresses the band and sends it over the wire, and the band gets rendered on the page. This process is repeated until the entire page is processed. Then the printer gets told, "Go ahead and eject the page; get ready for the next one."

It's a nice architecture. The display driver is the only piece of the system that pushes pixels around.

RESOURCES

Topic	Resource
Current list of supported micro-processors	*http://www.microsoft.com/windowsce*
Windows CE system integrators that can help port the OAL and device drivers	*http://www.microsoft.com/windowsce/ embedded/partners/sysinteg.htm*
Detailed procedures for porting Windows CE to a new device and using the porting debugging tools, including developing the bootloader, developing the OAL layer, and profiling system performance	Microsoft Windows CE Embedded Toolkit for Visual C++
Detailed procedures for developing and configuring native drivers and stream-interface drivers	Microsoft Windows CE Device Driver Kit

7 Communications

T *he Microsoft Windows CE development group was formed from the merger of two groups working on mobile computing devices. One group worked on a consumer device that offered wireless communications, while the other worked on a business device, a Microsoft Windows desktop companion.*

This organizational history meant that from the very first version, Windows CE supported a rich mix of communications options for both consumers and business. As additional interfaces became popular or were supported by other Microsoft operating systems, the development team created Windows CE versions for those interfaces as well, adding such options as infrared communications and Internet standards and protocols.

The Windows CE architecture includes a wide variety of communications and connectivity options, providing subsets of all major Microsoft communications programming interfaces. The modular design of Windows CE allows OEMs and third-party developers to easily add drivers and protocols, to enhance and even replace the supplied communications components.

The communications API options are best described in layers, working up from the lowest level that communicates with the hardware to the higher levels that represent more abstract services.

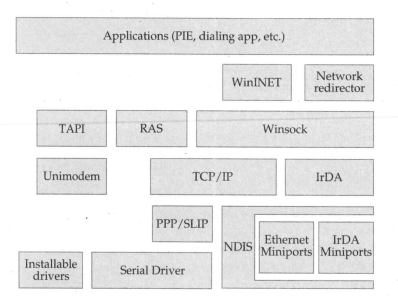

Windows CE offers a variety of communications options based on subsets of the standard Win32 API.

At the lowest level, Windows CE offers support for serial connections through the Win32 Serial API to the serial driver; local area networks through a subset of NDIS to Ethernet drivers; Infrared Data Association (IrDA) standards through IrDA to the infrared driver; and fax and modem support via TAPI and Unimodem to installable PCMCIA fax/modem card drivers. At the intermediate level, Windows CE supports Remote Access Services (built on the serial connection) and Winsock, which uses the TCP/IP and PPP/SLIP modules to communicate via either serial, Ethernet, or infrared. At the highest level of the communications programming interfaces, Windows CE supports the WinINet API, which provides FTP and HTTP services and access to a Common Internet File System (CIFS) redirector for access to remote printers and files. The highest level also includes the Windows networking API, which enumerates network resources and manages connections. Both the WinINet and WNet interfaces are built on top of Winsock.

Version 2.10 also includes support for secure communications at all levels of the model. At the lowest level, Windows CE offers data-link authentication using Password Authentication Protocol (PAP), Challenge Authentication Protocol (CHAP), and Microsoft CHAP. At the intermediate level, Windows CE offers secure socket connections through the Winsock and WinINet APIs over any of three provided security protocols: SSL 2.0, SSL 3.0, and PCT 1.0. At the highest level, Windows CE supports the Microsoft CryptoAPI. These API functions allow applications to manage data encryption, decryption, and the certificates used to exchange encryption keys.

In this chapter, Mark Miller, the Windows CE communications lead, offers perspective on the choices made by the Windows CE developers and discusses some possible directions for the future. David Kanz describes the Ethernet networking support. Bill Mitchell, who leads the Mobile Computing Products team, and Charles Wu, who developed the desktop connectivity interfaces, describe the ActiveSync interfaces and the extensible Windows CE Remote API (RAPI). (Windows CE also defines a set of file filter interfaces to transfer files between the desktop and the device.)

In addition to the communications capabilities provided by the Windows CE operating system services, Microsoft exposes an authoring interface for its Mobile Channels viewer application. Mobile Channels is an extension of Internet Explorer's Channel Definition Format (CDF), which gives content providers a way to efficiently deliver data to mobile devices. Jay McLain, the Mobile Channels development lead, describes support for standard HTML authoring and for the new advanced authoring model.

Mark Miller

I worked on Pulsar, which was a predecessor project to Windows CE. Pulsar was supposed to be an inexpensive, portable consumer device with wireless communications and a touch screen, no keyboard. The average person on the street could use the device to get general information. You could walk into a strange city and say, "I'm interested in Italian food." Because the device has GPS, it knows your location. It answers, "Oh, you want to go to Tony's around the corner; it's a great place and here's the menu with the prices."

We tried to build a device in the $250–$300 range that would be an *unconscious carry*. The concept is that you'd get up in the morning, pick this device up off your dresser, and put it in your pocket. I don't think I've ever left the house without my wallet, keys, and glasses; the Pulsar device was meant to be like your watch—pretty much always with you.

Mark Miller

TCP/IP

In terms of communications Pulsar was a wireless device, so we worked on a generic Winsock-like provider. We had a TCP/IP transport stack that worked with paging devices. After we started working on the Handheld PC, we decided that because the device was a desktop companion, we had to have a protocol stack that could talk to the desktop and that was compatible with Windows 95 and Windows NT. So we decided to go with the TCP/IP stack from Windows 95 and Windows NT. At that time, it was called the "Rhino" stack.

We tried to look down the road, and we thought TCP/IP was a platform that we could leverage to do other things. We were very conservative about our ROM size. If we had written a proprietary protocol and somebody else added TCP/IP, we would have wasted ROM space by having two protocols.

The original plan for Pulsar didn't include an Internet Explorer and a Pocket Mail component. This was before the Internet craze. At that point TCP/IP wasn't even the Microsoft standard. The standard at that time was whatever was on corporate LANs—NetBEUI, NetBIOS, and IPX. But even back then, when we first started, we liked TCP/IP, and some people in the group really believed it had a lot of support in the industry.

At a previous job, I worked on an application that broadcast stock data on a network of Sun workstations. I had all of my processes linked together using TCP/IP, giving me 24-hour reliability. If my main big processor died, I needed to be able to run pieces of the whole system on various workstations in the office and link them all together using TCP/IP—you know, brute force multiprocessing. We had some experience with TCP/IP and believed it was the right thing to use. And we had a fallback. Because it was supposed to be used only for desktop communication, if TCP/IP didn't work out, we could in effect hide our decision.

We did make a number of changes to the TCP/IP code. In the desktop environment you don't worry as much about how much memory your stack is using, whereas in our environment the user sometimes is working with a big spreadsheet or Word document and memory has to be available. So we freed memory when the stack wasn't using it instead of caching it for use later.

We also removed some features. Some were #ifdef'ed out because they weren't needed for the first generation of the product. We're adding some of those features back in as the OS adds more support.

THE WINSOCK API

We also looked at how the protocol was exposed to the application space. The Winsock API set was originally derived from the requirements of getting TCP/IP to work on a Windows 3.1 system. Windows 3.1 wasn't really multithreaded (it used cooperative multiprocessing), and Winsock was an extension of the Berkeley Sockets API, which supported this cooperative multiprocessing model.

In Windows 3.1, you couldn't block on a receive because you wouldn't get any mouse or keyboard events from the user. You had to indicate to the protocol stack that you wanted a packet so that the stack could send you a window message when that packet was available. Your main thread processed the window messages.

Why would you ever want to do that in a true multiprocessing system, where you can spin a thread? From a pure protocol perspective, that message is just additional overhead. A message comes up and has to go through some message path to be able to get to my application. Threads aren't free, but they're certainly more lightweight than messages.

So we decided to completely cut the asynchronous functions and really focus on the core Berkeley Sockets implementation: *socket, recv, send*. The implementation is compatible with Winsock in that it's a subset, but the async APIs are not supported. This saved ROM space. If we had supported the async APIs, we would need a thread to manage the receive packets and send back window messages.

Windows CE Winsock Functions		
Supported		**Not Supported**
accept	*ntohl*	*AcceptEx*
bind	*ntohs*	*EnumProtocols*
closesocket	*recv*	*GetAcceptExSockaddrs*
connect	*recvfrom*	*GetAddressByName*
gethostbyaddr	*select*	*GetNameByType*
gethostbyname	*send*	*getprotobyname*
gethostname	*sendto*	*getprotobynumber*
getpeername	*setsockopt*	*getservbyname*
getsockname	*shutdown*	*getservbyport*
getsockopt	*socket*	*GetService*
htonl	*WSACleanup*	*GetTypeByName*
htons	*WSAGetLastError*	*SetService*
inet_addr	*WSAIoctl*	*TransmitFile*
inet_ntoa	*WSASetLastError*	all other WSA* functions
ioctlsocket	*WSAStartup*	not listed as supported
listen		

Windows CE implements the core Berkeley Sockets API functions, but does not implement redundant functions and does not support the asynchronous functions.

The Windows NT group has now extended the asynchronous capability to use events, which makes more sense for a threaded model. My thread gets a pretty lightweight, efficient event mechanism to notify me that a packet's available. For a future generation of the Windows CE sockets implementation, using events makes a lot of sense, although it does mean that people who have applications running on Windows 95 or Windows NT with the window-based messages might need to change their code somewhat. At least they'll end up changing their code in a way that should be more efficient.

IrDA: INFRARED COMMUNICATIONS

We also added IrDA support. IrDA was being used in Windows 95, and we investigated using it but actually decided pretty early on that trying to port the Windows 95 code wouldn't work for Windows CE. A better approach would be to start from ground zero. So we had IR, and we had this concept of squirting data to exchange information.

From the beginning, the group was separated into the OS team and the applications team. In my role on the OS team, I really wanted to provide an infrastructure that made the most sense. So the team came up with the raw IrDA protocols to enable IrDA communication. In each release, we've improved some of the low-level features in the protocol layers.

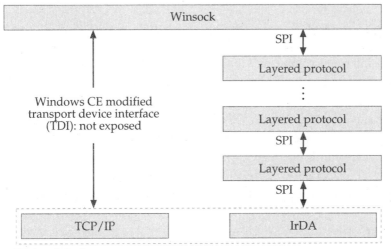

Protocol stacks

The Windows CE implementation significantly changed the transport device interface (TDI) and so does not expose this layer to developers. Developers should instead use the Winsock 2.0 layered protocol service provider interface model.

The IrDA stack plugs in under what's known as the TDI interface, which is between the protocol manager layer and the protocol stack. The TDI interface is a somewhat complicated interface, and because we really wanted to get the product out in a certain time frame, we consciously decided not to expose the TDI interface. We're still a small team at Microsoft, especially in terms of external support, and we want to think carefully about the APIs that we expose. We always have to ask ourselves, "Can we adequately test this?"

Our TDI interface is modified, and it works differently from the original TDI interface in a number of ways. So it wouldn't be that simple to port existing TDI code from Windows NT to our modified TDI interface. We're trying to concentrate on developing areas where people can add value, which is why we've gone to the Winsock 2.0 model. It has a layered service provider interface and a way to install additional stacks.

THE WIN32 SERIAL APIs AND TELEPHONY APIs

About midway through the project, we decided to add support for modems and more Internet connectivity applications. The whole reason we put TCP in the software was to enable that support, and now we were actually taking advantage of it.

We really focused on the minimum features required for the first-generation product, the H/PC. The features that made sense to include were modems, Internet Explorer, and mail. The H/PC would have a modem that could dial out, but we couldn't imagine anybody taking an incoming fax or telephone call on it. Because we didn't have staff, we said, "What's the minimum we can do that doesn't make us miss our schedule?"

We had already decided that Win32 interfaces were the way to go. Rather than inventing a new API, we used a subset of the existing API so that people could use existing applications with some changes. When we come up with our next version, developers will need to extend their applications only slightly to get a whole lot more functionality. So you start thinking about what you are going to expose: a subset of Winsock? That makes sense. The serial APIs? Those are pretty much identical to the Win32 API set. And the telephony API—TAPI—is also very similar to the Win32 API set.

TAPI was an obvious choice for talking to modems. TAPI is a very robust API, and for 1.0 we really focused on what we needed to call out. Through the service provider interface and through the generic Unimodem, TAPI provides an extensible solution for supporting modems.

We made our Unimodem very robust. It supports most of the available PCMCIA card modems without having to be modified. We actually got away with one standard setting in the Modem.inf file, and although you can override it if you want to take advantage of your particular modem's features—by entering your particular modem settings in the registry—in general, you don't have to think about it.

Basic Telephony Services Category	TAPI Function
TAPI initialization and shutdown	*lineInitialize, lineShutdown*
Line version negotiation	*lineNegotiateAPIVersion*
Line status and capabilities	*lineGetDevCaps, lineGetDevConfig, lineSetDevConfig, lineSetStatusMessages, lineGetID, lineConfigDialogEdit*
Opening and closing line devices	*lineOpen, lineClose*
Address formats	*lineTranslateAddress, lineSetCurrentLocation, lineGetTranslateCaps*
Making calls	*lineMakeCall*
Call drop functions	*lineDrop, lineDeallocateCall*
Location and country information	*lineTranslateDialog*

TAPI illustrates how the Windows CE team selected subsets from the Win32 API: focus on the functionality that is appropriate for the device and minimize memory use. From more than 100 Win32 TAPI functions, Windows CE initially implemented the basic telephony services for outgoing calls.

In version 1.0, we focused on outbound data modem support. In our 2.0 release, we exposed the TAPI service provider interface so that a third party can create its own service provider. If third-party developers want a soft modem, they can support something other than the AT command set. Our modem knows only how to send ATDT-type commands and a phone number.

And now, as more people request dial-in support for various products such as faxes, phone terminal devices, and other phone products, we'll be adding more and more TAPI extensions—the TAPI functions that deal with terminals, phone terminal devices, and inbound calls.

But you know, if I were to develop a phone device today on a standard Windows CE system, I don't know if I'd really want full TAPI support. TAPI makes the phone hardware available to a large number of apps and helps manage the users of that hardware. But is that functionality really in the spirit of the devices that Windows CE is targeting? There's no reason why the app can't handle its voice call operations by talking directly to the phone hardware. You need TAPI only if you have two phone apps that need to be able to communicate with the hardware.

I don't want to restrict people, but adding generic support means more code, greater size. If we stop worrying about the size, we could potentially blow up the OS infinitely. And that's something we do want to avoid.

COMING FULL CIRCLE: WIRELESS

Back when we were working on the Pulsar project, the market wasn't really ready for the paging capability and the wireless features. The infrastructure wasn't in place; the costs associated with it just didn't make sense.

We're now revisiting these features and capability in the context of the Palm-size PC project, so we're kind of coming full circle. And all that work we did four and a half years ago—I was in the Research team then, and now that research is finally becoming a reality. The infrastructure is a little cheaper; we can send more data; the backbone has higher data rates; and the hardware costs and power requirements have improved. So looking back, I'd say that pausing Pulsar then was exactly the right thing to do; we're starting it up again now and taking some of its ideas into the Palm-size PC.

NETWORKING

David Kanz

We have a new client component on Windows CE that lets you browse network resources on Windows 95 and Windows NT machines. You might be in your hotel room and realize you forgot a file, and you can call RAS and access your corporate server and get the file to your device. The device supports the Windows NT (Lan Manager) SMB spec, with long filename and Unicode support. It's important to note that all system files on Windows CE support UNC names; the network resources use strings rather than drive letters.

David Kanz

In Windows CE 2.0, we added an SMB redirector that was leveraged off the Windows 95 redirector. That redirector uses NetBIOS, but we didn't want to have a supported NetBIOS interface, so we created a pseudo-NetBIOS that's used internally by the SMB redirector. Developers should be writing to Windows Sockets.

NDIS (Network Driver Interface Specification) provides a generic interface between a transport and a low-level driver that talks to an Ethernet adapter. The miniport for any adapter is written such that it is operating system–independent—all the operating system–specific support is encapsulated in NDIS calls. Our interface is just like the Windows NT version of NDIS, but with the current limitations of Windows CE: having only the TCP/IP transport and supporting only Ethernet.

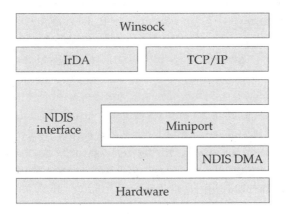

Windows CE implements a subset of NDIS 4.0 to support miniport drivers. To validate miniport driver ports, Microsoft also provides a test tool called Ndistest that performs functional and stress testing.

NDIS supports Ethernet miniport drivers that are source-level compatible with Windows NT. You can perform all of your driver development on a Windows NT machine, change your driver to a DLL, and the driver should work on Windows CE. We ported some Windows NT miniport drivers for Ethernet adapters, mostly for proof of concept so that other independent hardware vendors (IHVs) could then port their drivers. I actually ended up porting three or four miniports that the IHVs are now responsible for maintaining and distributing.

CONNECTING TO THE DESKTOP

Bill Mitchell

There was a huge difference of opinion over what we should do for the desktop connectivity software for version 1.0. It was going to be a key bit of functionality, but what exactly should it do? At the time, no one in the market had created anything that had real file synchronization or PIM data synchronization. One group of people said, "All we need is file transfer; we don't need PIM data." Another group said, "Forget about Pocket Word and

Pocket Excel. We don't need to move those files back and forth, all we need is PIM data sync." Then there were the unified field theory people who said that what we needed was a grand scheme to sync all types of data, whether files or finer-grained data.

Bill Mitchell

Synchronizing all kinds of data was a beautiful idea, but there were a ton of issues, both with architecture and with presentation in the UI. Think about what happens when you round-trip the data, when you send it to the device and then back to the desktop. We can round-trip PIM data: when we synchronize, an appointment makes it back to Microsoft Outlook with all the data it started with and we don't lose any of the information. But when a Pocket Word document is moved from the desktop to the device, we prune off all the OLE embeddings. When the file goes back to the PC, do you really want it to write over that original document?

Ultimately the 1.0 team took a very pragmatic and unpopular approach: "Hey, two different types of data—let's treat them separately." We synchronized only the PIM data and let you drag and drop other files using a little Explorer window. It was an unpopular approach internally because it wasn't as elegant and perfect as the sync-everything vision. So we kept working on the architecture, and we persevered and delivered a very clean design that can handle all kinds of data: ActiveSync.

THE ACTIVESYNC ARCHITECTURE

Charles Wu

The ActiveSync architecture allows synchronization of any kind of data between any Windows CE device and desktop application. We already have ActiveSync for Microsoft Outlook, Schedule Plus, the Windows CE file system, and Active Channel, and we're looking forward to ActiveSync becoming available to more apps as ISVs synchronize their own particular applications.

Charles Wu

This architecture requires ISVs to develop two components: one on the desktop and one on the device. The desktop component is an OLE in-process server that exposes two interfaces, *IReplStore* and *IReplObjHandler*, which I'll talk more about later. As long as those two interfaces are fully implemented, the ActiveSync engine on the desktop asks the components to enumerate the objects, request changes, and so on. If the engine sees that the object is to be synchronized down to the device, it asks the ActiveSync component to serialize the data—in other words, to convert the object into a series of bytes in any desired format. The engine then sends the bytes down to the device. The ActiveSync component on the device takes serialized data and converts it to the corresponding object on the device.

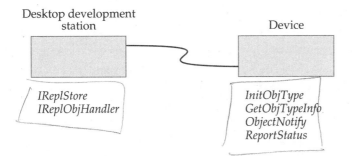

By implementing two interfaces on the desktop and four functions on the device, the developer is able to use the common services provided by the ActiveSync engine and offer data synchronization with a minimum of development work.

Synchronizing Outlook or Schedule Plus appointments requires tasks that are common to both apps:

◆ Transferring the actual appointment data

◆ Providing a mapping between the appointment on the desktop and the appointment on the device, which usually involves maintaining a table

◆ Detecting conflicts, when you change an object on either the desktop or the device before you synchronize

All these common services—data transfer, table management, and conflict resolution—are managed by the ActiveSync engine. For example, the ActiveSync engine automatically detects the conflict, gets a description of the two objects, and presents these descriptions to the user, who can choose either object.

The ActiveSync engine also supports remote synchronization, in which the device dials into the desktop. Let's say you're in a hotel room, and you want to synchronize. You hook up your modem by using your hotel phone and dial into a desktop in your office a thousand miles away. Or you dial into your corporate RAS server, establish a network connection, and synchronize there. You don't have to worry about whether you're talking over the Internet, infrared, or a serial line. The remote synchronization uses all of the communication options in Windows CE, and the whole process is totally transparent.

You don't have to reinvent the wheel. The design abstracts all of the common services into one place—the ActiveSync engine—enabling you to focus solely on your own data. That saves you a lot of time.

If you think you have perfect, lossless conversion, all you have to do is move the data back and forth. But if your conversion process is imperfect and data can be lost, you have the option to, say, pop up a message box stating that the user risks losing some of the data by transferring. We give ISVs a lot of freedom to design their own UI, their own options, their own settings dialog, and their own data transfer dialog. The ActiveSync architecture handles every kind of data; the ISV just has to implement the interfaces to support it.

THE ACTIVESYNC INTERFACES

On the device, the ActiveSync component exports four functions: *InitObj-Type*, *GetObjTypeInfo*, *ObjectNotify*, and *ReportStatus*. If those four functions are fully implemented, ActiveSync serializes or deserializes the data going back and forth, reads the registries for options, and so on.

As mentioned earlier, on the desktop you have to implement two COM interfaces, *IReplStore* and *IReplObjHandler*. *IReplStore* is the interface that deals with the collection of data. Its methods can be organized into these categories:

- ◆ *Object enumeration.* You have to be able to tell how many objects are in the store and be able to retrieve them.

- ◆ *Object management.* The ActiveSync engine gives the component a piece of data—a checksum, a timestamp, a change number, anything you define—and the component decides what this piece of data is. By comparing this piece of data with the existing data, the engine knows where the change occurs.

- ◆ *Data conversion and validation.* The validation methods ask the component whether a piece of data is valid. This is important because you could have an invalid timestamp, for example.

◆ *Option setting.* Options are set in an ISV-defined dialog, which offers a lot of freedom. An ISV can do anything it wants in its UI. For example, the ActiveSync component for Outlook can display a dialog that allows the user to sync all appointments starting with those that occurred two weeks in the past and ending with those scheduled in the future.

◆ *Folder-management, store-management, and miscellaneous.*

IReplStore Function Categories and Associated Methods

IReplStore Category	Methods
Object enumeration	*FindFirstItem, FindItemClose, FindNextItem*
Object management	*CompareItem, IsItemChanged, IsItemReplicated, UpdateItem*
Folder management	*GetFolderInfo, IsFolderChanged*
Store management	*CompareStoreIDs, GetStoreInfo*
Option setting via end-user UI	*ActivateDialog, GetObjTypeUIData*
Data conversion and validation	*BytesToObject, CopyObject, FreeObject, IsValidObject, ObjectToBytes*
Miscellaneous	*GetConflictInfo, Initialize, RemoveDuplicates, ReportStatus*

IReplObjHandler is the main interface that communicates with the desktop store, which is a collection of objects on a desktop: a Microsoft Outlook store, a Schedule Plus store, and an Internet Explorer store. This interface deals mainly with serialization, deserialization, and deletion of the object.

How does this interface work? The ActiveSync engine realizes that an object needs to be updated and calls *IReplObjHandler* to serialize the data. The ActiveSync engine sends this byte stream to the other party and calls its *IReplObjHandler* to deserialize the byte stream—that is, convert the byte stream back into an object.

The beauty of the design is that the ActiveSync component has total freedom to define the format of the byte stream. The ActiveSync engine doesn't care about the format of the bytes; it guarantees that whatever it gets from one end will be received in exactly the same order on the other end, with the same number of bytes. There's absolutely no limitation on the size or the form of the byte stream. That gives the ISV maximum flexibility to serialize its data in any convenient way it wants. You can share code on both sides because you design your own format.

These interfaces are all just standard public COM interfaces. They can be used not only by Windows CE services but by anyone who chooses to support them. The ActiveSync component can be reused as long as the user follows the interface requirements. The ISV can also develop the container that controls all the ActiveSync components, so it can write any program it desires to enable it to talk to the ActiveX component. All that's kind of cool.

We'll try our best to make sure that future versions of ActiveSync are compatible with version 2.0. But we cannot guarantee object code compatibility—you know, that this DLL, without any changes, can be reused in the next version. We cannot promise that. You might need to recompile your module or update header files. But we can guarantee that most of your intellectual property can be reused in the next version.

REMOTE API

In addition to the synchronization, we have an extendable Remote API (RAPI). So if all you really want to do is make a simple call from a desktop to query some data or to retrieve some status information, you can use the Remote API instead of using ActiveSync.

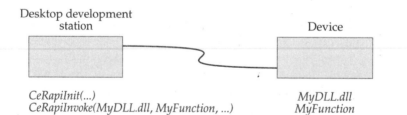

Desktop development station   Device

CeRapiInit(...)   MyDLL.dll
CeRapiInvoke(MyDLL.dll, MyFunction, ...)   MyFunction

The Windows CE Remote API (RAPI) supports its own flavor of remote procedure call. The RAPI function CeRapiInvoke lets you specify the DLL, function, and parameters to call that function on the remote device. Sample code is provided in the Windows CE SDK.

RAPI offers a very small, nonstandard RPC (remote procedure call). It's not the standard RPC that Windows NT is using. We don't provide the MIDL compiler and those tools. It's our own version—a very lightweight, simple version of the remote procedure calls because the device has limited memory and limited support. ISVs are allowed to develop on the device their own functions that can be called freely from the desktop. Basically, ISVs are responsible for their own parameter marshaling.

But if you're developing an application, you have a piece of data on the desktop, just want to get it down, and don't care about the current state or whether the data was changed, the Remote API is probably what you want. For example, if you wanted to find out how many applications are running on a device, you'd just want to use simple RAPI.

MOBILE CHANNELS

Jay McLain

We certainly handle plain HTML, and people can author web sites to be viewed on these smaller devices. But because most people aren't designing their sites with these devices in mind yet, the smaller Windows CE form factors don't really lend themselves to Internet browsing. The displays are very small, and without a keyboard, you can't navigate easily by typing in URLs.

Jay McLain

So in addition to handling standard HTML, we added some advanced features that people can choose to take advantage of. We developed the offline Mobile Channels reader—the Channels application, which introduces the idea of offline reading or viewing of content.

The Mobile Channels mechanism is a pretty convenient way to access data. You can give users some general information, such as news, stocks, sports, and weather; or local information that changes frequently over time, like movies and restaurant reviews. For intranet scenarios, you might have vertical information such as sales tracking and routing.

Channels are a feature of Internet Explorer. The Mobile Channels extend the Internet Explorer architecture. We leverage the CDF standard, not only for describing a web site but also for updating its content. We've taken the 1.1 version of the Pocket Internet Explorer control, moved that into the Palm-size PC device, and built the Channels application around it. The Mobile Channels technology is based on the XML and CDF standards.

If you want to go beyond standard HTML and use this advanced authoring scheme, you want to start to think about your site in terms of *view* and *data*: How do you want users to view the data, and what data do you want them to view? And you want to organize the hierarchy of data that you are going to show the user.

Using this type of authoring, you can define the hierarchy in the .CDF file and define the presentation in the form of mobile channel script (.MCS) files. The only part of the channel that will really change over time is the data, which appears in the mobile channel data (.MCD) files.

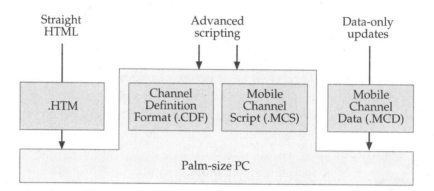

In addition to standard HTML, the Mobile Channels technology supports advanced scripting for smaller form-factor devices. One of the authoring designs extends the Internet Explorer CDF standard and represents the data structure, data presentation, and the data itself in different files. This design minimizes the transmitted data.

You can associate scripts with the channels and the data items that you are presenting to the user. You can have different scripts per channel or different scripts per item, so you don't have to present the same layout to the user all the time.

We also support logging and tracking on the device, in case you're interested in knowing what items or what pages the user views the most often. For example, if you display advertisements on your web site, we can tell you which advertisements are displayed most frequently. We can track the hit information on the Palm-size PC device and migrate that hit information to the desktop during synchronization. Then, when the Mobile Channel is finally updated on the desktop, that updated information is transmitted all the way back up to your server.

Another cool thing we've added to the mix is notifications. Notifications allow you to set up a page that refreshes when its data changes. For example, you can associate a database with a URL that is updated when the database changes. Or you can use notifications on the Active Desktop to refresh your current day's appointments.

You can see how powerful it is to separate the data from the view. If you choose to use this advanced method, we don't always have to download a whole bunch of new HTML code; we just download the new data.

RESOURCES

Topic	Resource
Communications API, writing your own file filters, synchronizing data with the desktop using ActiveSync, writing your own remote API, developing a TAPI service provider	Microsoft Windows CE Toolkit for Visual C++
Mobile channels	Microsoft Windows CE Mobile Channels SDK

8

User Interface and Shell Services

A *shell is a set of user-interface components and underlying support routines that translates user input into useful operating system actions. Each Microsoft Windows CE device can have its own unique shell, developed and customized for that device and its target audience. Creating a shell is one of the greatest challenges facing embedded systems designers.*

Version 2.10 of Windows CE offers several modules and components that support UI and shell development. These include the base functionality needed by GWE; common controls and dialogs; shell-related APIs such as shortcuts and notifications; the control panel; and a console, or command window. The embedded toolkit does not currently include a complete ready-made shell, except for a minimum implementation offered as a sample. The complete Microsoft-developed shells are currently offered only as part of complete devices, such as the Handheld PC (H/PC) or the Palm-size PC.

In addition to the visually-oriented "point and click" interface, some Windows CE–based platforms developed by Microsoft also support alternative methods of interaction, such as rich inking and voice commands. For example, handwriting recognition components are used in the Palm-size PC and in Far East versions of the H/PC. Voice recognition and text-to-speech (TTS) components are used in the Auto PC.

In this chapter, Tandy Trower, Microsoft's senior UI design specialist, provides an introduction to the general principles used in UI design. Sarah Zuberec, Tony Kitowicz, Scott Shell, and William Vong, all part of the Handheld PC 1.0 team, describe the design of the H/PC shell. Steve Masters describes the voice recognition components that ship with the Auto PC. Greg Hullender describes the design of the handwriting recognition components used in the Far East versions of the H/PC. Roberto Cazzaro explains the process of "localizing" the system and applications— that is, making them suitable for use in different languages, countries, and cultures. Arul Menezes, the shell developer in the Windows CE Core OS team, describes the components available to OEMs interested in developing their own shells.

GENERAL UI DESIGN CONSIDERATIONS

Tandy Trower

As the senior user-interface design specialist for Microsoft, I'm responsible for reviewing and critiquing ongoing work on the products. I'm also responsible for providing to third parties our guidelines for designing applications.

Tandy Trower

I put together the book *The Windows Interface Guidelines for Software Design* (Microsoft Press, 1995), which is about how you should design your applications—what controls you should use under what circumstances. It contains fundamental information about basic user-interface design principles: the importance of consistency and simplicity, and the importance of keeping the user in control of what's going on in the interface.

A section in *Windows Interface Guidelines* talks about basic design methodology and the process that a product team should follow in designing an interface. I highly recommend using an iterative design process, in which the UI is designed not only as the product is being defined but throughout the development cycle. After the team investigates basic issues such as how a user performs a task, it puts forth a design prototype followed by a cycle of usability testing to find out what works and what doesn't. The team takes the results and cranks them back into redesigning the product. The team prototypes and tests again, and it follows this testing cycle through the entire design process to improve the product. I'm really focusing on just a part of the whole design cycle. The book provides much more detail at each step of the way.

The Windows CE Handheld PC team came to me early on in the development process. The device had a smaller form factor and used stylus input rather than a mouse. The team asked me if I could work with them in extending the standard Microsoft Windows guidelines to include the Handheld PC platform. For example, to enhance the required interaction with the stylus device, the team was interested in reducing the number of double clicks required to perform tasks. With the Internet and Microsoft Internet Explorer integrated into the Windows interface, the trend now is to require only a single click to open a window. So in some ways, the H/PC design foreshadowed the direction that the desktop Windows operating systems were going.

USABILITY TESTING

Sarah Zuberec

Our products are interesting because we leverage the Windows concept, but some of our devices have smaller screens, so we have to modify the design. Our modifications sometimes deviate from Windows, and we have to determine whether they still make sense. We sometimes have quite a few hard problems to solve because we can't cram everything onto the tiny screen.

We perform what is called iterative testing. I sit with the team, so I have a pretty good understanding of the work that goes on day to day and know when features are ready to test. We get a build from the developer, test it, and report needed changes. These changes go back to the program manager and the developer, and a month later we test again.

Sarah Zuberec

Back in the beginning we wanted a finger-accessible device. We thought about the same types of applications that we did eventually ship on the H/PC—Microsoft Word documents, Microsoft Excel spreadsheets, email—but our original product design had silk-screened buttons that you tapped with your finger.

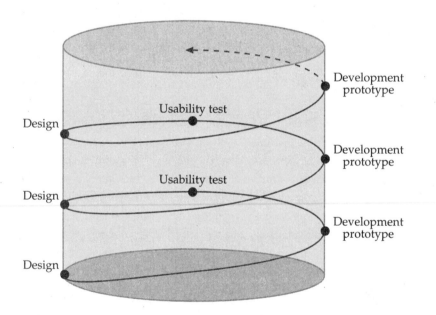

The user interface design process is iterative. The developers create a prototype that is subjected to usability tests, which in turn provide guidance on how to improve the design, leading to a new prototype and more usability tests.

When we started developing the Windows 95–like interface with the taskbar, I performed a usability test to determine the smallest area a person could accurately hit. The usability test subjects hit a button—a little "x" target—to start the timing of the application. If they couldn't hit the target in three tries, we went to the next-sized target. We just collected a whole heck of a lot of data about using different-sized targets from a lot of people. It's been good data because we've shared it with other groups designing touch screens and have used it in products throughout the company.

We realized that the targets were just too small for a finger to hit accurately, so we adopted a keyboard/stylus-based design. I just looked at the results of the second usability test: [reading from the report] "Overall recommendations for Windows 95 similarity. The Handheld PC should be designed to incorporate the necessary features of Windows 95, but at the same time optimize the design." I wrote this report in May of '95. So by that date, we had become Windows.

In June 1995, we had a really good outline of all our applications, and I started testing the address book and the calendar. By then, we already had the command bar. Microsoft Office adopted this concept. They liked the way we combined the menu and the buttons. We argued a lot about whether the buttons should have labels on them. A lot of research indicates that showing text plus a picture is the best way to go, but because we were so constrained by space, we were able to use only the picture.

We made a radical change with our OK and X buttons and put them in the upper right corner of the command bar. Jeff [Blum] and I always joked that we were going to get fired because this was such a non-Windows standard. But we tested it, and it was marvelous and worked really well. It saved us all that space in the interface.

Wherever possible, wherever it made sense for a handheld product, we tried to leverage the desktop. All in all, I think developing the similar interface was the right thing to do. It's very interesting—you can give a person a Handheld PC device or a Palm-size PC, and the interface is enough like Windows that, in a matter of seconds, the person knows how to use it.

THE FAMILIAR WINDOWS INTERFACE: THE H/PC SHELL

Tony Kitowicz

Originally, we had a social interface and we weren't getting anywhere. It just seemed like every month we were changing the UI focus. The software wasn't getting anywhere; nothing was getting done.

Tony Kitowicz

Win95 was going to ship that summer, so around the end of February I wrote a small Microsoft Windows NT application that looked like the Win95 desktop. It had a hokey little taskbar on it with a Start menu and a little Explorer-like window. And I made the mistake of showing it to Bill Mitchell! [laughing] The application was pretty simple. It was just like Win95, which was about to ship. People could pick it up and, if they used the desktop computer, already be familiar with it. So I wrote this little thing that worked, and I think that started other people thinking. The personal information guys started thinking, "Well, let's start looking like Microsoft Schedule Plus or Microsoft Outlook. Let's just go for it."

It had a window the physical size of our screen, which at that time was 320 pixels by 240 pixels. It displayed four shades of gray, and it actually explored a hard drive using the Win32 *FindFile* APIs. It was real code. I didn't see any point in just throwing up bitmaps. It was a lot easier to just write the code to allow you to actually manipulate things. That code became the demo for BillG, and it became the code base for the real shell.

On Memorial Day weekend we had the BillG review, and Thomas Fenwick, Mike Ginsberg, and Sharad [Mathur] got a kernel working with a small window manager and a very limited subset of GDI. I got the shell working and provided enough controls to actually give us a real Win95-like shell, limping along. It was actually pretty cool. It took about 1 MB of ROM and used 1 MB of RAM.

And at that point everyone said, "Okay, let's just copy the desktop." The usability studies helped us out a great deal. In our first version, our basic font was too small and hard to see. I wrote a test program that blasted a lot of different fonts to the screen, and Sarah [Zuberec] tested the fonts with users. The tests proved that we needed a bigger system font. And in the second version, the screens became a lot more readable. We also learned that we should hide the taskbar to get more screen space, so version 2.0 allowed that.

I think our approach served the version 1.0 product very well. Of course, the Version 2.0 product went beyond copying the desktop. We went ahead and modified our shell to provide seamless integration so that you can browse the web and browse the file system in a single window.

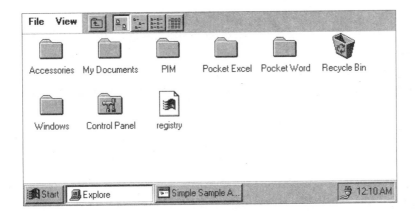

The prototype that Kitowicz wrote for the Bill Gates project review incorporated the taskbar along the bottom, and the command bar, which combined the menus and toolbar, at the top. Both features shipped in the final Handheld PC user interface.

We have several different components in the H/PC shell:

◆ *The common controls.* Windows CE has the same common controls as Win95. It has the rebar control (which some people call the "little bar"), the tree view control, property sheets—all those things. It is its own little independent portion of the shell.

◆ *An HTML control.* We separated the HTML control so that in the future ISVs can write applications that use it. One example of this type of application is our own internal help application, which loads help just like the rest of the desktop systems, through the HTML control.

◆ *A forms package that provides containers for COM objects.* The file system browser and the web browser are doc objects. The appropriate browser is loaded into the container based on which addresses you're trying to browse.

◆ *The Explorer* puts the form together with the necessary toolbars and loads the appropriate browser into the form.

◆ *Standard control panel applets and a control panel browser.* The architecture is very similar to what's on the desktop now. But to make the code fit on the device, we wrote the code (except for the common controls) from scratch.

◆ *The taskbar.*

For version 2.10, we also did the real componentization of the shell to make available to embedded developers more shell functionality as optional components.

One pretty cool result was that when we shipped V1, a lot of people thought we just used the Win95 sources, but we didn't. It was all from scratch, brand-new.

INTERNET-ACCESSIBLE SHELL COMPONENTS

Scott Shell

I was on the shell team, working on common dialogs and *ShellExecuteEx* and fun stuff like that. Harel [Kodesh] sat with me and Tony [Kitowicz] at lunch one day and said, "How hard would it be to display web pages?" So I sat down that weekend and started hacking together the basic pieces of a browser.

Scott Shell

Originally the thought was, "OK, HTML is really simple; we'll just strip out all the HTML tags and display the text." I quickly got carried away and decided, "You know, this stuff isn't so complicated—I'll just render the HTML. And OK, sure, we'll display images." We threw something together and Bill Mitchell decided to take it to the BillG review, and BillG said, "Cool, great, you have a web browser. Ship it." [laughing] I thought, "Wait! This is a little side project! I have other work to do!"

Though the web is very simple, the way it has evolved has made it the essence of anarchy. Everybody comes up with their own way of doing things. People write specs that try to coalesce the nature of things, but the pages that exist out there violate every spec ever written. It's a practice in deviance— how badly everybody can write everything. Eventually Tony took over all of my shell work and I started working on the browser full time. I spent two years keeping up and adding new features.

The basic architecture from V1 had two separate pieces: the web browser window with its command bar; and the HTML control, essentially like any other Windows control, which the window creates in its client area. For the first version, we ignored color. All backgrounds were always white; all foregrounds were always black. For Pocket Internet Explorer 1.1, we added security via the secure channel.

One of the big challenges in V2 was to support color. People also wanted frames, which divide up the web page, creating two or more independent HTML areas in the window. And we wanted to combine the shell and web browser, as was done in Internet Explorer 4.0.

The new infrastructure, based on ActiveX and the document object model, is hooked together in essentially the same way as the desktop web browser: you plop in an ActiveX control, and the ActiveX control does everything itself. If you click on a link, the ActiveX control handles the click internally and knows how to navigate the web.

The ActiveX controls provide a whole new programming interface. I started completely rewriting this new interface when somebody said, "What about backward compatibility?" The HTML control in V1 was such a nice tool for laying out HTML that we exposed it to ISVs. So we had to continue to support that in V2, not only for ISVs but also for our own help program, which used that HTML interface. This support created another level of complexity in the architecture in V2. The new HTML control is basically ActiveX, so I created a wrapper container to export the old interfaces. The window control creates the HTML control inside the container and exports the old interface on top of the new interface. Their roles are reversed: the new interface is now the primary way of talking to the HTML control, and the old interface is the external interface.

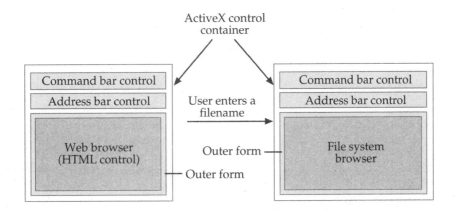

The H/PC 2.0 browser architecture uses ActiveX controls. The container swaps in either an HTML control or a file system browser, depending on whether the user enters a web address or a filename.

Tony wrote the piece that hosts controls. The asForm component is an ActiveX forms package that knows how to contain ActiveX objects. When the web browser gets created, it creates an instance of the form—an outer form—that hosts exactly one thing: another form, exactly like itself, that manages the ActiveX controls. The text and the pictures are treated as the background of the form. The form says, "Yoo-hoo, HTML control, please paint all of this background."

If you enter an address that needs a file system browser instead of a web browser, we delete the entire web browser and then insert into the form a different ActiveX control, Tony's shell. Explorer manages the top-level complexity such as the Back and Forward arrows, the history list, and the favorites list. It creates a list view window for displaying icons and basically runs the shell.

So basically for free—well, by using Tony's component—we got ActiveX hosting and the ability to contain objects. That's how the H/PC shell pieces fit together.

William Vong

After the demise of Pulsar and WinPad, Steve Isaac hired an outside firm to come in and participate in what we called a "UI camp." We were to sit in a room for a week and design from scratch what we now know as the Handheld PC. We were going to totally revolutionize the design. Our team consisted of Sarah [Zuberec], Lila Silverstein, Lisa Dreger, Jeff [Blum], Adrian Wyard, Michael McDevitt, Cathy Linn, and myself.

At first the UI was a hybrid of the WinPad and Pulsar model. We envisioned a device with a silk-screen area on the left side of the display containing the labels Menu, Help, Applications, and so forth. The device had a four-way navigation pad with action and exit buttons. But this very new, proprietary design was not expandable at all; we couldn't change the silk screen. The labels were printed on the device. We eventually realized that the silk-screen area, which behaved like the Start button and the taskbar, wasn't scalable enough for our needs.

I wanted to promote really good industrial design to make these products part of our everyday lives. That's why we incorporated the notification LED. The LED feature addressed the personal and portable aspect of the design. It was positioned to be visible in all orientations, whether it was open, closed, on, off, in your pocket, or on your desk. This feature is still used in almost all of the Windows CE devices.

During this time, Tony Kitowicz prototyped a Windows 95–like shell and presented this to the team. Tony planted a seed, and Marketing backed it up; they really wanted to leverage the Windows 95 affinity. Users could look at the interface and say, "I know how to use this. I can leverage whatever I know from the PC and take it to this H/PC." We started by prototyping a taskbar. The more we went along, the more we adopted the Windows 95 look—the annunciator tray, the start menu, the toolbar—and it cascaded from there.

A cornerstone of the H/PC was to provide the best PC connectivity on the market. At that time, data synchronization between a PC and a handheld device was a relatively new notion.

We conducted a considerable number of usability studies. Sarah [Zuberec] developed a lot of touch screen metrics. We learned that if we wanted a finger-accessible design, we would sacrifice a lot of the screen real estate due to the size of the controls. So we started moving toward adopting the stylus. We were also aware of the difficulties with handwriting recognition at that time and opted to include a hard keyboard.

My first prototype was a device oriented like a tablet, but with a keyboard that slid out underneath the LCD and tilted like a small laptop. I presented this concept to one of our OEMs. The OEM liked the idea but said manufacturing it would be too hard and too expensive. I moved on to promote a clamshell design with a basic keyboard, touch screen, LCD, and stylus.

Using my hardware prototypes and bitmap storyboards, we demoed this product to mobile professionals across the country. These focus group tests were the first simulations to incorporate PC synchronization, infrared capabilities, and the clamshell design with the touch screen and keyboard. They ate it up! The focus-group testing reinforced our thinking about connectivity and the need for a stylus and a keyboard.

OPTIMIZING THE UI FOR SMALL DEVICES

We leveraged the Windows 95 UI, but we made a conscious decision to deviate where appropriate. There are some noticeable differences between the Windows 95 desktop and the Windows CE interface for the Handheld PC.

A major design accommodation was the command bar, which munges the menu bar and toolbar into one control. The menu bar was designed in white and bordered by a single black line to promote legibility and contrast to the toolbar. In V2, we added a gripper control that allows you to stretch or grow either area at the expense of the other. You can also drag the toolbar off the command bar for placement below the menu bar, similar to the Microsoft Office toolbar model.

All primary windows were full-screen. Only secondary windows floated. We removed title bars from the primary full-screen windows to save real estate. Secondary dialog boxes such as option dialog boxes still had the title bar. However, in the primary window we rely on the taskbar to provide title bar information. In the secondary dialogs, to conserve dialog space, we deviated dramatically and placed the OK and X command buttons in the title bar. Using the X button as a "Cancel" function breaks the Windows UI guidelines. We consulted with Tandy [Trower] about this, and he was very much against this feature, but we had to deviate to save space in both the title bar and the dialog areas of the UI. The word "Cancel" was just too large for a button. This might still be a sore point with Tandy today.

Primary windows can not be resized or restored. We put the minimize and maximize window functionality into the taskbar so that if I press the taskbar button for an open window, the window is minimized. That behavior was unique at the time, but IE 4.0 also added it.

We increased the contrast for the 2-bit-per-pixel displays for version 1.0. On the Windows 95 desktop, dialogs and text are gray. To make our text more legible, dialogs and windows were in white, and any text displayed on gray was bold. We designed a 3-D common control scheme that used dark gray instead of light gray for all the highlight edges. On the Win95 desktop, light gray is used as the outside border to provide the three-dimensionality of buttons, edit boxes, and combo boxes, but a single pixel line of light gray on white is very hard to see.

We added different file formats, including 2-bit gray format icons. I took all the color icons and mapped them down to four grays. The amazing thing was that they translated really well. All of our ICOs have both the color and 2bpp gray resources in them. We made other small changes, such as the way icons display in the annunciator tray on the taskbar. Instead of a gray recessed well, the tray was painted white to increase legibility and contrast for text, icons, and application buttons. I argued left and right with dev to get that in white.

Gripper control   Command bar

The command bar shows the addition for version 2.0, a gripper control that lets you increase the size of the menu bar or toolbar at the expense of the other, or drag the toolbar below the menu bar. The floating secondary dialog shows the OK and X buttons in the upper right corner.

We incorporated animations to show where items were coming from, particularly on the taskbar. When you selected a particular program on a taskbar, an animation showed it growing out of the taskbar to give the user a sense of origination.

By default, we played sounds for daily PIM and clock alarms, which are all tied into the notification APIs that wake up the device, flash the LED, and play a particular wave file.

Cascading lists weren't implemented due to time constraints. This was a huge loss for me; I pushed for this very hard. My friend Tim Sharpe decided to do this on his own time and this feature was eventually packaged in the Power Toys.

DESIGNING UI FOR THE WINDOWS CE FAMILY

You will start seeing a variety of devices powered by Windows CE. The challenge is to design each product to be the best in its category, while still retaining the Windows CE affinity. In the end, people buy individual products because those products address utilitarian needs. Our challenge is to address the utility of the product but still allow for cross-product synergy. I think we can only go so far in pushing the Windows 95 UI into new products such as the Auto PC and Palm-size PC. You will start seeing the slow divergence of the UI in terms of the look and feel of various products, but we're hopeful that devices will retain the same interoperability and usability.

You can see an evolution from the H/PC shell to the Palm-size PC shell. The Palm-size PC shell has a taskbar, which accommodates a start button, a soft input panel (SIP) button, and an annunciator tray that provides the time, the date, and any annunciators for your appointments, battery status, or connectivity status. The SIP button allows you to toggle your keyboard or your particular input modality on and off.

Keyboard button not depressed

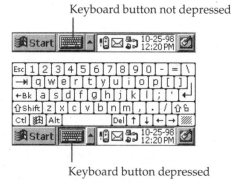

Keyboard button depressed

An icon on the Palm-size PC taskbar lets you choose to enter input through the soft keyboard or one of the other built-in soft input panels (SIPs). Developers can also add their own input panels.

We have hard up-arrow and down-arrow buttons to scroll within a list, hard enter and exit buttons to confirm or exit a task, and hard program buttons to quickly switch you to the applications—functionality that's very much like the taskbar's.

Because this model is considerably smaller and more task-based, we removed the X [close] button from each window. You should be able to move between tasks by simple clicks with one hand.

With the Auto PC, you need hard button navigation. So we provide a Start button that brings you to the shell, which is a circular list of icons presented horizontally. We've gone with the center-focused model, which allows the user to look at a single location every time he wants to see what he has selected. Text-to-speech and voice recognition are also very important components of the design. We offer prompts and voice queues so that you can get to applications by saying only the application name.

VOICE INTERFACES

Steve Masters

On the Auto PC, we support a discrete recognizer as opposed to a continuous recognizer. A continuous recognizer is always evaluating the spoken audio stream and trying to pick out commands, whereas a discrete recognizer requires some amount of pause, or white space, around the command. When you say the word "radio" and then the word "on" with distinct pauses in between, the discrete recognizer picks it all up and processes the words as a single command.

Steve Masters

One reason that we support the discrete recognizer rather than the continuous recognizers is memory constraints. Continuous recognizers require much larger data dictionaries and larger grammar databases. Another reason is CPU power. People do not tolerate radio or CD playback interruptions that occur when they issue commands or touch buttons. We wanted to limit how much CPU bandwidth the recognizer would use.

Ours is also an independent recognizer, meaning that it functions independently of the individual user. So it's very likely that somebody from Boston or Atlanta or Albuquerque can say the same word and be recognized without any training. The speech vendor that provided this particular engine recorded over 500 voice samples of each word in the command grammar: 350 samples in an office environment and 150 samples in a car with road noise built in. The car samples included what it would sound like sitting in a car in a parking lot, with the engine running, with the windows up, and with the fan on; and driving at 35 miles an hour and 60 miles an hour. The vendor also tried to get people of different genders, ages, and other demographics.

We can also train words. If for some reason the system just doesn't recognize you, you can add a new template with your speech pattern. Because both the default speaker-independent template and your template are active, the system has good recognition accuracy for both you and for others using the independent template; accuracy is not degraded.

Category	Recognized Words Stored in ROM
Global commands	Start, AutoPC, Help, Mute, Volume
Start menu	Radio, CD Player, Address Book, Navigate, Wireless, Audio, Settings, Next, Previous
Radio	AM, FM, Preset, Next, Previous, Review, numbers 0 through 9, Stop, Seek
CD player	Play, Pause, Delete, Next, Previous, Random, Review, Disk, Stop
Address Book	Locate, Next, Previous, Skip, Dial, Repeat, Review, Select, Letter, Home, Phone, Office, Cancel, Back
Navigate	Next, Previous, Review, Repeat, Cancel
Wireless	Next, Previous, Review, Repeat, Skip, Read, News, E-mail, Traffic

This table lists some of the words that will be recognized by the Auto PC's discrete recognizer. These words will be present in ROM and available to application developers. The Auto PC SDK will also include additional words, and developers can add their own.

The Auto PC system will ship with about 50 words in ROM; these are the words we need to run the main system functions. The development kit will include another 150 words that we think cover a pretty broad spectrum of tasks in the application suite: words needed for controlling a security system, moving the windows up and down, locking and unlocking the doors, and running the heater and air conditioner. We've even put in words for games: hearts, spades, clubs, deal, draw, spin, roll, and pull. We tried to anticipate which applications interact with car systems, and we tried to encompass information access—the words needed to receive and parse through email or paging messages. We prerecorded the words that we anticipated developers would need and provided them in the SDK. And of course other words not in the SDK can also be added.

Those 50 words in ROM are required in every system—that's part of the Microsoft license agreement. You need to guarantee that those 50 words are on every system and have the given functionality. I need to know that on any system, I can say "start radio" and the radio app will launch.

We also use various spoken output methods. The main output is text-to-speech (TTS). Any application can be built to pass a textual message through the Speech API (SAPI) to the TTS engine and transmit that message as speech to the user. We also support prosody. The TTS output strings can contain embedded control tags—for example, to add emphasis to certain words.

TAGS ENABLING CHANGES TO PLAIN TEXT

Prosody Command	Description
Com	Comment: embeds a comment in the string
Emp	Emphasize: emphasizes the next word in the string
Pau	Pause: pauses speech for a specified length of time
Pit	Pitch: changes the average pitch of the TTS speaker
Prn	Pronounce: specifies how a particular word or phrase is to be pronounced
Pro	Prosodic rules: activates or deactivates prosodic rules
Prt	Part of speech: indicates the part of speech of the next word
Rst	Reset: resets all tags to the engine's default settings
Spd	Speed: changes the average rate of speech
Vce	Voice: selects a speaking voice, either "male" or "female"
Vol	Volume: changes the average volume

We're also using recorded speech in some areas. Recorded speech sounds nicer than TTS, but it takes up a lot of space and it's not very dynamic. I don't see any way to record a bunch of words and store them in some library that an app developer could then call to cobble together some sentence. The library would be too big, and the speech just wouldn't sound right. We use recorded speech to traverse the shell, to tell you which application you're currently focused on.

One of the goals of the Auto PC was to enable you to operate the system while keeping your hands on the wheel and your eyes on the road. With TTS output and a speech interface for command and control, you can run in a hands-free, eyes-free environment.

HANDWRITING RECOGNITION

Greg Hullender

On Windows CE devices for the Far East, the user provides most of the input by using electronic ink to write on the device. The handwriting recognition components turn electronic ink into Unicode strings. As an input method for 6600 characters, handwriting is a lot more feasible than a 106-key keyboard.

Greg Hullender

The best way to think of electronic ink is as a collection of strokes, where a stroke is an array of points. You've got a big array of x and y coordinates that correspond to the points that, when written out, look like a character.

Now Windows does not have a "get ink" call. The obvious way to collect ink is to use the mouse move events; the left button down and left button up events correspond to the stylus touching the surface and the stylus coming off the surface, respectively. The problem is that Windows coalesces mouse move events. If you get two or more mouse move events in the queue at the same time, Windows throws out the older ones. Applications just want to put the mouse cursor in the correct final position, so it throws out intermediate positions to prevent them from filling up the queue. This isn't a problem for the mouse; the user just sees the mouse cursor position jump. But this is a problem for electronic ink, because if the intermediate points are eliminated, your chances of getting the character you wanted are slim to none.

To solve this, Windows CE provides a new API called *GetMouseMovePoints*, which gives you all the missing points at digitizer resolution. The recognizer performs better with higher resolution, especially if it has all the points. So calling *GetMouseMovePoints* is critical.

Our API set is a small, simplified subset of the old Pen Windows API. Pen Windows provided about 100 APIs because it had to do several different things to get around the fact that it had very little support from the operating system, but we've boiled the necessary APIs down to 11. We have OS support; we're integrated into the Input Method Editor (IME).

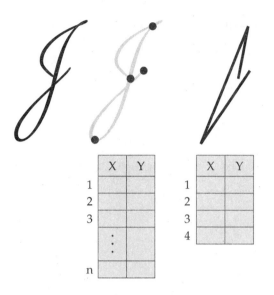

	X	Y			X	Y
1				1		
2				2		
3				3		
⋮				4		
n						

To show handwriting, Microsoft Windows must save all the input mouse move events. They are represented as an array of x,y positions. This illustration shows the input points for a cursive letter J; the far right shows how the information would be lost if it had been coalesced into four points.

The original Pen Services offered five services:

◆ *Pen as mouse.* It provided services to enable the pen to act like a mouse. Obviously, any Windows CE device has to do that.

◆ *Pen events at digitizer coordinates. GetMouseMovePoints* provides both this service and the pen as mouse service.

◆ *Ink data type.* This data type had a lot of interesting functionality, but to reduce the number of APIs, we dropped support for it. If you really need this, you can accomplish pretty much the same functionality by maintaining your own array of strokes.

◆ *Data squirted into the app.* The app didn't have to be pen-aware; as long as it had an edit control, you could get ink input into the app. Now, with Windows CE, we assume that input goes through the Input Method Manager (IMM); the app thinks it's getting keyboard input. The way all this works is a whole different discussion, but basically, you have an intermediate buffer between your app and its input with a UI that consists of a few boxes and buttons. Your inking appears in one box; your translated text appears in the other box. The application sits in the background and when you're done; you hit a button and the text is squirted into the application.

◆ *Handwriting.* We support about a dozen APIs. The full reference is in the SDK documentation.

An application that handles handwriting usually has an initialization phase and a loop:

```
// initialization phase
HwxCreate(...);
HwxSetGuide(...);
HwxALCValid(...)
// get ink and process ink
while (...) {
    HwxInput(...);
    HwxProcess(...);
    HwxResultsAvailable(...);
    HwxGetResults(...);
}
```

The initialization phase has three steps:

1. *HwxCreate.* Create a handwriting recognition context, an HRC, which is like a file handle.

2. *HwxSetGuide.* Give the handwriting recognizer the GUIDE structure. The GUIDE structure defines the coordinates you're using and the boxes the characters are going to be in so that it can tell one character from another. That's how it performs character segmentation. We tend to use only two or three boxes, and as you pen down in the next box, the user interface clears any other boxes that have ink in them. That's how it knows you're finished writing the character. The problem with other UIs was that you constantly had to say, "OK, I'm finished," which was distracting. This sort of UI, where you write in multiple boxes, lets you write and write without pause. It's very popular in Japan.

3. *HwxALCValid*. Set an ALC (alphabetic code) structure to describe the alphabet that's allowed. The ALC tells the recognizer which character set to use. For English, typically the character set is either everything—digits, uppercase and lowercase characters, punctuation, math symbols, and white space—or only digits. But you can restrict the set in different ways if you have a special field.

After the initialization phase, the code enters a loop where the user adds ink that is constantly fed to the recognizer. One immediately apparent effect is that adding the ink and getting the results are asynchronous. A user might add a lot of ink and get nothing, and then add just a little bit of ink and suddenly get a whole bunch of characters. That happens because the user finally entered something that resolved an ambiguity.

The recognizer refrains from giving the user results until it's seen something that clarifies what's going on. Consider two strings: "007" and "OOPS". After the first two characters are entered, the system doesn't know whether those characters are digits or letters. After the third character is entered, the system can tell what's going on from the context.

At the point where the user is constantly writing and you're updating asynchronously, the app needs two threads: one thread to handle the inking and another thread to handle the actual handwriting recognition. We've got a sample that shows how to do that.

The loop has these calls, basically in this order:

1. *HwxInput*. This call adds ink.

2. *HwxProcess*. This call tells the system to go ahead and recognize as much as it can. If *HwxEndInk* hasn't been called, more ink might still be coming.

3. *HwxResultsAvailable*. This call tells you how much you can retrieve at this point. It actually gets you the count of characters. If there are none, it just returns 0. So then you know exactly how much space to allocate.

4. *HwxGetResults*. After *HwxGetResults*, the loop returns back to *HwxInput*.

HwxEndInput means no more ink is coming. You generally call it when the user clicks a "done" button in the user interface. Otherwise the system still has the last little bit of ink hanging out there. For all it knows, the user got up, will be back in five minutes, and will write some more. The system might not be prepared to give a response, but when you call *HwxEndInput*, you tell the system that nothing more is coming and to make up its mind based on what it has.

Other than making the user write into a box, we're a lot more generous with what we'll let people write than almost any other system out there.

DEVELOPING INTERNATIONAL APPLICATIONS

Roberto Cazzaro

I'm responsible for the localization strategy for all the Windows CE–based products. Many people are approaching the international market cautiously, thinking that it's too hard to develop for. You don't really need to invest a lot of resources up front to get into international markets.

You don't need to do everything at the same time; localization can be handled in stages. I usually define it in four steps:

1. International enabling, or writing the code so that it can handle different formatting conventions everywhere in the world

2. Writing the code in such a way that simplifies localization, which means making it easy for a non-technical person to change the user interface

3. Localizing the system—that is, actually translating the software to other languages

4. Developing specific products for target local markets

Let's analyze the four steps one by one. The distinction between the steps is mainly academic, but you might find it helpful to visualize the resources required. In real life, the four steps are usually happening at the same time.

STEP 1: INTERNATIONAL ENABLING

The first step, and by far the most important step, is international enabling, that is, writing code in such a way that people in different countries with different conventions can use your software. The set of conventions for a country is called the "locale," and it specifies the country's date format, number format, currency format, currency symbols, alphabet, and sort orders.

Western World Enabling

Western world enabling is obviously the simplest kind of enabling. Systems that are candidates for this type of enabling use the same United States character set and system functionality but recognize different locales—different date formats and currency formats. If your code just supports local conventions, you can sell the untranslated United States version abroad. You can target niche markets in foreign countries just by enabling locales, especially if you target technical users, where the level of English knowledge is usually pretty high.

Eastern European Support

Eastern European scripts are still simple left-to-right scripts, but the alphabets are completely different. Often, when we talk about Eastern Europe, we mean Russia, all of Eastern Europe, and also Turkey and Greece, which geographically are not part of Eastern Europe but share technical issues: You need different glyphs for the Greek alphabet and for the Turkish alphabet. If your font supports multiple glyphs (called "fat fonts" in our jargon), you can support all those countries at the same time. Windows CE, for example, supports all the glyphs for these countries.

Far East Support

The Chinese language and the Japanese language each have around 6000 kanji, more or less—that's 6000 characters—and a character is a word or a concept. You need big fonts to support these 6000 characters, and unless you've got a 6000-character keyboard, there's no way you can input characters except by using a trick called the input method editor (IME), or handwriting recognition.

An IME is an application that enables you to "build" a kanji character in two different ways: either by "spelling" the kanji sound and then selecting the correct symbol from a list of similar sounding symbols or by "building" the kanji from the root symbols forming that concept. For example, the kanji for "flower" is a combination of the symbols for "grass" and "change."

One interesting aspect of the Japanese system is that everyone learns how to write a kanji character in exactly the same way, with the same type and number of strokes. This means the character recognizer can achieve a very high recognition rate. Moreover, a symbol is a whole word or concept, making it easier to fully recognize a full sentence. A full English sentence might be formed by, say, 50 different characters, and each one has to be correctly recognized, even when handwriting styles vary a great deal. A full Japanese sentence can be only four or five symbols, all written by individuals in exactly the same way. Handwriting recognition programs are very common in Japan and have great success.

Bidirectional (Bi-Di) Support

The Hebrew and Arabic languages are written from left to right for characters, from right to left for numbers, and also in both directions at the same time. If you are writing a name and then a number, you compose the name from left to right but the number from right to left, and the system has to be smart and figure that out on the fly. Moreover, Arabic has ligatures, and glyphs change according to the characters that follow them. We display a glyph one way if it's a standalone glyph, but if the glyph is followed by another, the preceding glyph changes its form.

Issues to Consider

You don't want to limit yourself when writing software. You want to write software that can run anywhere, so never think about just one language. Think about a family of languages. Every time you write software for one specific language, you can assume that the other languages in that family are free apart from the translation cost. Let's say that you have a business case to sell a product in Germany; Germany is a pretty big market, but writing code that will work only in Germany turns out to be a pretty bad idea. With the same effort that you will apply to the German market, you can also target other Western European countries, like France, Italy, and Spain.

You cannot assume that *locale* conventions are the same as *linguistic* conventions. Just think of a French product that can be used both in Canada and in France, and then remember that the conventions in Canada differ from the conventions in France. If you assume that every single French user will run your software with French settings, well, users in Canada will be very upset. Even people in France who need to do business in, say, Belgium, will not be able to use your software—the currency symbols are different.

Format Conventions

Language (Country)	Currency	Date	Number
English (USA)	$1000.00	10/12/54 Tuesday, October 12, 1954	123,456.78
French (Belgium)	1000,00 FB	12/10/54 mardi 12 octobre 1954	123.456,78
French (Canada)	1000,00 $	54-10-12 12 octobre, 1954	123 456,78
French (France)	1000,00 F	12/10/54 mardi 12 octobre 1954	123 456,78

Conventions for displaying currency, dates, and numbers can change not only between languages, but within a single language as it is used in different countries. The NLS API supplies the appropriate formatting for the specified locale.

The Windows CE operating system has what is called national language support (NLS), which is full support for character set, sort order, date format, and currency format. NLS is written specifically to support international code. If you use the NLS APIs properly, all the formatting work is done for you. You don't need to worry about supporting different date or currency formats or about how numbers are going to be displayed. You don't have to write an extra line of code; you just use the correct NLS call and your code will work everywhere without needing changes from you. Windows CE supports an almost complete subset of the NLS APIs that are supported by Windows NT, simplifying the porting of international code between platforms.

Windows CE is also Unicode-based, meaning everything—the file system, the registry, databases, everything—is based on Unicode. Unicode is a linear space of 65,535 characters; all characters can be encoded with just 2 bytes. Unlike Windows 95, which had a "code page" concept with only 255 characters (or more, for FE countries, where a very complex encoding system called DBCS is used), Windows CE is very easy to write for. Basically you can have any character you want. All you need are the fonts.

We have input method editors and input method managers for Far East support, and we will be supporting more and more locales. We are targeting Eastern Europe and are thinking of adding bidirectional support for Arabic and Hebrew. So very shortly you will be able to write on the same platform all over the world.

STEP 2: WRITING CODE THAT CAN BE LOCALIZED

Now that we have written our software to work in different locales, we want to go one step further and make sure that we can translate our software. The second step is to make a system that is localizable. Making it localizable means making it easy for a nontechnical person to change the user interface. Basically, if you can separate the user interface completely from the code behind it, all you need is a tool that strips the U.S. face and puts another face in its place. Ideally, you develop in Esperanto, which is a completely neutral language, and then put on the U.S. face and all other faces as a localization step. This way, from the very beginning, everyone focuses on making localization an integral part of development, rather than as an add-on. Sometimes, just for fun, I suggest that we develop the original version in Pig Latin.

To limit the time hit for test and development, you want to write code that works everywhere in the world without needing to be recompiled. Don't use language-specific #ifdef's because, for example, if you have #ifdef GERMAN and #ifdef FRENCH, every time you work on another language, another developer has to change the code and recompile for you. If you have to recompile, you must build an environment for every new language, and instead of incurring a small incremental cost, you will incur big up-front costs to rebuild, retest (because you might introduce bugs), and ensure that the software is ready to ship. At Microsoft, we use a "no-compile" strategy. No-compile means, "I don't need a developer to translate the software; I just need a person who knows how to translate the language." At Microsoft, when we ship the American product, we know that product is capable of being localized and shipped anywhere else in the world.

Satellite DLLs

You can localize your code at different levels; the way you write your code determines how localizable your product is. For example, you can hard-code the strings but you won't be able localize them later. Moving strings into resources is a reasonably good strategy but still goes only halfway. Having separate DLLs for each language with only resources, not code, is the way to go, because testing is easier. The phrase we use to describe this is "resource satellite DLLs." If you want to change languages, all you have to do is recompile with a different satellite DLL.

The nice thing about satellite DLLs is that you can have many of them in different languages resident on the same system, which is very important for consumer devices. By flipping a setting in the registry, you can change the language on the fly.

Let's say that you have a bug fix. If you have code and resources tied together, you will have to relocalize the bug fix in 20 languages. But if you're using satellite DLLs, you issue a bug fix in the code, and that bug fix will work in all the languages.

The other advantage to this approach is that you usually freeze the user interface much earlier than the code, so you can localize a month in advance and then keep on working and churning out code. The moment the code is ready, you have 10 languages ready at the same time. No wasted time. If you don't use this approach, and the code and the language are closely tied to each other, you have to wait until the product is done to start localizing. And then you have two weeks or a month of wait time, which is something we try to avoid.

STEP 3: TRANSLATING THE CODE

Once your code is able to work everywhere in the world, you are ready to have it translated. This is the third step. In this stage of the localizing process, you find someone with linguistic skills and the right tools to put a new face on your software and test it. You are also trying to make the software feel more natural to the user so that it will be perceived as "right."

When software uses standard terminology, the user finds the product much easier to use. Microsoft is pretty successful abroad, so by now people are really used to Microsoft terminology. We put our international glossaries on the web for other developers.

Art

One frequently overlooked item needing localization is art. Too frequently people design art that uses conventions that are very well known to North Americans, but that don't make sense in other markets. You want to be wary of art that can be offensive in some countries. Some art might also be confusing. For example, the mailbox symbol is well known in the U.S., but for most people in Europe, that icon looks like a barn with a flag. Localizing art is much harder than localizing software or localizing strings because you need a skilled artist, not just a translator.

STEP 4: DEVELOPING SPECIFIC PRODUCTS AND FEATURES FOR THE LOCAL MARKET

The last of the four steps is the most costly step and the one that requires more research, but it is also the one that can have a big payoff. With international software, you have to think, "How can I sell the product in a particular country?" You want to make your product more interesting for that selected market.

Let's look at a few examples. If you're working on a phone for the European market, you work on GSM-specific features. If you're working on the Auto PC for Japan, however, you have to completely change the maps and the navigation engine because the Japanese people don't use street names. The U.S. navigation engine is based on a grid: "Go to Main and Fifth." But in Japan, there is no Fifth. The code needs to be reworked to say, "Turn right after the yellow post box next to the red brick building." This translation process is the most expensive step, and so unfortunately, not many people are doing it yet. You usually need people in the target country to help you understand specific feature requests.

So where is Windows CE in the international market? Windows CE is still a young operating system; it's still growing in international support. Yes, Windows CE supports Unicode. Yes, you can process any language you want on a Windows CE device, even Russian or Japanese. But there's still other work to be done to enable all the tools to be fully Unicode-compliant. If you want to ship in Arabic or Hebrew tomorrow, well, we're not quite there yet. We will be soon. But I would say that Windows CE is a very solid foundation on which to build real international applications in the future. If you invest in Windows CE now, everything will eventually be available so that in the future, you can ship in any language you can think of.

DEVELOPING YOUR OWN SHELL FOR WINDOWS CE

Arul Menezes

Before Windows CE was fully componentized, some of the shell-related APIs weren't available to embedded developers because they were implemented only in the H/PC shell. If the H/PC shell was missing when third-party apps called the shell APIs *ShellExecuteEx*, *SHGetFileInfo*, *SHCreateShortcut*, *SHGetShortcutTarget*; the notification APIs; and a few other miscellaneous shell APIs, the calls failed in a not very clean way. GWE was also affected because it depends on a blank desktop window for proper repainting of the background and for hiding windows. Without the shell, the afterimage of the previous window would remain displayed until something else was drawn on top of it. This window and the shortcut keys Alt-Tab and Ctrl-Esc were also originally implemented in the H/PC shell.

So we moved these system services and the background repaint and shortcut keys into a set of OS modules and components to provide minimal shell functionality. We created several shell modules so that you can choose whether or not to include each module in your operating system configuration.

Arul Menezes

Shell-Related Module or Component	Description
Commctrl	Common controls
Commdlg	Common dialogs
Console	Command window support
Control	Control panel support; also includes the individual control panel applets: system, screen, passwrd, sounds, main, comm, intl, network, dialing, and power
Fileinfo	*SHGetFileInfo* API support
Notify	GWES component that contains the notification API support, such as *CeSetUserNotification*
Shcore	Core Shell support used by Shexec and Shmisc
Shexec	*ShellExecuteEx* API support component
Shmisc	Misc Shell APIs component; supports *SHLoadDIBitmap* and *SHShowOutOfMemory*
Shortcut	Shell API support component; supports *ShCreateShortcut* and *SHGetShortcutTarget*
Taskman	Task manager functionality (launching and switching between active applications); also manages desktop painting, the desktop bitmap, and battery warnings

The shell modules, new to version 2.10, support embedded developers who are creating their own shells. The full list of system modules and components is provided in the embedded toolkit.

The module that glues all the other shell services together is the "taskman" module. It provides the hidden desktop window that repaints when windows are hidden or closed, and taskman also registers the window that GWE uses for shortcut keys. Pressing Alt-Tab and Ctrl-Alt-Delete brings up the Windows CE task manager, which provides the ability to switch between apps. We also added a Run button, which gives you a very rudimentary version of the functionality you get in the Start/Run dialog.

Some OEMs want to develop a real shell. You will be able to pretty reasonably produce a device for a vertical market if you want to run just one app or a couple of apps. An OEM or a third party can easily take these components and add in a fixed set of icons that launch the apps. With these new components, it won't be hard for them to implement a usable shell.

RESOURCES

Topic	Resource
User interface design	*The Windows Interface Guidelines for Software Design*, by Tandy Trower (Microsoft Press, 1995)
Enabling systems and applications for other countries and markets	*Developing International Software for Windows 95 and Windows NT*, by Nadine Kano (Microsoft Press, 1995)
International glossaries for software development	*ftp://ftp.microsoft.com/developr/msdn/ newup/glossary*
Win32 resource files and satellite DLLs	Microsoft Visual C++ product documentation (Resource Editor)
Developing your own shell	Windows CE Embedded Toolkit for Visual C++
Developing voice-aware applications for the Auto PC	Microsoft Windows CE for the Auto PC Software Development Kit
Developing handwriting-aware applications for Windows CE; using the Input Method Editor and Input Method Manager	Microsoft Windows CE Toolkit for Visual C++ 5.0
Windows CE Power Toys	*http://mscominternal/windowsce/hpc/support/wce1/powerr.htm*

9

Testing Your Embedded System

A lthough Microsoft tests a set of OS configurations for each Microsoft Windows CE OS and embedded toolkit release, embedded developers are responsible for providing quality assurance (QA) for their final Windows CE–based systems.

This chapter describes Microsoft's internal QA efforts as a way of providing general guidelines that can be adopted by embedded systems developers working on their own products. This chapter focuses on Microsoft's approach to testing multiple versions of the componentized OS, highlights the management strategies that can ensure successful QA efforts, and describes some test resources that are available to embedded developers in the embedded toolkit.

The principal function of a QA or Test group, writes Jim McCarthy in his book, **Dynamics of Software Development** (*Microsoft Press, 1995*), "is to continually assess the state of the product so that the rest of the team's activities can be properly focused." QA keeps a team in touch with reality. It provides "a comprehensive list of tested and missing functionality, bug count sorted by severity, bug arrival rate, bug fix rate, projected total bug count, and the other vital metrics." QA provides information so that it is obvious to the entire team when the product is ready (and not ready) to ship.

As Windows CE team members point out in this chapter, customers expect higher quality from consumer electronics and from embedded systems than they expect from PCs. Success in these new markets will require rigorous testing and the adoption of a broad set of project management and QA initiatives across the development process.

The Microsoft development team members emphasize the importance of working in a layered, bottom-up fashion, starting with hardware testing to establish a common, "blessed" hardware platform; testing the drivers; and then working up to higher levels in the system, such as the shell and applications. They describe the benefits of a test harness that can run automated tests in different sequences and combinations. Other important steps include establishing a physical (or a virtual) test lab that can run regular regression testing and ensuring timely communication among the team members. The Microsoft team uses bug databases, intranet web sites, and email to share the latest build, test, and product bug status information.

This chapter features Anna Boyd, test lead for the Handheld PC 1.0; Sharad Mathur, the core OS development lead; Bryan Trussel and Patrick Copeland, the former and current core OS test leads, respectively; and Kieu Nguyen, who established the Windows CE OS Test Lab and acted as program manager for the Device Driver Test Kit (DDTK).

The device driver tests and test harness created by the Windows CE QA team are available to embedded developers in the DDTK, which is provided as part of the Windows CE Embedded Toolkit for Visual C++. The NDIS Test tool provides validation of NDIS miniport drivers.

Embedded developers can accelerate their system software development and QA efforts by using one of several reference platforms that operate with the Embedded Toolkit. These development platforms, such as the Hitachi D9000 Development System and the CEPC, a standard PC-based hardware development platform, are configurable so that embedded developers can simulate different target platform capabilities.

Independent test organizations are also available to validate some or all of the Windows CE software and hardware as part of the Windows CE logo program. For more information, see http://www.microsoft.com/windowsce/logo/.

———◆———

TESTING STRATEGIES

Anna Boyd

With the Handheld PC, we started out with some very broad test responsibilities because we had so few people: one person on the OS, one on replication, one on applications; I was going to own all the device drivers. As things progressed, I started taking on bigger and bigger responsibilities, and eventually I took over Testing. I ended up hiring a lot of temps into the group and built the team up to about 40 temps.

Ideally, we have a lot of test automation so that we don't have to manually go through every build and every release candidate (RC), but we started running out of time. We had commitments to OEMs and reached the desperation point where we said, "OK, we need as many hands as we can to get pounding on the device." We needed to know: Does the Handheld PC device work? Does it work as advertised, with the different applications? Overall, we did a pretty good job of getting that product out.

Back in the 1.0 release, we used a lot of reference platforms from the OEMs, and they all worked differently, and they were all getting revved. We went through this hassle where we were fighting broken reference platforms along with build problems. We didn't know what to trust. Finally we said, "OK, you reference platforms have to pass minimal functionality tests before we'll let you come into the lab with the rest of us." So before the team ever saw a platform, Kieu [Nguyen] ran through these basic tests. If a platform passed all the tests, the rest of the team was allowed to have it. Even so, we dealt with several flavors of devices right to the end. Because the OEMs shipped only about 20 devices for both dev and test, everyone worked with a different one. I was managing not only people but also devices. I had to figure out which testers needed hardware with a PCMCIA slot.

OEMs usually develop device drivers on some kind of reference platform. You can probably get 80 percent of your testing done on the reference platform. We use the D9000 for the platform and hook up a Microsoft Windows NT station for debug and logging. But you definitely want to check out your actual final device before you ship your product out the door. If you use a different CPU, and especially if you have PCMCIA slots, you'll probably get much better results using the actual device.

When testing an upper layer, the software layer, the number one thing to test for is memory leaks. I also recommend running your application on as many different CPUs as you possibly can, because CPUs vary so much in speed. For the most part, people are writing in C, so they don't really care about the CPU, but they should care about the speed differences. You could really throw some tiny, tiny timing loops. Page size can really make a difference too. When you're allocating memory, you can run out of memory much faster on a system with 4-KB pages as compared to 1-KB pages.

As an embedded systems developer, you can set up two test teams: the "component test" team, which tests the specific device driver, and the "system test" team, which tests the whole system. If you had, say, a Palm-size PC device, ideally you would know which apps were added onto it. You'd test each of those applications to find out what impact the device driver had on them and on the overall device. You might not think you'd find any interaction between an app and the driver, but you'd be surprised. That's where things tend to break down. The OEMs usually test their components pretty well, but we do find some problems during system testing.

You can use the Microsoft Windows Hardware Quality Lab (WHQL) for verifying your device drivers. We are also using the National Software Test Lab (NSTL) for the logo program.

Tools for the Componentized OS

Sharad Mathur

With version 2.0, one of our big challenges was figuring out how to test the OS configurations. Many of the automated tests were monolithic tests that assumed the presence of lots of components. The tests weren't actually componentized, so we ended up running most of our stress and integration testing on the monolithic configuration, which has almost all the components of the OS.

Sharad Mathur

We still needed to test whether a component's behavior differed from one configuration to another. To do that, we tried to figure out, given our entire universe of tests, which test could run on that particular configuration. We realized we needed automated tools in place to try to help us keep things sane, so we started work on a tool, named Coffup, which could grunge about all of the .OBJs and all the executables, derive dependencies between components, and verify that everything was right.

This tool is still a work in progress, but it's pretty amazing. It reads all the .OBJ files and derives all the exports and imports for every library. It creates a database and does cross-matching so that it can figure out which APIs and what other components each component needs.

Among the very practical functions Coffup performs is to take a test, figure out which APIs it needs, look at a configuration file, and spit out whether or not the test will be able to run on that particular configuration. Coffup also enables us to come up with the list of APIs that are exposed by a particular configuration and a list of all APIs that *should* be exposed by a configuration. We populate a small Microsoft Access database, which is also used by the doc team to make sure that all the exposed APIs are documented. So you take what's being exposed from the .DEF file and you check to make sure that the same APIs are being exposed from the header file.

This tool can do all kinds of cool work for you. In its ideal form, the tool would output a dependency graph for all components in the system. It would be able to verify that the exposed header files and APIs are consistent, that the import libraries are consistent, and that a configuration is self-consistent. If you want to use component A, which needs component B, Coffup would warn you when you specify A without also specifying B.

We could also come up with a tool to allow you to create configurations. You could say, "I want this component," and based on the generated component dependency graph, the tool could say, "Okay, you're going to also need this component, and these are the APIs that you're getting, and here are all the sizes." You could very easily use this tool to plan your ROM. All you'd have to say is, "I have 2 MB and I want these features," and you could trade off features and sizes until you have what you need: "Okay, this is my configuration." Boom! There it goes: you have your header files, your import libraries, and your OS—you can start developing for it.

We have invested a lot of time and effort in making these tools work with componentization. During 2.0, we put a lot of the framework in place. And this is going to be a big thrust for us as we go forward—adding more stability and making the componentization process a lot easier.

THE CHALLENGE OF TESTING OS CONFIGURATIONS

Bryan Trussel

For Windows CE 1.0, our entire goal was to ship a working H/PC. That is a much easier task than shipping a generic embedded OS to OEMs who are going to build something we've never seen, with a variety of hardware, for all of these fundamentally different devices. For Windows CE 2.0 we said, "We'll make the OS generic, and we'll let people build doorbells and fire alarms and factory automation controllers and game consoles and TVs and whatever they want."

I don't know whether anybody at Microsoft had ever done that before. To complicate matters even further, we are in ROM, so if we have to update the software, we can't mail out a floppy or tell users to download a patch from a web site. The ROM has to be replaced, and the users aren't necessarily knowledgeable enough to do that. So we've got this super high quality bar, a super high risk for potential bugs, and a super serious situation if we ship with a bug.

We can't apply to Windows CE too many of the lessons we learned from all our experience in the desktop PC world. The consumer electronics market has a really quick turnaround time, and the quality has to be much better for consumer electronics products than for the desktop. People tolerate application crashes every once in a while on the desktop, but on VCRs and TVs—well, our customers are going to expect those products to behave like VCRs and TVs.

If you're shipping Microsoft Word or Windows NT, you're shipping on a PC. That means you know who the target audience is and you know what you want. With Windows CE for embedded systems, we had to guess what the product would be, guess who the customer would be, and guess what the demand for the quality level would be. I think this is the most complicated test matrix anybody has at Microsoft. We have the platforms times the processors times the componentization, which is a huge number.

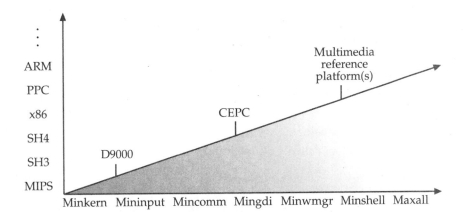

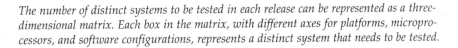

The number of distinct systems to be tested in each release can be represented as a three-dimensional matrix. Each box in the matrix, with different axes for platforms, microprocessors, and software configurations, represents a distinct system that needs to be tested.

We had five processors; the most we ever had before was probably three, and that was for Windows NT at its peak. We had various hardware platforms too. We had the D9000 development platform, the CEPC, and the multimedia reference platform.

The componentization was the most technically difficult piece. You can have a system with window messaging but no display, or a system with no network, or a system with a network and some UI and no keyboard input. We thought, "OK, we'll have 200 components and it will be like ordering off a menu in a restaurant. You can just say, 'I'll have that, that, and that,' put them together, and build a product." We were naive, but that's what we thought we were going to do. When we saw how hard achieving that goal actually was, we thought, "Look, we're on a schedule, let's just get out the most important configurations: a kernel that has no UI, a kernel with communications." We ended up with the seven configurations that are in the embedded toolkit: minkern, mininput, mincomm, mingdi, minwmgr, minshell, and maxall.

Most of the bugs that we find aren't componentization bugs; they are in the API. So we grabbed what we call the "monolithic configuration," which has all the components, and that's where we ran all the tests, every day, on every processor, thinking that 95 percent of the bugs fall under that category. We hammered on the other configurations on a rotating schedule. It took about two weeks to cycle through and exhaustively hit all the configurations on all the CPUs on all the platforms.

Another big challenge was our tests, which were all written to this monolithic H/PC version 1.0 configuration. The test harness assumed there was a UI; the GDI tests assumed the network was there for logging. On all these configurations where the guts were yanked out, and suddenly there was no communications support or no graphics support, we tried to run our tests but they wouldn't run. And given that we were trying to ship again in a matter of months after 1.0, we couldn't possibly modify all of the test code that we had been developing for two years.

We wrote a tool called Coffup, and that ended up working out pretty well. When you go back and look over the database, plain vanilla OS bugs accounted for 85 percent of total bugs, platform bugs accounted for 10 percent, configuration bugs equaled 2 percent, and the rest were CPU related. I don't know whether we got lucky or just thought hard enough about it, but it turned out about how we'd expected.

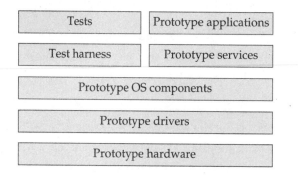

At some point in every Windows CE product development cycle, many of the layers in the system represent prototypes—both hardware and software. The QA team took a divide and conquer approach, verifying each layer independently and building up the layers to help isolate bugs. The use of reference platforms and a hardware validation process helped isolate hardware issues.

Originally, the H/PC hardware manufacturers provided us with prototype hardware, so we had prototype drivers, prototype OS, noncode complete applications, and our tests. And when the system blew up, we had to guess which of those pieces didn't work. It was just murder there for a while before we got the reference platforms because we couldn't lock onto anything. We made the lab a choke point before any code went to Test. We said, "Before the hardware goes out to anybody it goes through the lab." We either wrote low-level tests or designed manual test procedures to flush out hardware and driver issues. That helped because we were all on the same hardware. We knew it was blessed; we knew it had some level of functionality.

When we went to 2.0, we didn't want to go through that pain again, so we came up with the D9000 reference platform. The OS testing for 2.0 never actually tested H/PC devices. The OS was completely platform-independent; the H/PC was only one of many platforms, and it didn't make sense to concentrate on only that. We moved to a tiered system with quality checkpoints all the way along. The OS test team said, "We know the OS works on this processor with our drivers on the reference platform." So the H/PC lab had a basic assumption of what was working and could build on that by running its BVTs for the H/PC platform before releasing to the team.

But we did bang on it hard. We had a lot of people working really, really hard at the end. The saying is true: *You can't test quality into a product.* Don't expect Test to find everything and work it all out. But this effort came as close to actually doing that as any similar effort I've seen. We banged on it from every angle, and we actually did test a fair amount of quality into the product.

The big challenge going forward is more CPUs. We shrank the configuration matrix down, but now the CPU matrix is exploding, and that means more cross-compilers.

Patrick Copeland

The Microsoft way of testing is to do a lot of black box API-level and driver-level testing. The main objective is to find a lot of bugs. In other companies, testing is not as rigorous: "Let's do a pass and make sure everything works." But at Microsoft, our testers are software developers, and QA is our secret added advantage in the market.

Patrick Copeland

Our OS QA group writes code focused on making sure the OS works. We don't test the OS on the shipping platforms but on the reference platforms. After we deliver a working OS, the H/PC group, Palm-size PC group, or Auto PC group picks up the OS and augments it. They write code on top of the OS, and then they test those augmentations. By doing that, they provide additional testing for the OS too, because they find a small number of OS bugs that somehow made it through. And so they throw those bugs back over the wall to us, and we investigate those.

We try to model the configurations that we test, so we look at the scale of what we're supporting. We scale from a full-blown version of Windows all the way down to just a kernel, and we pick slices in there that are close to existing configurations. For example, one picks a configuration that's like an H/PC and one that's like the Palm-size PC, and we push those configurations through the lab. The lab has two reference platforms, and we try to pipe all these configs through all the chips and run all the tests.

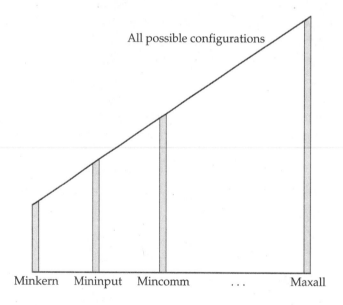

All possible configurations

| Minkern | Mininput | Mincomm | . . . | Maxall |

The Windows CE OS QA team examines the entire spectrum of possible configurations and chooses slices along the spectrum that correspond to systems that embedded developers are most likely to use.

Think about the number of permutations in componentization. GDI alone has thousands of different permutations—it's got 17 different components and exclusive OR relationships in which you can have this component but not that component. Take all those combinations and combine them with the rest of GWE, with COM, with the file systems, and with the kernel, and that total number of combinations is just impossible to test. We have to be smart about how we pick the configs.

Our first decision was to keep our existing tests. We didn't try to componentize the tests because that would have taken probably six months to a year. We decided instead to use Coffup to see which tests we could run and then fill in the holes. First we got the picture of what the Swiss cheese looked like and then started filling in the holes. We wrote component verification tests (CVTs) to touch every single API in a way that would not require any other component.

We then took all that information and maintained a database with all the tests, components, owners of the components, and people testing those components. That database enabled me to hit a button and list all of the APIs for a tester, or tell the lab which tests run on a given configuration, tell them the command lines for all those tests, where the tests are, what component they're testing. Part of the challenge is documenting what's going on because you don't want to miss any components. So we look through the whole source tree, through all the APIs, and then I create another list and say, "Component *A* isn't covered well enough." The process puts a spotlight on where the problems exist.

We also have a group that does backwards compatibility (BC) testing. We have people who are really good at running through apps on a Version 1 and a Version 2 device and then comparing the two. We're constantly thinking about potential backwards compatibility effects.

PLANNING FOR QUALITY: PROCESSES AND TOOLS

We try to incorporate QA objectives throughout the development process. For example, whenever developers create a new feature, they write developer regression tests (DRTs), which are like code specs. We can take a written DRT and augment it or say, "Here's what Development tested, so we'll go in this other direction." It gives us an idea of where to start.

We've invented some new processes. Windows CE is special in that we have to worry about the hardware and the kernel ports and the reference platforms. We have to worry about all these other partners, all the CPU vendors, and make sure they come in exactly on time. If they don't come in on time, we won't have enough time to stabilize the kernel port—we won't have enough time to make sure that the chip is working correctly. So we defined a new milestone called "Initial Integration Period" that marks the time when we expect CPUs to start arriving at our lab. We have acceptance criteria, meaning we accept a CPU in the lab if it meets these minimum requirements: it boots, you can load it, you can run a small set of tests on it. We also added a "Final Integration Period," which means that if the chip doesn't arrive by a specified date, we're not going to test it.

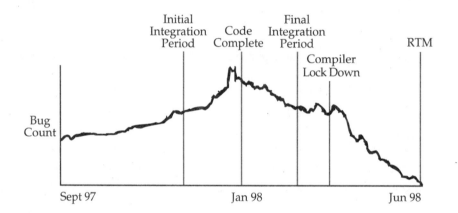

The Windows CE QA team augmented the Microsoft software development model by adding milestones to integrate the new CPU and its compiler.

THE TEST HARNESS

We try to create tests that Development can run. Whenever we write a bug, we have to write our command line for the test, and then make it easy for Development to go grab that test and duplicate the problem. One way we make it easier is to use a test harness. It simplifies the process. We just write test code in one area, and the test harness can run the test, manage permutations, and run multiple threads. It can load suite files that run certain combinations of tests. To test for a specific condition, we write special suites that create the proper preconditions.

A test harness can be something as simple as an .EXE that loads DLLs and provides a common interface—for example, a common command line specifying the way that the DLL talks to an .EXE. Our test harness is called "Tux." It's a very simple program. You pass Tux a DLL on the command line, and Tux calls *LoadLibrary* on that DLL. That DLL is expected to include a table with entry points. After messages are passed between the .EXE and the DLL, the .EXE can start running the first test.

We used to have three or four different harnesses for testing, and we've now moved to supporting Tux. We had to rewrite some tests, but we saved time. Tux is the test case launcher, and Kato is a generic logging engine that we use to enumerate, select, and launch tests in an automated way. Tux and Kato really have a very low memory footprint, so they wouldn't interfere with your hardware platform. If you are just getting started with the DDTK, you can use the Tuxdemo sample to learn about its capabilities.

CKato Method	Description
BeginLevel	Begin a new level in the logging hierarchy
Log	Log a string to the current logging level with a specified verbosity level
Comment	Log without recording the verbosity level
GetItemData, SetItemData	Allow applications to retrieve and set a 32-bit application-specific data with the CKato object
SendSystemData	Send a buffer of raw data
GetCurrentLevel	Get the current logging level of the CKato object
GetVerbosityCount	Query the number of times *Log* was called with the specified verbosity and logging levels
EndLevel	End the current level in the logging hierarchy

The Kato client class library lets you create a hierarchical log with multiple levels of test reporting detail, called "verbosity levels." The log can be filtered by hierarchical level, verbosity level, or by a 32-bit data item defined by the test application. This item typically specifies a time, a process, or a computer data stamp. In addition to being provided in the class library, Kato API functions are provided in C.

As the OS evolves, the tools have to evolve. We try to take advantage of all the newest features of the OS. For example, as Ethernet support came online, we were able to control D9000 reference platforms across the net wherever they are connected to a PC. So I can control all the test platforms in the building, and I can tell them all to run tests and report back what's going on. At night, we convert the whole building into a virtual lab.

QUALITY METRICS

You also want to be able to track how the project is going. I watch the bug counts to determine if we're on track to ship. We want to control the period when new features come in because getting a bug fixed takes a while. For version 1.0, the mean time was four days and the average was about seven days to fix any given bug. We have a milestone called "code complete," which means the developers think that they're finished with the bulk of the coding for their features. We try to hammer everything down and close down shop early, which gives us time to go through code finding bugs. It also gives Development time to go back and start closing out all the bugs.

We use charts to track all these metrics. We're pretty chart-happy; every component is charted. We chart size and performance over time. We write benchmark tests that call a specific API for 1000 cycles and time its performance from the beginning to the end, to figure out how much time it took per cycle. It's kind of an early warning signal that something's going wrong, and you can go back and adjust it before it shows up in other tests.

THE OS TEST LAB

Our OS test lab is a regression lab, to run the tests across all the CPUs and all the reference platforms, and then report what happens. The lab actually files bugs against our tests so we'll know which things to fix. If a test breaks, it gets fixed. It's just like the relationship with developers. A testing group doesn't have any benefit unless it's finding bugs and the bugs are getting fixed. The lab is our client, and they report back to the whole group about what's going on.

The test owner writes a test and hands it to the lab. The lab reports a failure back to the test owner. The test owner looks at the log. When you look at the big picture for the day, you can tell: "Okay, a lot of the BVTs failed on one chip but not on any other chips. This looks like the compiler or a chip problem as opposed to an OS problem. An OS problem would go across all the chips." Having a good reporting mechanism helps us to visualize what's going on. For example, we'd get a different idea of what's going on if everything were failing: the problem would either be an OS bug or a test bug.

Testing is a complicated process because we are not only dealing with chips but with reference platforms, cards that are written on the chips, tools, the kernel, and the compiler. We try to identify each kind of failure. Basically, there are five variables: the compiler's broken, the chip needs a rev, the reference platform is screwed up somehow, the tests are broken, or there's an OS break.

We test with multiple configurations by using our monolithic tests and our CVT tests. And after that whole combination of tests, we come up with an OS that is fully tested. We don't claim to test more than we do. We just say, "This is how much we test. You can build your own config, and we think that will work." But we're not to the point yet where we randomly create a config, test it, and see that it works.

Kieu Nguyen

My background is working with the low-level network architecture. Testing the OS is pretty cool, it's low level; I love that. I remember back in October 1996, Bryan [Trussel] was saying, "We need an OS lab; we need to test all these CPUs—it's yours." That's how Bryan and I work together: he just says, "This is yours." I'm learning now that when he says, "How busy are you?" I need to look at him and ask, "Why?" [laughs]

Kieu Nguyen

I'd never done anything like this kind of testing before. So I went with Callie [Wilson] to look at the lab and opened the door. It had been a game room and somebody had just moved out. There was a lot of junk in there and the lights were broken. There was nothing. That's how the OS lab was. And from there we ordered benches, stole hardware left and right, and collected all the cables. We built it from scratch. So when I think of that lab at the beginning, I feel like saying, "Oh, what a nightmare!" But I'm really very fond of it because we built it from scratch.

You surely need a lab where you can run automated tests. During the OS testing for the Handheld PC, I dealt with the OEM platform and hardware issues, the driver issues, and automation. Basically I was the customer for the testers who designed and wrote the test code. I took what they wrote and ran the tests.

We had a tremendous challenge because we had CPU issues, hardware platform variations, and different configurations. And for us, the tests themselves created a fourth dimension. So it was a tremendous challenge. We cannot test everything every day, so we came up with this scheme to rotate through the tests, and set up an internal web page to report the test results. When we click on a build version, the web page comes up with the latest results for any configuration based on the last time the tests were run.

The hardest part about testing an OS is that you can lose your focus on the customers, the real people using it. For example, maybe an SRAM card doesn't get detected all the time. When you look at the whole OS, that's not such a big deal. But when you think about somebody buying a Handheld PC and paying 200 bucks for an SRAM card that doesn't work, you realize that your customer would be pretty steamed. I think it's crucial to make sure that your test team remembers the customers. Look at what you're trying to build. Break it out into components as fast as you can and see how you can test each component independently. Use people who know how to test your system as components and people who know how to test the whole system. When you hire people, you have to realize that testers are different. In the same way developers have different strengths, some testers are good at low-level testing and some are good at high-level testing.

Make sure you have tests for troubleshooting the drivers. Find a way to test those drivers immediately. With the Handheld PC, we first developed manual driver verification tests. Once you know those are working, then build up to the next layer. Don't start by building the whole thing together and testing all of it at once, because you won't know where the heck things are going wrong. The DDTK can help you.

THE DEVICE DRIVER TEST KIT

I was in charge of putting together the Device Driver Test Kit (DDTK). We took our driver tests, cleaned up the source code, and made sure that developers could build in the Embedded Toolkit environment. For version 1.01 we provided only a few drivers, but we shipped out more with 2.0, and we're adding more and more. We have tests for display drivers, keyboard drivers, audio, serial, PCMCIA, FATFS, and network communication.

The DDTK is self-contained and designed for running with the Embedded Toolkit. Basically, you download the tests to a device that boots and runs them. You can put them in RAM or Flash memory.

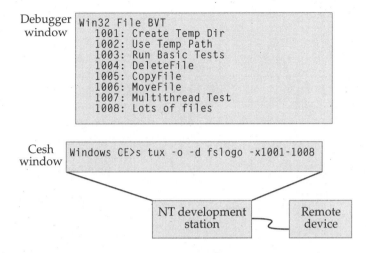

Debugger window

```
Win32 File BVT
   1001: Create Temp Dir
   1002: Use Temp Path
   1003: Run Basic Tests
   1004: DeleteFile
   1005: CopyFile
   1006: MoveFile
   1007: Multithread Test
   1008: Lots of files
```

Cesh window

```
Windows CE>s tux -o -d fslogo -x1001-1008
```

NT development station

Remote device

The Tux test harness allows you to launch different sets of tests and run them in different sequences. Tux is often used with another tool provided in the DDTK, the Kato logging engine.

These driver tests don't require any components for the window manager or controls; they just send their output to the debug port. You can view them on the desktop by using Windbg, which communicates with the device via the serial port—a COM port on your machine and a debug port on your device. We also provide a little tool called ComRoute, which captures the COM port on the desktop side. Windbg, you know, doesn't have a very big buffer, so ComRoute lets you save all of the output messages. That's how we do automation. You can run overnight, over and over and over, and ComRoute keeps on capturing. You can send the output to a file or to the screen.

The decision we had to make with the DDTK was how much of our test suite to ship. With drivers especially, there are so many timing issues. We ship the binaries of the test harness, Tux, and we ship the source code of the test DLL itself so that people can change it, modify it, and enhance it. The ideal situation is that we send out our set of tests to the OEMs, and as the OEMs enhance the tests, they send the enhancements back to us. That would be perfect. We're not there yet, but we're getting there.

RESOURCES

Topic	Resource
Certification and logo program	*http://www.microsoft.com/windowsce/logo/*
Development methodology	*Debugging the Development Process*, by Steve McGuire (Microsoft Press, 1997); *Code Complete*, by Steve McConnell (Microsoft Press, 1997); *Dynamics of Software Development*, by Jim McCarthy (Microsoft Press, 1995)
Hardware reference platforms: D9000 and the CEPC	Microsoft Windows CE Embedded Toolkit for Visual C++
The Device Driver Test Kit (DDTK), Tux, and Kato	Microsoft Windows CE Embedded Toolkit for Visual C++

10 Development Tools

*W*hile the development team was proceeding with work on the operating system and on the first Microsoft Windows CE–based products, two other teams were simultaneously working on development tools. One of those teams, under the guidance of Randy Kath, created the Software Development Kit (SDK) and the Device Driver Kit (DDK) for application and driver developers, while the other team, under Roland Ayala, created the OEM Adaptation Kit (OAK) to help OEMs port the operating system to their specific platforms. The strategy was to provide commercial development tools in three phases for these three different groups:

◆ *Microsoft Visual C++ application developers*

◆ *Microsoft Visual Basic and Microsoft Visual J++ developers*

◆ *Embedded systems developers*

The integrated development environment (IDE) on desktop products offered a popular GUI in which to write, compile, link, and debug applications. To extend this development model to Windows CE devices, Kath's team decided to offer emulation and remote debugging.

Using emulation, developers can simulate the appearance and behavior of some devices on the desktop PC. This enables much of the development to take place without a reference platform or Windows CE device. After debugging the application under emulation, the developer at the PC development station can use remote debugging to test the application and examine or manipulate the state of the remote device. The remote debugging technology allows all the standard operations on the remote device: single-stepping through code, setting breakpoints, and examining memory. Version 2.10 supports connections between the development station and the device via serial port, parallel port, or Ethernet connection.

The development products also include support for such programming models as COM, MFC, ATL, and ActiveX. Microsoft's language-independent Component Object Model (COM) extends earlier work on Object Linking and Embedding (OLE) to offer a standard for creating robust software components. These components, called COM objects, can be reused and assembled into larger systems. An ActiveX control is a specific type of COM object that exposes properties, methods, and events, so it can be driven by scripts in such languages as VBScript and JScript. In this chapter, Kenneth Macleod describes the underlying OLE/COM/ActiveX infrastructure in version 2.10.

Randy Kath explains the vision behind the first several offerings of the SDK and Visual C++ toolkits for application development. Chris Stirrat and Keith Szot explain the Visual Basic and Visual J++ products, respectively. Roland Ayala walks through the command-line development environment used to build the OS from its components. These tools were originally packaged as part of the OAK and are now available in the Windows CE Embedded Toolkit for Visual C++. Scott Horn, the program manager responsible for the embedded toolkit, describes these tools and future directions for the graphical IDE.

———◆———

PHASE 1: SUPPORTING VISUAL C++ DEVELOPERS

Randy Kath

In the world today, 4.76 *million* Win32 developers use Microsoft Visual C++, Visual Basic, Visual J++, and other tools. Those developers represent a tremendous human resource. We recognized that if we could get them to apply their Win32 skills to this new category of non-PC devices, we would essentially jump-start a new industry, enabling many experienced developers to extend their skills and products to the new devices.

Randy Kath

We began by building Visual C++ for Windows CE. Windows CE works with many new processors. Our strategy was to build cross-compilers and host all these different architectures out of Microsoft Visual Studio on the x86 desktop—the same environment that developers work with today in building applications for Microsoft Windows NT, Microsoft Windows 95, and Microsoft Windows 98. By doing this, we really felt like we were enabling people to develop everything, from device drivers and the OEM adaptation layer all the way up to third-party applications.

We worked on remote debug, auto-download features, and some niceties to integrate our environment as seamlessly as possible with the desktop environment. People liked it, but when they started to look more carefully at Windows CE, they said, "Hey, we can build apps, but where's MFC and where's Visual Basic and where's Java?" We realized we had to complete the offering and produce the rest of the tools that Win32 developers are used to working with. So we expanded the Visual C++ product to include support for new OS features like COM and ActiveX controls. The corollary in Visual Studio is ATL, which gives you very good support for ActiveX control development.

PHASE 2: SUPPORTING VISUAL BASIC AND VISUAL J++ DEVELOPERS

Phase 2 of the strategy was about building Visual Basic and Visual J++ for Windows CE. Visual Basic was an interesting challenge because on the desktop, it has all the client/server work, really great database access, and lots of different controls that just drop in to enable easy development. In the Windows CE environment, however, much of this functionality doesn't work in the same way. So we spent a lot of time thinking, "What is the best way to offer VB in the Windows CE environment?" Although a lot of people have VB language expertise, they're not necessarily going to build the same kinds of applications for these devices as for the desktop.

The key was to build a run time [library] that enabled developers to apply their language expertise and experience to this new category of computers. So we built what I would characterize as a very small, lightweight run time and a very minimal object model. We leveraged the extensibility of ActiveX controls so that developers can build everything, from tiny but very effective applications that literally take only a week to build, to very big, scalable, or distributed applications with a robust set of ActiveX controls that require a lot of time to build.

If you stop and think about a more commercial or industrial environment, such as a factory floor, you see that the challenge is in building the software to run systems like automation controllers. Suppose the developers said, "Let's control this factory floor with a lot of microprocessors. We'll install embedded versions of Windows CE with the Visual Basic run time and then add some RAM so there's some room to work. And we'll network all these together using TCP/IP, which is built into Windows CE. We could boot up all the systems, and they could communicate very easily."

With Windows CE, a team of IS developers who are familiar with Visual Basic can build the ActiveX controls and Visual Basic scripts necessary to control the factory floor. The developers can build all this functionality in a lab and deploy the apps across their distributed solution. The system is very flexible, easy to develop, and easy to modify. If for example, the company wanted to change the order in which events occur on the factory floor, the developers could very easily change the logic of the script. VB makes the system very flexible.

In fact, most of the requests for Visual Basic weren't from people prototyping the UI but from people on the manufacturing side of the business who wanted to reduce the amount of time they spend scripting systems like factory automation systems. It was really very interesting—Visual Basic adds value to our system differently from the way it adds value to the desktop.

With Visual J++, we offer the same benefits as Visual C++ and Visual Basic: remote debugging, downloading, and an SDK that allows you to choose a component set of the class libraries rather than the whole set. We spent a considerable effort enabling the Java virtual machine (VM) to run on Windows CE, getting the class library, and defining how the VM would best work in the environment with smaller memory footprint.

Suppose you want only the I/O class from AWT. You can reduce the footprint substantially by picking and choosing just the I/O class component. So again, we're taking advantage of the knowledge developers have about the desktop development environment, but we're adapting the non-PC device environment to reflect what developers are trying to build and what Windows CE brings to the table.

PHASE 3: SUPPORTING EMBEDDED SYSTEMS DEVELOPERS

Along the way, we also introduced a new product—the embedded toolkit. Initially, we didn't envision needing this, but as we got more and more involved in the embedded industry, we realized it was necessary.

We originally had a kit called the OAK—the OEM Adaptation Kit. We took everything we used to build the system, put it all in a box, and said, "Here, embedded systems engineers. Go figure it out. We figured it out; you can, too." The kit provides all the enabling technology, but it doesn't make development any easier for them. Maybe only one or two thousand developers in that 4.76 million can actually overcome such a steep learning curve. We need hundreds of thousands of developers picking this up and running with it. So we invented the Embedded Toolkit product to encapsulate what the OAK was delivering and bring it into the Visual Studio development environment.

Embedded development is full of complexity. The engineers might be working with a VME bus from AMD with their special processor and a whole new set of peripherals. To get all the hardware working, they have to write some drivers and build a ROM image and flash the image into ROM and see if it works. And they'll probably encounter a couple of hurdles along the way where they're performing some very painful kernel driver debugging. Even today, when Thomas Fenwick and Mike Ginsberg bring up a kernel on a new processor, they use LEDs to get hex numbers to walk through the code—really rudimentary debugging techniques.

The embedded community is very fragmented, with lots of different tools and operating system options. Developers and others in that community are plowing forward on their own with very few standards. The desktop is much more mature at this point. It has standard APIs, standard object models, and even standard programming languages. The desktop PC is a much more standards-based environment. We're trying to bring that same model to the embedded community.

For us the holy grail was getting the IDE debugger to debug remotely so that developers using Visual Studio could use the exact same debugging methodology they use on the desktop. The only perceptible difference between the two is that remote debugging is a little bit slower because it is running over a connection to the remote device; otherwise, it works the same way.

REMOTE TOOLS

Tool	Description
Windows CE Spy++	Graphical tool used to display information about a window and its messages (all messages or selected types)
Windows CE Registry Editor	Manages the desktop, emulation, or device registry
Windows CE Process Viewer	Examines detailed information about processes, threads, and memory on the remote Windows CE device, and modifies many settings
Windows CE Heap Walker	Examines the contents of system memory
Windows CE Zoomin	Examines the contents of the device display
Windows CE Remote Object Viewer	Examines files, registry entries, or database objects in the object store on the remote device

This debugger is really cool. Even though you're debugging against different remote RISC targets, the debugger knows what type you're debugging against, and the RISC target information is available. For example, the x86 and R4300 register sets are nothing alike; the number of registers each has is different and they have different register names. But in either case, you work with the debugger in exactly the same way, and the debugger takes care of all the hardware specifics for you.

We adapted the Windows NT kernel debugger, Windbg, as a remote debugger for Windows CE. We allow you to debug over a serial port, parallel port, and Ethernet connection. You can also have multiple ports so that you can debug over one while using the other, which becomes critical when you're performing tasks like debugging the serial driver. You know, if you set a breakpoint on the driver for the debug port, well, you kill yourself.

The architecture is transport-independent today; all we're doing is writing more transports. And as we add new transports, we'll make sure the tools for VB, VJ++, and VC++ will work on all of them.

So our challenge is to allow developers familiar with existing systems to continue working with what they know. If you want to set a breakpoint on some kernel-level driver, you shouldn't have to learn a new debugger and a new way to set that breakpoint. You should be able to use the tools and strategies you already understand. You should be able to apply the exact same technique to a problem. Whether that technique is JTAG or EJTAG (IEEE Standard 1149.1), BDM (background debug mode), or anything else, you shouldn't have to know which processor or which board you're working on. We are now working very closely with our semiconductor partners to integrate capabilities such as hardware or system debugging.

ENABLING EXTENSIBILITY: OLE, COM, ACTIVEX

Kenneth Macleod

Our requirements were to support ActiveX controls, which you can use with your Visual C++ and Visual Basic apps; support Microsoft Internet Explorer 4.0; and support desktop compatible storage. And that's what we got. We support the basic COM infrastructure, automation, and storage.

On the desktop are a container and an object, and in between them is OLE. When you use the apartment model, or make a call to an object in a different process, OLE is always in between the container and the object.

But on Windows CE, we support only in-process servers and the free threading model. So we went into the code and thwack! [Macleod draws lines through the OLE block to indicate removing it.] Because it's just left over from Win16, right? I mean, Win16 had this horrible crap where OLE was putting messages into the message queue, and it had all these OLE APIs for message handling and message filtering, which we don't need for Windows CE. So OLE on the CE platform never gets in between your calls. The calls just go straight through. OLE is a bunch of APIs and a bunch of interfaces, but it never gets in the way of things.

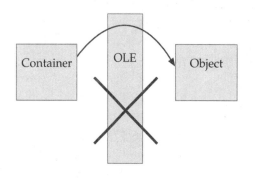

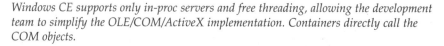

Windows CE supports only in-proc servers and free threading, allowing the development team to simplify the OLE/COM/ActiveX implementation. Containers directly call the COM objects.

The most commonly called API is *CoCreateInstance*. For Windows CE, the implementation is just this huge *LoadLibrary*. A programmer passes the class ID to *CoCreateInstance*. We fish for the DLL in the registry, then call *LoadLibrary* to spin up the DLL and hand back a pointer so that the developer can talk directly to the object. The developer's thread does direct jumps into the other code, straight through.

The object needs to be thread-safe. It needs to be able to handle as many threads as the container spins up. We tried to drive that point home. In fact, before we shipped Windows CE, we stripped out the code for *CoInitialize* and

OleInitialize and replaced them with *CoInitializeEx*, which forces you to pass in a flag that says what thread model you support. We accept only the flag for multithreading.

The desktop's version of the storage code was ported and then ignored. We wrote our own version of desktop storage, which is about 150 KB. Storage itself is optional—I believe the Palm-size PC is dumping OLE storage altogether—but if you use storage, you have to select all of its components.

OLE32 Components	Description
com	Basic COM support, including *CoCreateInstance*, *CoInitializeEx* and the *CLSIDFrom** functions
docfile	Desktop storage; supports the docfile implementation for Windows CE
exp	Desktop storage; supports the *Stg** API functions
msf	Base desktop storage support
ole232	ActiveX and embedding support
oleaut32	Automation support; includes all functions relating to variants and typelibs

Desktop storage is optional, but when desktop storage is selected all three components must be present. The full list of OLE/COM-related modules, components, and API functions appears in the embedded toolkit.

The desktop's version of the automation code was ported and shredded. Well, some of the automation stuff is genuinely based on the desktop. We analyzed that and rewrote some of the fundamental APIs and then rewrote the type library code because it's sort of the top level of functionality.

THE WINDOWS CE TOOLKIT FOR VISUAL BASIC

Chris Stirrat

We want to enable the millions of VB developers to program for a handheld device with a minimal learning curve, and the way to do that is to add tools that integrate as seamlessly as possible into the VB environment. VB has a new project type called the Windows CE Project. You lay out your form and put code behind it the same way you would in VB. The new Windows CE–specific project properties indicate the target environment, *emulator* or *remote* for the remote device, and indicate the build type, either *debug* or *regular*.

Chris Stirrat

When you want to run your application, you click the Run button. The tool then automatically compiles to the Windows CE file format, sends the file to the device, and starts the file on the device for you.

We support full remote debugging so that you can remote debug to your device from your desktop. The debug environment has all the same debugging tools that you'd expect to see in VB: step into, step out of, step over, looking at variables, the watch window, and the immediate window. In addition, we support remote tools such as Zoom, Spy, Heap Walker, Process Viewer, and Registry Editor (for remote registry editing). There is also a Control Manager to help you keep track of which controls are available for the desktop and the remote device.

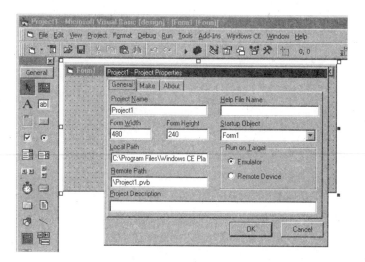

The new Windows CE project properties let you choose whether to build for the emulator or build for the remote device. You can also click the Make tab to select debug or retail builds. The Windows CE menu added to the Visual Basic menu bar offers access to the remote debugging tools.

We also have full support for an emulation environment that ships with the product. It's the standard Windows CE SDK emulation environment, which allows you to emulate a Handheld PC, so you can lay your forms out and see what they look like. Essentially 90 percent of your development can be completed in your emulation environment without even using a device.

The Windows CE version of Visual Basic is a subset of the desktop version. Because Windows CE is designed to run on small devices without the CPU or memory power of a desktop, we had to find a compelling subset of the language and forms package. The forms package is a subset of VB5.0 that contains the objects you would expect to see, such as forms, controls, and error objects. The actual language support is a subset of VB5.0. One key difference is that all VB for Windows CE variables are VARIANTS and cannot be typed. Some of the language statements are also not supported.

We took what we thought was a good subset, put it on the device, got customer feedback, and tailored it based on the feedback.

In the run time, we give you the objects, forms, and controls. We provide you with the intrinsic controls, which are always available with the run time: the buttons, check boxes, list boxes, and combo boxes. Then if you want to add functionality, our extensibility story is to use ActiveX controls. We shipped five ActiveX controls to cover additional functionality that people wanted to see and released six more controls in our control pack. We will soon be releasing an ADO (data access) control. We have a pretty rich set of controls, each componentized and packaged separately so that you can manage your RAM space.

ACTIVEX CONTROLS IN WINDOWS CE PRODUCTS

Product	Controls
Microsoft Windows CE Toolkit for Visual Basic 5.0	Intrinsic controls and five ActiveX controls: picture box, image, Winsock, file system, and serial port.
Microsoft Windows CE ActiveX Control Pack	Six ActiveX controls: grid, tabstrip (for tabbed dialogs), tree view, list view, image list, and common dialogs. (The ADO control will be added as soon as it is available.)

DESIGNING VB APPLICATIONS FOR WINDOWS CE

A lot of people say, "I want to take my VB app and compile it for Windows CE." We can't really do that today. Porting existing applications directly to Windows CE would be tough. We can't anticipate which of the controls that you depend on might not exist for Windows CE. It really makes a lot more sense if you think about it this way: You have a desktop application connected to a network, you have a handheld device, and you want to take some of your users mobile. Instead of porting the whole application, you probably really want a piece of that application to be local on the device.

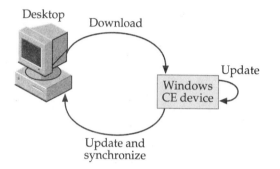

To take users mobile, VB developers should use a slightly different application model than is used on the desktop. The application should contain the smallest amount of code needed to create or update data in the field. The mobile device and desktop are synchronized to share data updates.

You want to send some data to the device, disconnect, take the device with you in the world, use the data, display it, capture more data, and then sync back up at the end of the day. You want to take a subset of the application functionality, reimplement that functionality in VB for Windows CE, and put it on the device. The key part of this whole process is moving the data.

ADO is the standard Windows database API, so we will have an ADO control that makes the object store on the device appear as an ADO recordset or as a database. Your desktop application will have programmatic access to the data on your device so that you can synchronize data between your desktop and device. And we'll also offer automatic synchronization to Microsoft Access and Microsoft SQL Server databases through Active Sync: you can drag an MDB file into your synchronize folder, and we automatically build the tables on the device and keep them in sync.

Every developer we talk to loves VB and is totally sold on the fact that developing with it is easy. Developers also like that it's processor-independent. The PVB app that you write will run on any device as long as it has a VB run-time library. Right now, we support VB for Windows CE on the H/PC device only. As we move forward, we will start releasing on more platforms and CPUs—for example, the Auto PC, PC companion devices, and custom devices. Then we will make VB available to all embedded developers as components in the embedded toolkit. This will allow OEMs to create "open" devices so that others can add value for that platform. This will give the OEMs access to a large programming community to create applications for their custom devices.

We have a flexible run-time architecture because we can't anticipate what your platform is going to look like. If you can picture the difference between the UI on an Auto PC and the UI on an H/PC, you can picture a completely different paradigm. We will have the flexibility in the run-time architecture to handle custom forms packages. That's definitely the direction we're going.

WINDOWS CE TOOLKIT FOR VISUAL J++

Keith Szot

You have to think about supporting the Java programming language from two perspectives: providing the appropriate development tools and providing run-time support on the actual platform. A lot of people ask, "Why do I need a toolkit for Java? If I have a desktop compiler that creates Java bytecodes, I can just put the compiled application on the device and run it." Well, that's true, you could do that, but you wouldn't have the ability to develop on your PC using emulation, and you wouldn't have the remote development technology. The remote technology enables you to download and execute an application on a device connected to your host development PC and to perform interactive debugging with control of the Microsoft virtual machine (MSVM) on the device.

That remote debugging and emulation is what our add-on product provides. The tools are fully integrated into Visual J++ and offer the same type of experience that a Visual J++ developer would have developing apps for the desktop. The learning curve for becoming productive in this environment is very low.

Keith Szot

We also support the Raw Native Interface (RNI) so that as a developer, you can take advantage of the unique functionality provided by the Windows CE platform. Let's say you want to take advantage of the Windows CE command bar or IrDA functionality that is not exposed to you through the JDK 1.1. You can use RNI to call directly to the Win32 API provided by the Windows CE OS. Or you could use RNI to call into your own DLL, if you have a fast routine in C or C++ or even assembly that you want to integrate with your application written in Java.

For the run-time library, not only is it important to provide the full functionality of JDK 1.1, it's important to make sure it works well in the resource-constrained environment of Windows CE. You typically have restricted RAM and ROM availability on the device; and the processors have lower processing power compared to the desktop. For example, you can't JIT—use just-in-time technology—on these types of devices; doing so would fill in all available RAM, which is impractical.

Corporations are very interested in the Windows CE–based H/PC products. Those wanting the benefits of programming in Java are looking to our toolkit implementation to bring the best of those two worlds together, to create corporate solutions written in Java running on top of the Windows CE H/PC platform. One of the features we offer is a componentization of the Java classes so that you can build custom DLLs with only the classes needed by your application: the application class files, the MSVM, and the associated native method DLLs. An ISV or corporation wanting to run a specific application on a particular device can provide that application in the form of a custom DLL. The DLL has the application's class file included, so it has everything it needs. Another nice feature of the single DLL is that it resolves the references to all those different classes for you; the classes don't have to be resolved at run time, which increases your performance and decreases your overall startup time.

Our complete implementation on SH3 is a little under 3.6 MB in footprint, and on MIPS it is about 3.9 MB. That's pretty dang good from a desktop perspective, because the typical desktop implementations are at least double that. We've done a pretty good job of slimming it down. The more choice and flexibility OEMs and developers have, the happier they are. Whatever we can do to minimize the resource requirements ultimately improves the developers' choices for minimizing the footprint.

We focused on Windows CE for the Handheld PC for the first release. Initially, we felt it was important to ensure that developers could get access to the Win32 API to get the full functionality and power of the Windows CE platform. Right now, we don't support J/Direct, but that's definitely something that we're working on for an upcoming release. And we will continue to integrate into future releases of the Visual J++ products. We will provide an add-on to Visual J++ 6.0 and extend WFC support to Windows CE so that developers making the move to Visual J++ 6.0 can be confident about carrying their new knowledge to Windows CE.

CREATING AN OS WITH THE TOOLS

Roland Ayala

The embedded toolkit was originally called the OAK, and that's exactly what it is—an OEM *Adaptation* Kit. It gives OEMs everything they need to *adapt* the Windows CE operating system to new hardware platforms—all the necessary compilers, assemblers, linkers, and debugger support.

We also provide a lot of sample code. The CEPC with the x86 architecture is a good example: CEPC users can see Windows CE come up as a working system fairly quickly because we have already ported to that standardized architecture.

Roland Ayala

The Windows CE command-line build environment that was in the OAK and is preserved in the embedded toolkit is almost identical to the environment used for the Windows NT DDK, so if you've worked with the Windows NT device driver kit, you'll feel very much at home. The environment is command-line driven and very arcane. OEMs who get the toolkit spend about a week getting comfortable with the build environment because we use so many switches and environment variables for the build tools. Many of those tools are set up automatically when you create your build environment using the Wince.bat file, but you can also choose different settings by manually setting environment variables—for example, you can switch from a debug build to a retail build. It takes time to learn them all.

We provide demo files with the toolkit for two reasons: to show the OS capabilities in different configurations and to give engineers a complete picture of system functionality. Seven different demos, each with its own configuration, can show you how to turn all the knobs to get the right effect.

SAMPLE CONFIGURATIONS

Configuration	Description
Minkern	Contains the kernel and the parts of Filesys needed to boot plus the registry and heap
Mininput	The Minkern configuration with minimal event system from GWE, offering user input and native driver support
Mincomm	The Mininput configuration with support for PC cards, networking, and serial communications including infrared
Mingdi	The Mininput configuration with graphics device interface (GDI) support
Minwmgr	A combination of the Mingdi and Mincomm configurations with window manager support
Minshell	The Minwmgr configuration with COM and shell API support; a nearly complete version of Windows CE featuring the task manager and command shell
Maxall	Includes nearly all available components (except those components with exclusive OR relations to other components)

Right now, we give you code for two sample platforms: the Hitachi D9000 development platform and the CEPC. Our directory structure, or build tree, is structured to include the directories for those platforms. OEMs can generally glean the information they need from these samples and apply it to their particular platforms.

THE PROCESS

An OEM first selects desired components by creating an ASCII batch file called Cesysgen.bat. This file is used in the Sysgen phase, which is the process of building the OS from the selected components. Right now, it's really arcane. An OEM has to know the components and the dependencies among the components. This process is typically iterated until the OEM can get a Sysgen that truly meets the product requirements.

Basically, an OEM edits Cesysgen.bat to set up a bunch of environment variables and then runs a batch file called Sysgen.bat that issues the command, *nmake sysgen*. As part of the make operation, the sysgen tools read the environment variables to understand how to link all the various components together to give you the desired OS components. We provide all the system libraries, and the OEM links them together to get one big final executable.

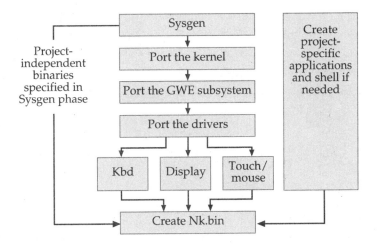

All embedded developers will perform the system generation step and port the kernel, and almost all will port the GWE subsystem. Driver development can be performed in parallel to save time. The final ported system software is combined with project-specific applications to create the system file, Nk.bin.

After selecting the components, an OEM implements the hardware-dependent portion of the kernel, the OEM Adaptation Layer (OAL), and links it with the Microsoft deliverable part of the kernel, Nk.lib. This is why an OEM has to use a supported processor: we provide debug and retail Nk.lib binaries only for the supported processors.

Most OEMs will want the GWE subsystem and at this point will start porting GWE. Ninety-eight percent of all systems are going to want to use the Windows event manager. GWE is highly componentizable. Like the kernel, GWE has a platform-independent portion and the OEM-dependent portion. The platform-dependent portion involves the drivers. The native drivers are the keyboard, the display, the video, the touch screen or mouse, the battery, and the notification LED drivers.

The OEMs will definitely parallelize their driver development efforts to get the products out their doors quickly. Drivers vary in complexity, but you can figure six to eight weeks of development time for each of these drivers. That's just Roland's rule of thumb. A really hot-shot developer or a developer working on a keyboard driver very similar to a PC keyboard controller will produce a driver in less than six to eight weeks. In fact, a developer working with the PC keyboard controller pretty much already has the driver from our samples. I'm talking six to eight weeks if the developer actually has to implement the PDD.

For the common drivers, Microsoft offers the MDD/PDD model. Unless an OEM has a compelling reason to avoid using our MDD, *not* using it is really silly because it comprises over 85 percent of the code. All the OEM has to do is worry about the platform-dependent portion.

When the driver development is all said and done, you take all the platform-dependent binaries, system-independent binaries, and project binaries—the apps—and roll them all into the operating system image file. (We name this file Nk.bin by default, but you don't have to use this name.) Nk.bin then gets loaded onto the platform. You could also load it all into Flash, a ROM chip, or RAM for development purposes. Windows CE is different in that you're not putting a bunch of system files on a hard drive. You're storing all the files into one big huge file—an image—and then loading that image into memory. Because everything is already in memory when you turn the system on, Windows CE boots and loads quickly. Boom! It's there.

SYSGEN AND BUILD

For componentization, we offer the Sysgen tool. For compiling and linking, we offer the Build.exe tool. Build.exe takes the Dirs file and Sources file as input. If Build sees a Dirs file, it walks into each of the directories listed in that file and looks for Sources files or other Dirs files. You can start at the top of a tree and then walk down to build everything under it by adding Dirs files. At the end of each path, a Sources file has to be present in order for the system to build.

You put a Sources file wherever you store the code for your module. The Build tool is really nice because you don't have to worry about questions like: "What are all the right linker options and switches and stuff for building for CE?" The tool makes your work very simple. You tell the tool, *target type=program*, or *target type=DLL*, or *target type=library*. You tell it the source modules. You can also pass additional parameters, too, if you need to.

Wherever there is a Sources file, there is also a local makefile. When you call Build, Build calls the local makefile, which includes Makefile.def. Makefile.def is this huge, long, five-page makefile with all the intricacies of the correct linker options, the correct compiler options, the directory structure, and so forth. This is the master makefile that really does all the work.

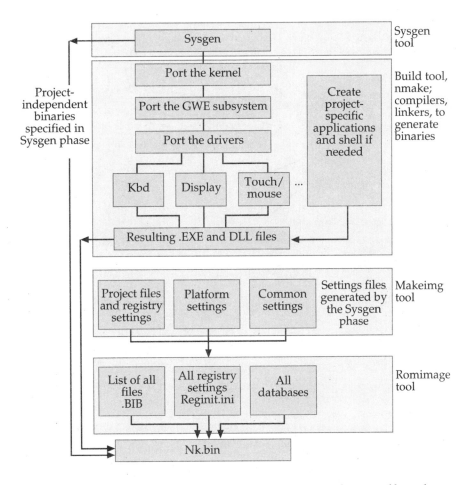

The Build tool, the compilers, and the linkers are used to generate the executables and libraries. The Sysgen phase generates the input files needed for the Makeimg and Romimage tools. Eventually, all the files are built into a single image file, Nk.bin.

This master makefile allows a few very knowledgeable people such as Mike [Ginsberg] or Sharad [Mathur] or Thomas [Fenwick] to say, "These are the correct compiler switches and this is how you need to link." If we check in a new compiler tomorrow, Mike changes the switches required for that new compiler, and business goes on as usual.

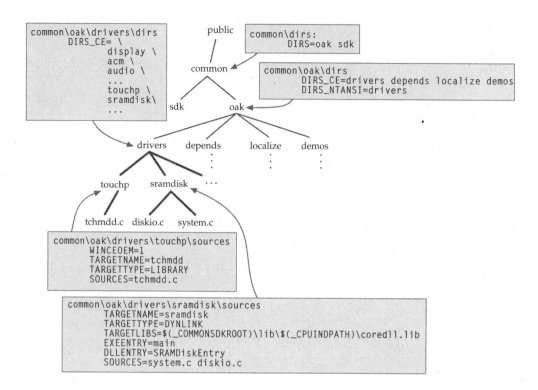

The Build tool traverses the directory structure beneath the directory in which it is invoked. For example, when invoked in the drivers directory, Build processes the dirs file, which directs it in turn to the touchp, sramdisk, and other driver directories. Those directories contain Sources files specifying the source files to be compiled and linked into libraries or executables.

Personally, I love Build. It manages the complexity. Even though a tree might have 15 different components in 15 different directories, you can go to the root of the Platform directory and just say "Build!" That's all you've got to do.

MAKEIMG AND ROMIMAGE

When your system is building cleanly, you need to use the Makeimg and Romimage tools to combine all the files generated by the Build process into one big file, Nk.bin. The Makeimg tool puts all the files in .BIB files, puts registry settings in .REG files, and puts databases in .DB files. The Romimage tool takes all the files that are specified in the .BIB and makes an Nk.bin for you.

Back when we released H/PC 1.0, we just had one big .BIB file, one big registry setting file, and so many #defines. We had to #ifdef this OEM's platform and #ifdef that OEM's platform. We were starting different projects, plus we had the Japanese version, and it was all totally insane! One project would change the .BIB file and break the builds for everybody.

That was why we organized the files and the registry settings as common, platform-specific, or project-specific:

◆ *Common files and settings.* These are set up by the Sysgen tool.

◆ *Platform-specific files and settings.* For any given platform, you need a specific version of the kernel. Some driver files and registry settings are always the same for that platform. For example, the platform-specific files for the CEPC platform never change from one system to another.

◆ *Project-specific files and settings.* Project settings change the most frequently. By breaking out the project-specific .BIB file, registry setting files, and database files, for example, you need to worry only about changing the .BIB file and registry settings for your particular work.

The Makeimg tool combines all the .BIB files (Config.bib, Platform.bib, Project.bib, and Common.bib) into one big Ce.bib file. You have the database files, Common.db, Platform.db, and Project.db. Makeimg also creates one big Reginit.ini file with the registry settings and compresses it into a file called Default.fdf. Do you know what .FDF stands for? Franklin D. Fite.

Makeimg performs some other functions for you too, such as localization. In your registry settings, for example, you can specify that you want to include a particular file that has some constants. When Makeimg sees that setting, it substitutes either the U.S. text or, say, the Japanese text.

After using the Makeimg tool, you need to use Romimage. Romimage collects whatever is specified in the .BIB file and puts it all into an image file for you. That's how you get your .BIN image.

CESH AND THE BOOT LOADER

We provide a tool called Cesh, and your Windows NT host development machine runs a service so that you can set up a two-way link between the development machine and the target platform to transfer files and communicate. The toolkit provides a boot loader that works with Cesh, which OEMs can port to their platforms. And generally that's what OEMs can use to port the kernel. Much of the platform-independent kernel boot loader is also used in the OAL.

The embedded toolkit Setup program configures Windows NT for you so that when you turn your target platform on, the Windows NT development machine sends an image file to the target device. The boot loader on the target device listens for this image file, and a little header in the image file tells the boot loader "Hey, I'm a bin image" or "Hey, I'm a Motorola S-file" so that the boot loader knows which file is being downloaded and its size. The boot loader performs some error checking to make sure the file is not corrupt. After the image is downloaded, it jumps into the kernel; the boot loader is gone, and now you're running the kernel.

You can then execute commands from the development host to see which processes are running. You can start processes, kill processes, view memory, and view debug flags (the *DpCurSettings* flags). Let's say you have a complete debug image running on your platform and you want to view only debug messages in your part of the code. When you write your driver, you can specify these *DpCurSettings* flags, and when you send a debug message, you can specify which flags you want associated with that message. When you're debugging you can configure these *DpCurSettings* from the Cesh shell so that you can turn them on and off: you want to see *these* debug messages, but you don't want to see *those*.

And what's really cool is, let's say you're iterating through your application, and you don't want to create and load the whole .BIN image every iteration. Loading a 4-MB image, for example, takes some time. So you don't include the application in the image; you use the Cesh *s* command to load only your application. If the kernel doesn't find the app in the image, and you're running Cesh, the kernel will attempt to retrieve it from the development host. That's really nice because you can try it out, and if it doesn't work, that's fine, because you can recompile it, build it, use the Cesh *s* command again to load the new version, and run the app. Getting the app from the development host is much easier than recreating and uploading new .BIN images every time you want to test a new version.

As we move forward with the ETK, we're working on making these tools very GUI-based and knowledge-based and on minimizing the learning curve.

THE EMBEDDED TOOLKIT FOR WINDOWS CE

Scott Horn

Learning about the kinds of devices people want to build is amazing—everything from bakery ovens to manufacturing automation systems to web phones. It's incredible. You have embedded developers coming from a UNIX background, and you have people from the Win32 desktop world who want to create versions of their corporate applications for these custom devices. Our challenge is to make it very easy for all of them to take their existing knowledge and skill sets into this custom device world.

The OAK required Microsoft to give its customers a great deal of attention and handholding. But we're seeing so much interest in the embedded market that we think potentially millions of people are going to want to build these custom devices, and we can't afford the same level of support for that many customers. So we built an Embedded Toolkit product that everybody can use easily.

The embedded toolkit, or ETK, makes these tools and the Windows CE OS bits available via the retail channel, which is a pretty different business model than you've seen before in the embedded space. You can walk into a store or call a number on a mail-order catalog and say, "Hey, I want to buy an ETK." The product cost is an order of magnitude less than what other folks are offering, and no restrictions apply. You can use the ETK for all of your development and testing, and when you want to distribute your application commercially, you can contact either Microsoft or an authorized distributor.

Another interesting feature of the ETK that differentiates us from other vendors is that few vendors out there support multiple chip architectures. We currently support five different chip architectures: the MIPS, the PowerPC, the x86, the SH3/SH4, and the ARM/StrongARM. We really are treating all chip architectures equally. Very few systems in this embedded space offer that kind of wide support.

And for the first time in the embedded space, people can use an x86 PC as a development platform. You know, typically in embedded systems, if somebody wanted a hardware reference platform, he'd have to spend between $5,000 and $10,000. We're enabling people to start developing on a 486 or a Pentium-class machine, which you can get for 500 bucks. We have prebuilt OS images for the PC-based development platform so that very quickly—within 30 minutes of buying the product—a developer, right out of the box, can read the *Getting Started* guide, load the prebuild images on a floppy, stick the floppy in the PC, and experience the OS.

We're actively working on the next release. Here are some of the challenges we face:

- *Providing developers with everything they need in a single product.* We want developers to have whatever they need to develop applications, the OAL, drivers, the OS extensions—everything—so the ETK also includes the SDK and the DDK. We provide the built-in drivers for standard device types, but we also enable developers to create completely different device types and drivers for those devices.

- *Improving our debugging support for issues like bringing up the kernel on a chip.* We want to help developers understand what's happening on the chip, for example, in the on-chip cache.

- *Enabling developers to figure out which APIs are supported by their OS builds.* As you know, Windows CE is a componentized OS, and you have a lot of flexibility in terms of the modules and components you can select. If you're an OS developer, you want to know which APIs are supported by the configuration and how much space the configuration takes. One component you add might also require another, so the OEM also needs automatic dependency resolution, which is something we're looking at intently. The application developer wants to know, "What's supported by this OS?" We want to enable a very easy handoff between the OS builder and the application developer.

- *Providing GUI versions of the OAK command-line tools.* Right now the ETK has some of the command-line flavor of the OAK. Some of our developers prefer that. We're also working to provide alternative wrappers in the IDE so that a developer has the option to build the OS in the IDE.

- *Providing a seamless handoff between the ETK and Visual Basic for Windows CE.* A seamless handoff means that an ETK developer can create an OS that includes the VB run time and hand it off to a person who has Visual Basic for Windows CE, and that person could write an app for the OS.

We know that the typical developers of embedded systems aren't Win32 developers, so we're trying to better understand their needs and make the ETK accessible to them. We want the Unix developer, for example—which is what I was before coming to Microsoft—to get comfortable with the Windows CE environment.

We're going to invest a lot of resources in the embedded space. We're going to sponsor magazines, developer conferences, web sites, system integrator networks, and distributors. We're building a whole network so that developers can choose from a rich set of resources. That network is another of our unique contributions to this embedded systems space. We're really good at partnering with a wide range of companies to support our development community.

RESOURCES

Topic	Resource
Using the embedded toolkit	*Embedded Systems Development with Microsoft Windows CE and Visual C++* (Microsoft Press, forthcoming)
Licensing Windows CE	*http://www.microsoft.com/windowsce/embedded/licensing/*
Developing COM and ActiveX controls	*Understanding ActiveX and OLE*, by David Chappell (Microsoft Press, 1996); *Inside COM*, by Dale Rogerson (Microsoft Press, 1997); *Microsoft Windows CE Programmer's Guide*, (Microsoft Press, forthcoming)
Makeimg, Romimage, and other embedded tools	Microsoft Windows CE Embedded Toolkit for Visual C++
Microsoft Windows CE ActiveX Control Pack	*http://www.microsoft.com/windowsce/developer*
Windows CE application development in C++, Java, and Visual Basic	Microsoft Windows CE Toolkit for Visual C++ 5.0, Microsoft Windows CE Toolkit for Visual J++ 1.1, Microsoft Windows CE Toolkit for Visual Basic 5.0

11

A Look at Some Windows CE Configurations

T his chapter describes several configurations of Microsoft Windows CE based on the core set of modules and components available in the embedded toolkit. Some are created by Microsoft, and others are created independently by embedded developers. Kimberly Gregory, group program manager for the Windows CE core OS team, describes work on such new devices for point-of-sale terminals and GPS-based automobile navigation systems. Gregory also describes how developers are installing specialized applications on the standard Handheld PC (H/PC) and deploying the H/PC as a dedicated vertical device. The versatility of the H/PC is demonstrated by the variety of vertical market customers: the Pittsburgh Police Department, Vail Resorts, the Seattle Mariners Baseball Club, and the United States Marine Corps.

In addition to developing the Windows CE OS and tools, Microsoft defines a base hardware specification for some devices, assists OEMs who are porting to that platform, provides a certification program, and creates all of the system software, including a specialized shell and an initial set of applications. The first two shipping devices of this kind were the Handheld PC and the Palm-size PC. The Palm-size PC always includes its shell and a baseline set of applications: Pocket Outlook, Voice Recorder, Mobile Channels, Note Taker, Calculator, Clock, and the game Solitaire. OEMs can also choose to include other applications, but customers know that, at a minimum, these Microsoft-developed applications will be present on all Palm-size PCs. A baseline set of applications is also defined and provided for the Handheld PC. Microsoft has also officially announced the Auto PC, a collaboration with Sega on the Dreamcast home video game system, and Windows-based terminals.

Roland Ayala describes the Windows CE terminal devices that connect to the Windows NT 4.0 Terminal Server Edition. Ted Kummert describes the Windows CE OS configuration used in the Sega Dreamcast home video game system. Patrick Volk was the senior program manager for the Auto PC and discusses its architecture and its core OS modules and components.

Dave Wecker served as development manager for the Palm-size PC and walks through its overall system goals and features. Because the Handheld PC has already been discussed in detail in other chapters, it is not described as extensively here. Robert O'Hara, one of the original members of the Windows CE team and author of Introducing Windows CE for the Handheld PC (Microsoft Press, 1997), and Cathy Linn, group program manager for Handheld PC 1.0, wrap up the discussion with their stories.

Several other Windows CE–based products under development at Microsoft had not been announced at press time. Watch the Windows CE web site, http://www.microsoft.com/windowsce, *for information on these additional devices.*

---◆---

EMBEDDED CUSTOMERS

Kimberly Gregory

A fair amount of confusion still exists in the marketplace when it comes to distinguishing the Windows CE *operating system* from Windows CE *products,* such as the Handheld PC, which are built on top of the operating system. Undoubtedly, the introduction of many more devices based on Windows CE will lessen this one-to-one binding in people's minds.

Kimberly Gregory

When I first started thinking about the embedded space, I used the term "embedded OEM" to describe the market that seemed most interested in our devices, but now I think I should really use the term "embedded customer." We have OEMs such as Radiant and Datus developing new devices, but we also have a lot of customers who *aren't* OEMs and *won't* be involved in creating the hardware and adapting the operating system to the hardware platform.

Meeting with this diverse set of embedded customers has been very interesting. We've seen Monsanto—one of the biggest agribusiness companies in the United States—and the Marine Corps, and we've seen police departments and baseball teams and ski resorts. I'm amazed by the variety of companies that are interested in using embedded systems, that can visualize how to use a commercially available system.

Most of the original customers who came to us back in 1997 were interested in adapting the Handheld PC for a particular vertical market. Some needed more capabilities than the H/PC provided at that time: color graphics and support for many different screen resolutions, more communications features, more networking capabilities, the Ethernet. Often they wanted to be able to consider an x86 solution. Interest in the Java VM and in our Visual Basic run time has been tremendous. You can run scripting languages either in Visual Basic script or in Java script. We provided all of these features in the version 2.0 OS, and in many cases, these customers have delivered on an H/PC 2.0 platform.

Many of these customers are interested in Windows CE–based devices as a way of reducing their overall system development cost. The U.S. Marine Corps is an excellent example. Their commercial off-the-shelf (COTS) initiative, started by U.S. Secretary of Defense [William] Perry, was really key to their decision to go with a Windows CE device as the basis for their field deployment.

ADOPTERS OF DEDICATED H/PC DEVICES

Organization	Windows CE Application
Seattle Mariners Baseball Club	Used to scout baseball players at many different game sites; allows standardized entry of scouting reports and transmission back to the front office
Hoeschst Marion Roussel	Provides information to 2,000 field sales representatives; records physician signatures on pharmaceutical sample deliveries
Pittsburgh Police Department	Enables more community-oriented policing; provides instant, secure access to city, state, and national databases
Vail Resorts	Matches customers with instructors and class times at the largest ski school in the world; operates on site on the mountain in all weather conditions
United States Marine Corps	Supports position location information (PLI) and small unit situational awareness; adds a ruggedized case and extra battery life for battlefield use

We're currently working closely with the Open Modular Architecture Controller (OMAC) Users Group. The manufacturing companies included in this consortium are the big-ticket manufacturers—big chemical companies, industrial companies, automotive companies. The OMAC group is evaluating Windows CE to benchmark real-time performance.

And these are just a few of the companies that are either planning to use or have already deployed Windows CE, typically with a single-purpose application on top of Windows CE.

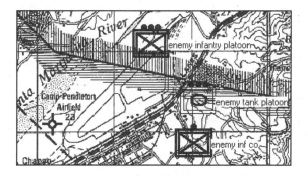

The Chesty, Jr. application, developed for the U.S. Marine Corps by Norman L. Hills of Casio Corp., allows friendly and enemy positions to be marked on standard topographic maps, resulting in accurate calculation of artillery range and distance values. Camp Pendleton, shown here, was the site of a joint exercise.

I also looked at some of the embedded customers who are building their own devices to determine why they were attracted to Windows CE. Here's what I learned they wanted:

◆ *Communication support.* Customers need quite a lot of communication support—this is true for many embedded customers I've come in contact with. We have a lot of comm stacks.

◆ *Data storage options.* Customers need to store data on nonvolatile media such as Flash, which we support. In our system, when your data is sitting out in Flash or on an SRAM card, the system automatically pages the data in for you. The process is seamless. You deal only at the file system level, and the system takes care of everything underneath.

◆ *Graphics flexibility.* Customers need some flexibility with graphics. Our GDI works with any pixel depth, from 1 bit per pixel all the way up to 32 bits per pixel. From a programmatic point of view, our GDI is just as easy to use as other graphics models.

◆ *Support for the Java programming language.* Some companies write all of their apps in Java. One that we've been working with is moving ahead with its apps while looking for the underlying OS solution. It evaluated some alternatives and found a great tool chain with Windows CE—one that integrated seamlessly into its existing desktop product. In version 2.10, we are supporting a 200 MHz processor and the StrongARM 1100 from Digital, and the customer feels that performance will be sufficient to run the interpreted code.

◆ *Rapid application development.* Another customer also wanted to script for rapid application development, so was looking for a system that would support Visual Basic.

◆ *An established object model.* Customers who rely on a component design methodology were looking for support for an established object model. Well, of course, Microsoft's object model is ActiveX and COM, and we support a sufficient subset to enable ActiveX development.

We can't speak about all of these companies because some of their systems are still under development. We are very excited to be able to talk about Radiant and Datus. Datus is producing an automobile global-positioning system device. It started all this work on its own; we first became aware of the company when it asked us what it would take to get the speech engine that comes with the Auto PC product.

Radiant is building a point-of-sale (POS) terminal. In fast food chains, for example, POS terminals, or *kiosks*, as you might call them, will be set up to expedite the order entry process. Someone going into that restaurant can enter an order at the kiosk using a very nice, colorful, intuitive, user-friendly, multimedia-based application.

After an order is placed, it is automatically relayed to a server that is tracking all orders and that can automatically update the inventory. Radiant has configured a fault-tolerant system such that, if its back-end Windows NT server goes down, it always has a redundant Windows NT server. The kiosk can ping using our UDP protocol to find the other server, then initiate wireless communications with it. In fact, Radiant has built a lot of expertise around Windows CE. They're very interested in Windows CE and are planning to use it in other systems as well.

What Windows CE can offer, first and foremost, is that it's a Microsoft system. That means the potential for interoperability with the desktop; being able to capitalize on—what is it Randy Kath says these days?—4.76 million Win32 developers; a standard tool chain; a single UI paradigm throughout your whole organization. The customer who can buy the operating system, the application suite, and tools that have been well tested and interoperate with other existing systems is going to be very happy.

MICROSOFT WINDOWS–BASED TERMINALS

Roland Ayala

It used to be that only one person at a time could sit down and log on to Microsoft Windows. With the Windows-based terminal, you can now go to another device, connect to the Windows NT Terminal Server, and experience the look and feel of the Windows NT machine. Just think of the network as a virtual cable for your monitor, keyboard, and mouse, where the server is just pumping all those bits over the network. This brings the Microsoft Windows experience to very low-cost hardware.

Most of the application processing is done on the server side. Obviously, the Windows-based terminal is processing the display and managing the keyboard input, but all the application processing is taking place on the remote Windows NT computer. Its official name is Windows NT 4.0 Terminal Server Edition, but most people know it by its code name, "Hydra."

Roland Ayala

The client program is a Win32 application, so you can connect to Hydra from Windows NT, Win95, or a Windows CE–based computer. The Windows CE computers are the most interesting because you can essentially create disposable devices. If one breaks down, you just put another one in its place.

Microsoft itself endorses a distributed computing model, but customers have been telling Microsoft that they want a solution that addresses total cost of ownership (TCO). You can imagine an insurance company or an airline that wants to bring the Windows experience to its task-based workers. They don't always want to deploy PCs because they have to worry about hardware problems or people installing unreliable applications onto the PCs. These Windows-based terminals are more reliable than PCs because there are fewer parts and because there's no way to install software on them. Here all of the software can be managed centrally. If administrators want to update software for the clients, they can do it in one place, on the Hydra server.

You can also use these terminals to connect to other servers. Our customers want to migrate to Windows, but they can't just throw away their infrastructure, so other terminal emulation packages are available to connect to their mainframes and all of their different systems.

This is the first Microsoft project to ship on Windows CE version 2.10. It uses a vanilla version of Windows CE—not a full OS configuration, scaled down a bit. There are a lot of GDI operations going on because you have to take those bits that come over the wire and turn them back into graphics.

Cesysgen.bat File for the Windows-based Terminal	
Windows-based Terminal Module	**Components**
coredll	coreimm, coreloc, coremain, corestra, fmtmsg, lmem, mgdi_c, rectapi, serdev, tapilib, thunks, wavelib, wmgr_c
filesys	fsdbase, fsheap, fsmain, fspass, fsreg, fsysram
gwes	accel, audio, btnctl, calibrui, caret, cascade, cdlctl, clipbd, cmbctl, column, defwndproc, dlgmgr, dlgmnem, drawmbar, edctl, foregnd, gcache, getpower, gsetwinlong, gwectrl, gweshare, gwesmain, hotkey, iconcurs, idle, imgctl, immthunk, kbdui, lbctl, loadbmp, loadimg, loadstr, mcursor, mcursor8, menu, menuscrl, mgbase, mgbitmap, mgblt, mgblt2, mgdc, mgdibsec, mgdraw, mgdrwtxt, mgpal, mgpalnat, mgrgn, mgtt, mgwinmgr, mnoover, mnotapui, msgbeep, msgbox, msgbox28, msgque, nclient, nled, oom, oomui, sbcmn, scbctl, stcctl, syscolor, tchui, timer, uibase, winmgr, wmbase
Other Windows CE modules	afd, arp, commctrl, cxport, device, dhcp, fatfs, ndis, netbios netui, nk, ppp, redir, shell, tapi, tcpstk, toolhelp, unimodem, waveapi, winsock

The Cesysgen.bat file used to configure the Windows CE OS for Windows-based terminals shows its extensive use of graphics and networking modules and components.

The official name for our display protocol is Microsoft Remote Desktop Protocol (RDP), also known as T.Share. It is an optimized version of the industry standard, T.120, and is the same technology that is used in Microsoft NetMeeting. The protocol is pretty smart about sending only the changing information. If you're typing in your document, the only region that changes is the region with the text that you are typing. Another popular client is the Citrix ICA.

This device uses a dedicated application for its shell. Actually, I wrote it myself. It is a fixed function shell by design because you don't want the users to load up and start all kinds of applications but rather use them as dedicated terminals.

I did some benchmarks and learned that the performance of these terminals is highly dependent on the processor speed. You'd think that it was dependent on the communications, but the client applications are very smart and do a lot of compression.

THE SEGA DREAMCAST HOME VIDEO GAME SYSTEM

Ted Kummert

We are providing a configuration of the operating system that provides the essential APIs for producing games. Mostly, that means providing a very lightweight configuration of Windows CE with a fully-featured implementation of the DirectX foundation components.

So we provide only what we believe to be the essential core functions:

◆ *The kernel, with its standard Win32 process and thread model.*

◆ *The file systems.* For the purpose of the file system, we needed

asynchronous I/O because you don't want the file system to block. If you're running a game, you don't want to be waiting for the CD. So we implemented async I/O, in much the same way it is implemented in [Windows] NT's Windows Driver Model (WDM). It is used by the core of the file system to enable overlapped reads from the file system.

Ted Kummert

◆ *GWE.* From User and GDI, we've provided just enough to do text output and just enough for application messaging to allow for input to the system.

◆ *Other modules and components.* We also support the core connectivity, the comm stack.

We can't really say much more about this system right now. The internals of Windows CE for the Sega Dreamcast system are only really available to you if you get a development agreement and nondisclosure agreement with Sega.

Dreamcast Modules and Components	
Sega Dreamcast Module	**Components Supported**
coredll	Supports IMM/IME (each game is responsible for providing the user interface for accessing system-level IME support). Supports standard C utility functions, string manipulation, math, exception handling, file I/O, and memory allocation.
filesys	Supports memory-mapped files and asynchronous I/O. ISO9660 Level 2–compliant. Provides access to Sega's CD-ROM; designed to allow the developer to fill the CD-ROM pipeline for better streaming performance. Very lightweight and block-oriented new API to manage NVRAM cards. A desktop version is also provided for emulation.
gwes	Supports loading and copying bitmaps, rendering text or DirectDraw API-based surfaces, input and message handling, string resource loading, and the Rectangle APIs. Other functions such as window management and cursors have been eliminated.
DirectDraw	Provides 2-D graphics facilities, including video memory management and palette management. Supports full-screen exclusive mode only.
Direct3D	The Direct3D API Immediate Mode supports transformation, lighting, and rendering of 3-D graphics primitives.
DirectSound	Supports digitized sound input and output. Interfaces with Sega ARM code to manage Dreamcast sound memory.
DirectPlay	Supports Internet and modem communications for multiplayer gaming. Provides APIs to enable online chatting, the sending and receiving of messages, and maintenance of game state among all players.
DirectInput	Interfaces to Dreamcast game controllers.
DirectShow	Supports digital audio and video playback and synchronization. MPEG1 encoded AVI playback is also supported.
Other Windows CE modules	Supports a subset of the Windows Sockets and RAS APIs, providing TCP and UDP sockets and PPP dial-up.

The Sega Dreamcast system uses fewer GWE components than the other configurations. It uses only what it needs from GWE to support the Windows CE implementation of DirectX.

THE AUTO PC

Patrick Volk

The base design for the Auto PC had a multimedia focus. Because the vehicle is such a difficult place to mount equipment, we wanted to take advantage of the standard space for mounting add-on entertainment equipment: the radio, the CD player, the cassette player. By targeting that one-din or two-din opening in the dashboard, we were committing to providing the same services that you are used to seeing there as well as all the other features offered by the Auto PC. Your information space moves into your car and you have access now; you can stay connected.

Patrick Volk

Because we moved the system into the dashboard, it had to be capable of full multimedia, with the ability to play the radio and the CD. We wanted to match the high-end systems, so we went with digital audio capable of surround sound and digital signal processing. This required isolating a lot of the data streaming for the speech input, speech recognition, audio input/output, and equalizer handling. We had to provide processing power external to the CPU because the device is for consumers and the price has to be suitable. The power management has to be suitable. The device has to be able to go into very low power mode and not drain the battery.

AUTO PC ARCHITECTURE: SEPARATE PCI AND CPU BUSES

We built our system around an internal PCI bus. The PCI bus is not designed to be an expansion bus but rather to allow us to move data without much CPU involvement. The CPU is isolated on its own local bus and can process speech recognition and the whole normal gamut of tasks that Windows CE needs to perform: graphics, visuals, the shell, controls. The PCI bus is the primary hardware differentiator.

The Auto PC also differs from the H/PC and Palm-size PC in its form factor and UI. We don't have a touch screen because while you're driving, it's not safe to focus your attention down and not pay attention to other cars and road activity around you. Same thing with the keypad. We don't expect people to type email while they're driving down the road. But we had to offer enough of a keypad to enable access to the system when voice control isn't working. Maybe the user has a cold or laryngitis that morning, or she rolls down all her windows or turns up her stereo system full blast. In a much noisier environment, activating the system via speech doesn't work as well.

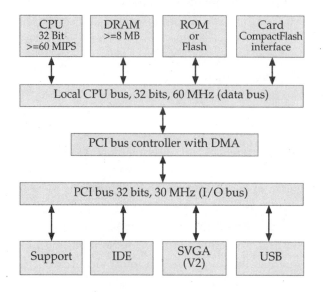

The Auto PC hardware design includes a separate PCI bus and CPU bus to ensure that the radio and CD player do not exhibit any performance degradation during peak periods of CPU processing.

So the CPU, the DRAM, ROM, and the Compact Flash interface are all on the local CPU bus, which is running at 60 MHz. All the other peripherals—the CD-ROM drive, the universal serial bus (USB), all the audio in the support module—are isolated on the other side of the PCI bus.

EXPANSION: USB AND COMPACT FLASH

Remember, I said PCI was not intended for an expansion bus in the system. People are not going to open up their chassis and expand their systems by plugging new hardware inside the boxes. They're going to have to plug them in externally. We use USB for the primary expansion capability—it can support 12 megabits per second. We'll use the USB to talk to the vehicle itself via a bridge to the vehicle bus. We have analog sensors, which can also be picked up by the vehicle bus and made available via the USB. A few direct digital input lines are available, too, so that the system can connect to the ignition and talk to the headlight switch and dim the system when the headlights are on. Just plugging in using this USB enables you to support CD Changer, a cell phone, and other USB devices.

The Compact Flash also enables expansion. This is a smaller form factor of a PCMCIA and uses the same standard adopted for the H/PC and the Palm-size PC. So customers will be able to plug in their wireless Compact Flash cards and stay in touch.

All of our device drivers are written to the Windows CE device-driver model. We added the CD file system to the Windows CE core set.

POWER MANAGEMENT

We've had to work through and solve a lot of automobile-specific problems. For example, although power management is built into Windows CE, we need to extend it a little bit because of the unique power system of a car. We have a 12-volt lead acid battery—a nice feature, but you don't want to get in your car after two weeks of not using it and not be able to start it.

When you're preparing to work on your car, the first thing the mechanic tells you to do is to disconnect the battery. Because of so many processors, airbags, and other systems on modern cars—systems that rely to some extent on power from the battery—the Auto PC system needs some kind of backup support, some kind of alternative power management. Let's say you've got wireless and you're going to receive a lot of your information overnight while your car is parked. The wireless needs to be able to wake up the system—but not fully, just partially. So we're working with the Windows CE core team to make sure that our environment meets the power needs of these devices.

SOFTWARE ARCHITECTURE: MULTIUSER SUPPORT

For multiuser support, the Windows CE kernel is intact; we don't do anything different with it. We're just building a layer on top of existing system layers. We've adopted the Win32 subset but we put a Forms Manager on top of GWE services: the event management, the focus management, and the window hierarchy management. The Forms Manager creates forms into which we put Auto PC controls and ActiveX controls. You can see that it's not an extensive layer we're building; it's a fairly tight, small layer, without a lot of overhead.

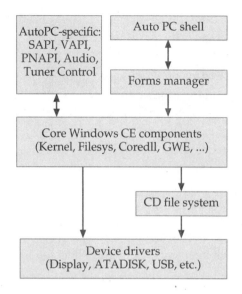

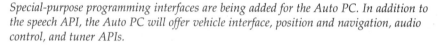

Special-purpose programming interfaces are being added for the Auto PC. In addition to the speech API, the Auto PC will offer vehicle interface, position and navigation, audio control, and tuner APIs.

In the car, we might want to have a multiuser station system, but GWE, like the Windows User32, is designed as a single-user system, with one window hierarchy and one frame buffer. With the Forms Manager approach, it's at least architecturally possible to replicate the GWE concept for multiple users.

Our Forms Manager gets a device context from the display driver, buffers it, and makes it available to the shell and the applications. The Forms Manager handles events from the keypad device driver that come through the standard Windows CE event manager, and it dispatches those events to the controls that have focus. This is functionality we're considering for future versions.

The Auto PC applications are on top of the Forms Manager. We don't think our Auto PC apps are the end-all and be-all of applications for radio, CD, navigation, contacts, and wireless communications, but they will give people a good grasp of what the platform is able to do for them.

Speech recognition is an important part of running this system. We want the system to make its best estimate of what a user says and means, but we don't want the system to be too aggressive in guessing: for a user, repeating a word to clarify a command is a lot easier than figuring out which application just started and trying to back out of it. I'm pretty excited about what speech can do now, but I am also very much aware that we need to make a lot of improvements. We need to increase recognition accuracy all the time.

Speech Categories and Words for the Auto PC	
Application Category	**Recognized Words Stored in ROM**
Global commands	Start, AutoPC, Help, Mute, Volume, Nomad
Start menu	Radio, CD Player, Address Book, Navigate, Wireless, Audio, Settings, Next, Previous
Radio	AM, FM, Preset, Next, Previous, Review, spoken numbers 0 through 9, Stop, Seek
CD player	Play, Pause, Delete, Next, Previous, Random, Review, Disk, Stop
Address book	Locate, Next, Previous, Skip, Dial, Repeat, Review, Select, Letter, Home, Phone, Office, Cancel, Back
Navigate	Next, Previous, Review, Repeat, Cancel
Wireless	Next, Previous, Review, Repeat, Skip, Read, News, Email, Traffic

Some of the proposed Auto PC commands that will be in ROM and available to application developers. The Auto PC SDK will also include additional words. This list of proposed command words is subject to change.

We talked to focus groups about different flavors of products, and people unanimously got excited about speech control. They were less excited about navigation, at least for North America. Maybe that's because in North America, streets are laid out in a grid and finding your way around might be a little bit easier. But being able to run radio with speech—that really caught their imagination.

New Windows CE API Sets

We've extended Windows CE with API sets that are either car-centric or necessary for the Auto PC. Some of them will migrate back into Windows CE and some of them will likely just stay with the car. Let me describe them to you.

Speech API (SAPI)

We ported the Speech API (SAPI) from the Research group, starting with SAPI 2.0. Now we're compatible with SAPI 3.0. We worked with an outside vendor to get the speech recognition and the text-to-speech engines into the Auto PC. It took some porting to make the engines SAPI-compliant and WinCE-compliant as well as compatible with the bandwidth that's left over in the CPU for speech processing.

Audio Control Manager API

The audio control manager API controls the audio source and destination, allowing you to perform sound mixing and to control whether the input source comes from the radio, the CD, a .WAV file, or from a microphone or aux input.

Tuner Control API

The tuner control API is flexible enough to tune any RF receiver, including a TV. In the car, we use it for AM/FM tuning and scanning. It gives you basic information about the tuner, such as its signal strength, and then reports on its other capabilities, such as whether it's got stereo, etc.

Position and Navigation API (PNAPI)

This is a port of an API that was first created on the desktop for Microsoft Expedia, Streets, and Trip Planner. We also allow navigation data content providers to build an engine that is compatible with the system so that others can participate in the market. Application developers can write applications without being concerned about specific data content providers. Both developers and providers gain flexibility. Each can increase the functionality of their products independently of the other. We're hopeful the whole market will be able to grow without the bottlenecks that come from being tied to a proprietary solution and proprietary data provider.

Vehicle Control and Information API (VAPI)

VAPI allows a developer to enumerate all of a car's data and controllable variables, such as the passenger environment variables. A lot of cars these days have buses and multiple processors—anywhere from 10 to 30 processors. The bus is either a CAN bus or an ODB II, a JNAT, or some other bus that vehicle manufacturers have incorporated or adopted. The Auto PC can't possibly define the interfaces for all those different buses and still retain general flavor. So again, we're making an API that isolates applications from all the complexity of the specific underlying hardware.

An IHV who knows the specific vehicle and the buses will build the device that provides a bridge between VAPI and the vehicle, and provide the information over USB.

Cesysgen.bat File for the Auto PC	
Auto PC Module	**Components**
coredll	coreloc, coremain, cryptapi, fmtmsg, lmem, mgdi_c, rectapi, rsa32, serdev, syscolor, tapilib, thunks, wavelib, wmgr_c
filesys	fsdbase, fsheap, fsmain, fspass, fsreg, fsysram
gwes	accel, audio, btnctl, caret, cdlctl, clipbd, cmbctl, cursor, defwndproc, dlgmgr, dlgmnem, edctl, foregnd, gcache, getpower, gsetwinlong, gwectrl, gweshare, gwesmain, idle, imgctl, kbdui, lbctl, loadbmp, loadimg, loadstr, menu, mgbase, mgbitmap, mgblt, mgblt2, mgdc, mgdibsec, mgdraw, mgdrwtxt, mgpal, mgpalnat, mgprint, mgrgn, mgtt, mgwinmgr, mnotapui, msgbeep, msgque, nclient, nled, scbctl, stcctl, timer, uibase, winmgr, wmbase
ole32	com, ole232, olemain
Other system modules	afd, atadisk, cardserv, cxport, device, fatfs, ircomm, irdastk, netui, nk, oleaut32, ppp, rsabase, shell, sramdisk, tapi, tcpstk, toolhelp, unimodem, uuid, waveapi, winsock

The Auto PC modules and components defined in the Cesysgen.bat file reveal that it features secure communications using the Microsoft CryptoAPI.

We want to work on other functionality for the vehicle in the future, and we can certainly support that because Windows CE is so flexible. The system is extensible. You can buy it today and you aren't locked into whatever set of knobs and functions you buy. You can keep current; you can plug something into your system tomorrow without having to buy and install a completely new system. You can add apps such as navigation systems—it's very flexible. If you don't like the software that comes with your system or, if three years from now, somebody has invented a much cooler interface or service, you can upgrade your system, find new software, and install it. Users are very familiar with this flexibility on the desktop; they're just not familiar with it in the car.

All this new software will change how people perceive time in the car and their commute. As services and applications become available, the car will become a much richer space than it is today in terms of how you spend your time and how you stay connected, entertained, and remain productive.

THE PALM-SIZE PC

Dave Wecker

Plain and simple, the Palm-size PC is a device you want to have with you at all times. You want to pull it out of your pocket or purse, get information, take quick pen notes or voice notes, and then put the device back into your pocket. It's not a platform for editing large Microsoft Word documents or working with Microsoft Excel spreadsheets; that's not what it's designed for. The Palm-size PC is a platform category of its own. One of the goals was to make it smaller and less expensive than the Handheld PC, to complete the Windows CE solution space—we now have solutions from the desktop all the way down through the palm-size devices.

Dave Wecker

The platform itself is, of course, based on Windows CE. The user interface is the Windows interface with some minor tweaks. Focus groups have shown a strong preference for the Windows UI. People don't like to learn something new if they don't have to. And down to about this size, the Windows UI still makes sense and people don't have to arbitrarily change to a different UI.

This is the first portrait-mode device we've created (as compared to landscape mode for the Handheld PC), so we don't use the H/PC shell; rather, we created a new Palm-size PC shell specifically for this device. The UI actually went through four major rewrites as we tried to make the most information available in the easiest way. We've done lots of little things to make the device much more efficient.

The taskbar looks like a normal Windows taskbar, but no tasks are on it because all tasks are always running. From the user's point of view, they are all running—apps don't have an exit button. The user just runs app after app and the shell manages everything. Since the shell is doing all this work, the user has a much simpler model.

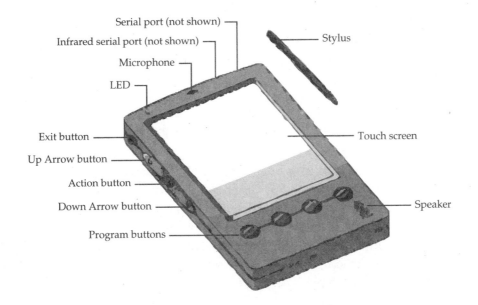

Serial port (not shown)
Infrared serial port (not shown)
Microphone
LED
Stylus
Exit button
Up Arrow button
Action button
Down Arrow button
Program buttons
Touch screen
Speaker

For selected platforms, Microsoft defines a hardware reference platform. The Palm-size PC, for example, requires a specific set of hardware buttons, but OEMs can place them in different locations on the device. This diagram shows one possible hardware design that meets the requirements.

Underneath, the Windows CE operating system is supporting a maximum of 32 processes, so Palm-size PC applications have to cooperate with this running application model. When the apps are asked by the shell to give back memory, they need to do that. If they are asked by the shell to shut down, they need to be able to save their state and shut down. In the background, the shell shuts down applications to make sure that you're not running out of memory or process space.

NATURAL INPUT MODES FOR THE PALM-SIZE DEVICE

For this size and form factor, we wanted to support the natural types of input to the device. We support voice input. We support rich inking. I like to scribble as I go; a lot of other people also prefer putting ink directly into the machine. So we use the Aha! technology, which looks at the ink as you enter it and figures out where the words are. You can cut, paste, and copy with ink: all the operations you're used to performing with standard text, you can do with ink. When we synchronize to the desktop, the ink becomes part of a Word document so that you can edit the text in Word. When you synchronize back down to the Palm-size PC, the text becomes ink again. You don't lose any information.

We have both handwriting recognition and the soft keyboard, or soft input panel (SIP). In fact, they're related. The hooks for handwriting recognition are the same as the hooks for the keyboard. Each is just an implementation of an input method. We provide two recognizers built into the device: the natural handwriting recognizer and a simplified character set recognizer.

Many people take notes using the soft keyboard, so we made a variety available in the device, plus you can add your own SIP. One of the things I like about the soft keyboard architecture is that you can turn anything into a soft keyboard and pop it in the device. The handwriting recognition plugs in as an input method, so your program sees only virtual keys coming back to you. Whether the input is coming from ink being recognized or from the keyboard itself, the application doesn't care.

The user never has to move the keyboard out of the way because all the applications use specific techniques to make sure they move themselves out of the way of the keyboard.

We have all sorts of communications channels. You can come in through the Compact Flash with modems. All the devices come with a docking cradle or a cable to connect to the desktop for serial synchronization as well as the standard Windows CE infrared.

On the software side, messaging and remote networking enable you to dial up to your RAS server. We have a new Active Desktop with Mobile Channels. A Mobile Channel is an Internet Explorer 4.0 channel designed for the Palm-size PC screen resolution. You can synchronize the Mobile Channel to your desktop (where it becomes a nice little desktop component) and synchronize it to your Palm-size PC every time you pop it into the cradle. You can use straight HTML or an advanced feature that runs scripting directly on the device, minimizing the amount of data you have to send and store.

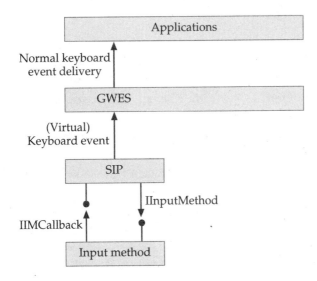

Touch panel events are received by the input method and handed back to GWE. The user input system then routes these "keyboard events" to the application, which can implement standard Windows keyboard handling code.

We allow for changes in devices over time. The Compact Flash interface is both flexible and compatible with the laptop and other computers with a PC Card slot. You can plug the Compact Flash into a laptop, an H/PC, and a Palm-size PC, spreading your investment to different types of devices across many different products. You can use a 56-KB Compact Flash modem or Compact Flash Ethernet adapter in your Palm-size PC, or plug the Compact Flash card into a PC Card adapter and also use it in your laptop. We announced a Compact Flash pager card with Motorola. Pop this into your device, and now you have paging capabilities—you can receive any information that anyone wants to send to you over a paging channel.

For the developer, the Windows CE APIs look the same as the familiar Win32 APIs, and the SDK is the same SDK. Developers will notice a few new APIs for the new hardware buttons and the new input methods, but for the most part the system uses the same Win32 API functions and Win32 programming model.

Robert O'Hara

When the WinPad project started, the intent was to ship a PDA as quickly as possible. We had a developers' conference when we had just a bare prototype going, at the end of September '93, and that, as it turned out, was way too early to host the conference—we didn't have any hardware. So the moral of that story was, don't have a developers' conference until you actually have hardware from the OEMs, because otherwise you're just touting vaporware. And we were dependent on Intel, which was building a low-power 386SX called Polar, which was behind schedule. By the summer of '94, PDAs had clearly *not* taken the world by storm, and our OEM partners realized that these devices were going to sell for close to a thousand bucks, so there were questions about whether WinPad made any sense at all. And then finally, Intel said, "We decided to get out of the low-cost 386 chip business. We want to sell Pentiums and not waste our fab plants making low-cost 386s." We would have killed it anyway, but that was absolutely the last nail in the coffin.

Robert O'Hara

In hindsight, we shot ourselves in the collective foot by adding more and more features; I think doing that hurt us. We could have been very hard core and said, "Let's get something lightweight shipped first." And so WinPad and Pulsar were basically thrown together right around Thanksgiving of '94. New management was installed. It was handled extremely poorly, but that's a nontechnical story.

You can see how these experiences shaped Windows CE. We didn't schedule our first developers' conference until we had hardware from vendors. We mailed devices to all the people who attended the developers' conference within two weeks after the conference. We were not going to put all our eggs in one manufacturer's basket, so from the very beginning, we felt that making Windows CE chip set–independent was imperative. We wanted to have a bunch of OEM partners in case one decided to pull the plug or otherwise faltered. As a reaction to all the negative publicity around PDAs, we had a stealth marketing approach—we did not promote this product at all. The goal was to underpromise and overdeliver.

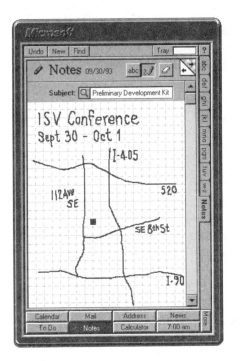

The original WinPad applications supported handwriting input. Byron Bishop, an early member of the WinPad team, kept a pad of notepaper, produced for the development team, based on this UI design. This screen shot appears in a history of the Handheld PC written by Robert O'Hara.

As we move toward developing smaller and smaller screens, I think we will diverge farther and farther from the Windows UI. The Palm-size PC creates a new form factor, a smaller size, with a portrait mode screen, no keyboard, and handwriting recognition, very much like a smaller version of what WinPad was going to be. The Palm-size PC is really back to what WinPad was going to be all along. The hardware's gotten smaller and more powerful and we're finally completing what we set out to do five years ago.

Cesysgen.bat File for the Palm-size PC	
Palm-size PC Module	**Components**
coredll	coreloc, coremain, cryptapi, fmtmsg, lmem, mgdi_c, rectapi, rsa32, serdev, tapilib, thunks, wavelib, wmgr_c
filesys	fsdbase, fsheap, fsmain, fspass, fsreg, fsysram
gwes	accel, audio, btnctl, caret, cascade, cdlctl, clipbd, cmbctl, cursor, cursor2, defwndproc, dlgmgr, dlgmnem, drawmbar, edctl, foregnd, gcache, getpower, gsetwinlong, gwectrl, gweshare, gwesmain, icon, idle, imgctl, immthunk, kbdui, lbctl, loadbmp, loadimg, loadstr, menu, menuscrl, mgbase, mgbitmap, mgblt, mgblt2, mgdc, mgdibsec, mgdraw, mgdrwtxt, mgpal, mgrast, mgrast2, mgrgn, mgwinmgr, moverlap, msgbeep, msgbox, msgque, mtapui, nclient, nled, oom, scbctl, startup, stcctl, tchui, timer, uibase, winmgr, wmbase
ole32	com, olemain
Other modules	afd, atadisk, cxport, device, fatfs, ircomm, irdastk, ne2000, netui, nk, ntlmssp, ppp, redir, rsabase, secur32, shell, tapi, tcpstk, toolhelp, unimodem, uuid, waveapi, wininet, winsock

The Palm-size PC configuration of Windows CE is very similar to the Handheld PC but does not include the OLE storage options or support for TrueType fonts.

The Palm-size PC is also the first Windows CE device to offer wireless communications. It will initially support one-way radios—that is, pager cards. We're not going to just handle simple messaging in which someone sends you a page and it appears in the Inbox as a message. We've gone beyond that functionality to create the Mobile Channels architecture for integrating web content and delivering web content updates via the pager card.

Right now we've got the one-way radio down. Give us time and we'll have two-way radios in the same form factor, which starts to get very, very interesting. You can find all the movies and starting times within five blocks of you, all the French restaurants in a particular neighborhood. I think this whole new location-based assistance has potential. You can have "to-do lists" based on place. The next time you walk into the hardware store, the device can turn on, beep, and say, "Remember, you wanted to buy nails." We can create spontaneous local wireless networks. So now when you're in a meeting, you can say, "OK, let's meet Tuesday afternoon at 3:00," and the other

Palm-size PCs—the other people in the room—become the default attendees. You can print to the nearest printer in the building, and the device will tell you where that printer is. These devices actually will become assistants and will make things easier for you by being aware of where they are.

THE HANDHELD PC

Cathy Linn

I had fun preparing for the first Handheld PC Design Review because I hadn't presented to a group in a while. I was working with Bill [Mitchell]. He was running the infrared demo where we transfer the business card information back and forth, and I was doing the talking. We practiced several times, and of course, nothing worked quite right. I was holding the H/PC that was being projected onto the big screen, and somebody was teasing me, calling me a great Vanna White.

This was our first public H/PC presentation, our first time showing external people what we had developed. We thought, "This demo is awesome; this will blow them away!" But when we actually gave the talk, we got an unexpected reaction. The audience was dead, completely dead. Now I've given enough talks to know that sometimes a speaker can be flat, but there was nothing wrong with this talk; it was a high-energy talk.

The Handheld PC 1.0 shipped with Microsoft Pocket Word, Pocket Excel, and Pocket Internet Explorer among its standard applications. Microsoft Pocket PowerPoint and Pocket Outlook were added for Handheld PC 2.0.

Cathy Linn

We discovered later, in talking to them, that they were all in shock. We hadn't participated in any pre-announcements or marketing, and nobody expected working devices. They figured it would take us another three years. And instead, we suddenly showed up with this device that had working apps and the SDK. The developers in the audience were stunned: "What are we going to do? We've got to rearrange everything we're doing now because we've got to have apps for the H/PC."

Our strategy was exactly the right approach because if we'd gone with vaporware, the attendees would have said, "There they go again; it's another WinPad." But our product was so far along and they'd never heard of it before, and that really blew them away.

When I first joined the team, I worked for Steve Isaac on the Pulsar, which was like the Star Trek communicator—way far out there, way cool, but not something you could ship in a couple of years. As we merged [with WinPad], we transitioned over several weeks and started to think about the standard Windows UI. The UI design strategy became: "How do you map Windows 95 onto a handheld device? How do you map a device that doesn't have a mouse but a stylus?" After a few weeks, we started getting very excited about it. Our attitude became, "We are so cool; we are Windows in your hand; look at this—we're Windows 95! You can take us with you, plug us in, and come back synchronized." Life became very productive at that point.

When I came to Pulsar, I was going to be a technical resource because the PM team at that time was very UI-oriented. Eventually it just became obvious that, OK, I'm the manager. That initial core group was really focused and so productive that from a manager's point of view, the group was ideal to manage. Everybody was great, incredibly hardworking. I used to be a professor, so I really liked watching the PMs grow. It was a lot like grad school, where you supervise your students and then you walk away and they can do it. That was fun.

Handheld PC Module	Cesysgen.bat File for the Handheld PC
	Components
coredll	coremain, coreloc, lmem, thunks, fmtmsg, wavelib, rectapi, wmgr_c, mgdi_c, serdev, tapilib, wavelib
filesys	fsdbase, fsheap, fsmain, fspass, fsreg, fsysram
gwes	accel, audio, btnctl, calibrui, caret, cascade, cdlctl, clipbd, cmbctl, column, cursor, cursor8, defwndproc, dlgmgr, dlgmnem, drawmbar, edctl, foregnd, gcache, getpower, gsetwinlong, gwectrl, gweshare, gwesmain, icon, idle, imgctl, immthunk, kbdui, lbctl, loadbmp, loadimg, loadstr, menu, menuscrl, mgbase, mgbitmap, mgblt, mgblt2, mgdc, mgdibsec, mgdraw, mgdrwtxt, mgpal, mgprint, mgrgn, mgtt, mgwinmgr, mnoover, mnotapui, msgbeep, msgbox, msgbox28, msgque, nclient, nled, oom, oomui, scbctl, startup, stcctl, syscolor, tchui, timer, uibase, winmgr, wmbase
ole32	com, docfile, exp, msf, ole232
winsock	sslsock
Other Windows CE modules	afd, arp, atadisk, cegsm, cxport, device, dhcp, elnk3, fatfs, ircomm, irdastk, ndis, ne2000, netbios, netdetec, netui, nk, ntlmssp, oleaut32, pcl, ppp, prnport, redir, schannel, secur32, shell, sramdisk, tapi, tcpstk, toolhelp, unimodem, uuid, waveapi, wininet

This list represents a Handheld PC based on the version 2.0 OS release. Not all OEMs offer products based on the 2.10 release, so you must examine each particular product to determine which OS version is supported.

We had a fairly technical PM team; it really does take technical expertise to gain the developers' respect. Jeff Blum was a key person, a very dedicated, intense, organized person with a strong technical background. Will Vong came in as our industrial designer, responsible for a tremendous workload not only for our product but for other products, too, and pulled it off. Kevin Shields didn't have a traditional computer science background—he got his degree in Political Science and had worked in Russia—but he had the ability to think analytically. And we told him, "Look, this is the type of person you're going to be working with and this is what you have to do." And he was able to gain the respect of the developers. Very diverse PM group, an incredible group.

We had that across the board. Laura Martinez is the type of person who very quietly gains your respect. She had the ability, in a very nonthreatening way, to ask exactly the right technical question. For a short time she was working with Dave Wecker, who's a fun, loud, off-the-wall, shouting type of guy, and that interaction was interesting to watch. Dave would have an idea, and without talking to anybody, he'd spend the weekend writing code and show up with it Monday morning. The code wouldn't have been spec'ed, and the UI wouldn't fit at all, and Laura would have to tell him to change things. He would yell and scream but then the next day he'd have it changed to what she said. Lots of different personalities and different techniques for interacting, and yet we all were able to pull together.

As I think back on it, the amount of work these people put in was incredible. I can remember leaving at 9:00 some nights, and I was the first of the PM group to leave. They worked incredible hours all weekend.

No matter how burned out and tired I was, though, when I started showing the H/PC to somebody else, the adrenaline started flowing. If somebody needed to know something about the H/PC, I gave them the short, 45-minute, in-your-office description; they'd say "Wow! Cool!" and everything would start flowing. I would be instantly reenergized. I wish the other PMs could have had more of that; we all needed that. The launch at Comdex was the ultimate experience. We were the busiest booth around, and people were coming from a thousand different directions, and they were so impressed and so positive about it that it was just a real high. I knew at the time. I said, "This is really exciting. This is why we did it."

RESOURCES

Topic	Resource
Selecting modules and components Input method manager (IMM) and input method editor (IME)	Microsoft Windows CE Embedded Toolkit for Visual C++ 5.0
Marketing case studies and Windows CE evaluations	*http://www.microsoft.com/windowsce/*
Windows NT 4.0 Terminal Server and Windows-based terminals	*http://www.microsoft.com/ntserver/*
The Sega Dreamcast system	*http://www.microsoft.com/windowsce/ dreamcast/*
DirectX programming	*Inside DirectX*, by Bradley Bargen and Peter Donnelly (Microsoft Press, 1998)
Using the Handheld PC	*Introducing Microsoft Windows CE for the Handheld PC*, by Robert O'Hara (Microsoft Press, 1997)
Developing for the Handheld PC and the Palm-size PC	Microsoft Windows CE Platform SDK
The Auto PC	Microsoft Auto PC Software Development Kit

12

The Future of Windows CE

*T*his chapter discusses possible future directions for Microsoft Windows CE. It doesn't need much introduction, except perhaps to explain why a chapter about the future contains so much about the past. As a famous writer once explained: "The past is never dead. It's not even past."

Frank Fite looks at the immediate future to discuss system software features in the next releases of Windows CE. Dave Wecker discusses hardware enhancements that we can expect to see in the next year or two. Harel Kodesh looks at the importance of TV-based devices in the home and the shift in Microsoft customer demographics from people who are computer-savvy to people who are intimidated by the computer. Brad Silverberg talks about the organizational and management challenges ahead for the Windows CE team. Tandy Trower describes current and future high-bandwidth social user interfaces. Microsoft architect Edward Jung discusses some of the ideas present at the birth of Windows CE that were ahead of their time and still await implementation. He also discusses the benefits of a single programming model for all Microsoft Windows and Windows CE devices.

---◆---

FUTURE SYSTEM SOFTWARE

Frank Fite

The next releases of Windows CE will have expanded processor support. Right now, we run on a good number of processor architectures and distinct chips, but there are many more we don't run on, and a lot of new features are coming out on processors that we can't yet take advantage of. Another big area for us in the future will be multimedia. As Windows CE is embedded in multimedia platforms, we'll provide more support for DirectX.

Frank Fite

Yet another area of growth for us is better and better connectivity. We have pretty good connectivity now with the basic protocols, which let you dial up or hook up to Microsoft Windows NT: TCP/IP, PPP, RAS. We have programs for the Windows NT side that enable you to access APIs on the Windows CE side and move bits back and forth. Connectivity right now is really good, but a lot of Windows NT developers want to use Windows CE clients in a spread-out network program that has object-oriented methodologies and tools that we don't yet support. Right now, we have COM support, but we support only those objects that are local on our machine and local to a process. With Distributed COM (DCOM), you can have all the objects throughout your network talking to one another. So we're currently working with DCOM and RPC so that in the future we can move to the new object model for Windows NT—COM+.

It is important to us to be able to hook into Windows NT BackOffice applications. We'd like third parties who work on other operating systems to connect their server applications to Windows CE too. We'd like Windows CE to work with as many systems as possible.

We already offer real-time, and we will be adding more features that customers of real-time operating systems want. Offering more components is always a good thing because we can provide more features, but helping people put the components together is really critical. We will be making componentization much easier for people. The tool set, which is critical for both componentization and for real-time functionality, should include support for enhanced debugging, better basic monitoring, and performance monitoring—all those perks that hardcore embedded designers really want. We can't provide all these enhancements by ourselves. We hope to get a lot of help through partnerships with third parties, who will see the value in our OS and make money selling their tools for our OS. We'll need all their help. The general-purpose embedded market is a big, varied market. Niche markets exist in there; people have expertise in different areas; tools are available for different kinds of products. We're not going to meet the need of every customer in every product area, but where we do, we want to have the best tool support possible.

FUTURE DEVICE HARDWARE

Dave Wecker

I'm principal engineer for all of Mobile Products, so I have technical and architectural responsibility for everything under Bill's [Bill Mitchell's] organization—the Auto PC, the Palm-size PC, the Handheld PC—anything not attached to a TV set. We're looking at how to add more storage to various devices.

The first of the storage options being made available is Compact Flash. These cards currently come in sizes of up to about 30 MB, and next year they will be up to 60 MB or so. A Compact Flash memory card is identical electrically to a PCMCIA card. It's missing eight data lines and eight address lines, but otherwise it's identical to the PC Card; the same driver works for both. It's fast, relatively speaking; it's nonvolatile; it doesn't need a battery. The problem is, Flash memory isn't cheap. When you get into 100-MB Flash memory cards, you get into a price that's a little more expensive than people would like.

Dave Wecker

In the Palm-size PC, the OEMs built a Compact Flash slot that has a bump. We've tried to promote a new standard—a Type 2 Compact Flash—that enables us to do a couple of things, the most important of which is allow wireless devices. The form factor of the current device, which is about 3.3 millimeters in height, isn't big enough. The new one, which is 5 millimeters, is actually big enough to insert electrical components other than memory cards. You can pop in a pager card, for example. Some companies are building modems, and we already have an Ethernet card that plugs in at the regular Type 1 form factor. If the Type 2 becomes popular, you'll see more and more devices. I think I/O devices in the Compact Flash form factor will be more and more interesting.

A new device named the Clik!™ drive from Iomega is 40 MB, and it will be out in a 100-MB size this year. It's very cheap, but you've got to spin the media, so drive requires more battery power and the access time is slower. We're talking dollars per disk at most instead of hundreds of dollars for Flash drives. The media and the drive around it is relatively large—the drive is bigger than the whole Palm-size PC device—so using this is more of a possibility in larger PC companion devices.

Some interesting products are coming in very small, fixed, optical drives. Hundreds of megabytes on a little piece of plastic that costs less than a dollar per media chip. One idea is to use this as a replacement for a Walkman because it has no moving parts, meaning that it is completely shock resistant. Initial drives will be read-only and probably fit in a Type 3 PCMCIA slot. Again, these drives aren't really applicable to smaller devices for the time being, but they will shrink dramatically. And if you increase the power—use a new technology or organic LEDs—you might be able to make the drives read/write. There's also new rotating optical media coming, which looks to be very high density.

BATTERY TECHNOLOGY

One of the problems is power. The problem with rotating media is you pay for it in power. For instance, the HP [Hewlett Packard] color H/PC has a lithium ion battery. It doesn't take size AA. So I think you're also going to see a lot more in the way of bigger batteries, especially in the larger PC companion devices. And as soon as you use bigger batteries because people want an 8-hour continuous run, you'll be able to put these little disks in a Windows CE device. I don't think it's at all unreasonable to expect to see bigger batteries within the next year.

In terms of the Handheld PCs and Palm-size PCs, battery life isn't as big a problem because most of them are going to rechargeables if they haven't already. Typically a user pops the device into a cradle to synchronize, and every time she does, the battery recharges. There have also been some very recent advances in zinc air battery technology, which offers five times the battery storage of alkalines.

WIRELESS

Wireless communication is also going to affect storage. If you can just pull the information you need off the Net or off the air as you need it, why should you locally store anything except the page you're looking at? This year we're supplying one-way communication, mainly because we want to fit the technology into the smaller size. I can put a one-way pager into the Compact Flash form factor. When you go into two-way, unfortunately things get big, and you need a transmitter and power for it.

But we will start growing these devices into phones. Either the Palm-size PC has a phone in it, or the phone has the Palm-size PC software in it—take your pick. In the future, you'll see both. Once you have that technology, you have full two-way capabilities: digital PCS services, short messaging services, and the like. As soon as I go to digital PCS, I can do full data up and down besides doing regular speech. And again, add more battery to the device and now you've got a full phone. There's no reason I can't browse the web, retrieve books, and do all this other stuff. Just grab what I need. We already handle email with two-way. Besides paging, we'll also do full wireless email.

The point is, with the OAL and the driver model we have, anyone can write a driver for these various devices. Software isn't holding them back, which is great. As soon as the technology is developed, we can enable it almost instantly. Also, once developers write a driver for one Windows CE device, the same core is underneath all the devices. The developers can run this driver in the car, on Palm-size PCs, on H/PCs—it doesn't matter; it's all Windows CE. The driver model is the same, which of course makes life much easier.

So, in general I don't think there's any problem with all these new devices coming. We support them; we enable them; and they're all Win32.

GROWING THE WINDOWS CE TEAM

Brad Silverberg

During the first few years, we were very conscious of staying focused. People came to us with all kinds of ideas: "Oh, let's do this thing" and "Let's do that thing." I vetoed all of them because I wanted the team completely focused on that first device. Staying on track enabled everybody to be totally committed and motivated, giving that initial device its greatest chance for success.

A good way to kill opportunities is to try to do too much too soon. You end up with too many teams that don't have enough people. You don't have enough resources; you don't have enough management; you don't have enough focus. You end up signing too many contracts, and then your managers are always flying around talking to this guy or that guy explaining why this is late or why we can't do that. You have to learn how to say no.

Brad Silverberg

You have to maintain a kind of iron-fisted focus on the initial devices and stay close to those OEMs. You just have to say, "Okay, let's get those first ones out the door. Let's make those successful, and then we'll broaden our focus."

It was tight. People worked really hard, but we made it, and I think it has proved to be an extremely high-quality operating system. Happy partners, you know. If you look back at the history of WinPad, you'll see that the partners weren't very happy. The products didn't get delivered; the products didn't meet expectations; we had to get out of a lot of contracts. We had to clean up a lot of messes. In contrast, the original partners of Windows CE are still around, and we have added new partners. People are pretty happy with the way things have turned out. And a lot of that success does come from a really clear sense of what we wanted to build, the initial project focus, the discipline, and learning to say no.

You know, Harel [Kodesh] is really the guy. I was around in the beginning to help put the WinPad and the Pulsar teams together. I was in the tough situation of having to name somebody to head the new group; both the WinPad guys and the Pulsar guys wanted to run the group. You just have to bet on one person, so I spent a lot of time with Harel and a lot of time with some of the other folks and decided to bet on Harel. I wanted him to do the job, and I was going to provide him with advice, feedback, direction, and mentoring; I wanted to help him grow: build the team, build the product, build the relationships, and grow. And I think that succeeded. He's got a very strong team with good products. Probably the most rewarding part for me is seeing how people exceed your expectations, even when you have high expectations.

It's gotten to the point now where Windows CE is a pretty hot part of the company to work in. It wasn't that way when we started. There were a lot of skeptics in the company who told us why we would never succeed. But today, you know, there's a lot of excitement. The quality of people working there is very high and they have the ability to attract even more good people. I think that's a testament to Harel and the job that he's done to stake out a vision, build a team, and provide real leadership. One indicator of successful projects is how many of the original people are still around—you can see how many people from the original team are still there.

I think the group has a really good sense of teamwork. You can identify with what I mean: a sports team can have a lot of talented players, but if those players aren't really dedicated to the team, the team doesn't typically end up winning. When members of the team understand that the team—the product—comes first, they experience a kind of selflessness. Whenever a problem comes up, anybody who can help just does whatever he or she can to solve it.

As we move into the future, our challenge will be to maintain that focus. Good managers should groom people underneath them who can take on individual projects and demonstrate the same level of focus and discipline. Managers need to be able to decide which projects to pursue while continuing to make the technology investments, both the conservative ones to ensure that the near-term and medium-term projects succeed and the more speculative ones that deal with concepts such as voice and handwriting recognition.

WINDOWS CE IN THE HOME

Harel Kodesh

Over the last few years, we realized that there are three distinct markets for Windows CE: embedded systems, the mobile area, and high-end graphics systems—TV screens.

Some of the design wins for embedded systems are going to be generic designs for us: We simply give people the embedded toolkit and let them build a system. For these generic systems, we don't provide any UI. You can do whatever you want with the shell. You can have our shell or somebody else's shell or no shell. But for the other markets, we realized that to be strategic we need to claim the domain. In the markets where we are 100 percent committed, 100 percent involved, we come up all the way from actually testing some of the devices to building the UI. For example, in the TV market, we are driving the strategy; this is where we just take leadership and really drive all the aspects of the business.

Harel Kodesh

The TV screen is the most prominent screen in the house, not just because it's a big screen—it's probably the only 20-something-inch screen that you have at your home—but because it's in a strategic place. The TV is almost like the fireplace of ancient times. It's a social event; the whole family gathers around. Even if the TV screen isn't perfect (it's interlace and not progressive scan, which is much more friendly for computers or consumer information appliances), it's still the only thing like it in the home and we're not going to start changing consumer preferences. Rather than just create another, completely different industry, we're going to work with the TV industry to provide data services.

The TV cable and the satellite cable are the two prominent, high-bandwidth inputs into the home, and we need an information appliance that terminates the network. There are a couple of ways to go about that. One is to take the PC and add TV-related features. The other is to subset the PC functionality for people who want to mix Internet with broadcasting or who want to play games. We intend to play a very dominant role in this market by making sure that we understand what consumers need, that these types of devices exist; and that we work with prominent players, everyone from game companies to cable companies.

We will take advantage of whatever technology is available for the transmission, whatever is developed for connectivity. Other groups at Microsoft are trying to advance the state of the world in that area. ADSL (asynchronous digital subscriber line) will be available; IP telephony will be supported on these boxes. But if for some reason ADSL doesn't come in the next three years, we'll still be able to get value out of Windows CE devices. We take the simple approach that we will work with whatever is available.

We also recognize the need to create new technologies and adopt existing technologies from Microsoft. So for instance, Windows CE is adopting DirectX, our game API. In our case, this is going to be optimized even beyond the PC. Because the device is an information appliance, we don't ship the same code to people using graphic accelerator x and people using graphic accelerator y. We can optimize the heck out of the software to work really well with a specific system.

The biggest question is how to make our software easier to use as the demographic landscape of users of Microsoft products changes. Our market is changing from computer-savvy people to people who are intimidated and don't know how to plug the various components together.

The way PC software is built today, everybody has to be a do-it-yourself mechanic. With PCs, you have to open the hood once in a while. With Windows CE, we don't require people to open the hood—ever. There is no hood. Our ideal model is service-based boxes, where somebody on the other side of the cable or wire makes sure that you get everything you need and that it is easy for you to use.

THE NEW INFORMATION ENVIRONMENT

Tandy Trower

With PC technology, we were limited to sitting at our desks to gain information. But Windows CE is now to the point where we're not limited. Wherever I am, I have access to information. Sitting in my car, walking down the hall, sitting down at my desktop, sitting at an electronic whiteboard—the information can move to any of those spaces. Before, I had to go to the information. Now the information is all around me; it can accompany me.

Tandy Trower

Technologies now exist that enable me to communicate on a larger bandwidth; I can send you a piece of mail, and you can receive it without going back to the office. All this means a very rich form of interaction, a rich convergence of information, coming in to the user as well as going out from the user. The Windows CE platform provides the potential to get to a place where my information space is ubiquitous.

I see possibilities where the appropriate information comes to me based on where I am and the task I'm performing and the device I'm interacting with. In my car driving down the road, I might want travel and map information, or hotel and restaurant databases. In the kitchen, I might get information on recipes or pull up my shopping list. In my family room, I have access to online videos or what's playing next. In other situations, the same information might be accessible to me but won't be the primary information. The information adapts to me and my environment.

Another interesting area for these portable devices is understanding how to display information that is appropriate for the devices. It's likely that portable and handheld devices will always have smaller screen capacities than desktop systems. Developers should be able to annotate objects for display so that an object, like a web page, will know where it's being displayed, automatically adjust itself to the form factor, and display appropriate information for the device. A *www.sidewalk.com* page on a large desktop screen knows it has a lot of room and knows how to lay out its objects; a page viewed under Windows CE automatically rearranges itself or scales down.

Getting to smaller screens isn't just a matter of scaling everything down, it's really a matter of asking: "What information is important to display in this form factor, and what is the best way to lay it out?" Microsoft is in the process of developing technologies that will help developers make those decisions.

LINGUISTIC INTERFACES

I can talk in general about directions that I think the Windows interface will go. The interface will support more modalities than the click-and-drag types of interaction we have today. Certainly, direct manipulation of the user interface has been a fundamental feature of the overall Windows interface.

This interface is very intuitive for the user. People understand how to click on icons and drag items in the interface because these actions relate to their real-world experiences.

This kind of direct manipulation isn't going away, but we're going to extend and enhance that interface and provide linguistic interfaces that take advantage of speech and natural language capabilities, and perhaps gesture and handwriting forms of interaction as well.

One of my ongoing projects right now is called Microsoft Agent. It enhances the modalities of the interface by allowing applications to create a sense of social presence on the PC. That major component of the human-computer relationship has been missing. We've focused on the cognitive aspects of communication—what we can remember, how we parse visual information. What this inquiry has totally left out of the picture, however, is an acknowledgement that human beings are *social* animals. When we talk with one another, we exchange nonverbal cues all the time. Like, I'm talking to you right now and you're nodding your head. If I was saying something that you didn't understand, you'd probably give me a puzzled expression. You might tense up. Your body posture tells me a lot about how interested you are in what I'm saying. We pass a whole set of social cues back and forth.

Microsoft's first attempt with the social interface was called Microsoft Bob. Although that product failed in the marketplace, its goal, I believe, was absolutely correct: to provide a focal point for communication between users and their PCs. The second-generation effort was the Microsoft Office Assistant in Microsoft Office 97. Microsoft Agent is the third generation, and it usually takes Microsoft about three generations to get things right. So being immodest for a moment, I think we're getting it right this time.

Microsoft Agent is an open system; any developer can write to the API, which is simple but very rich in that it allows developers to put interactive characters on the screen. Those characters can be used for any purpose: as a focal point for user assistance, like you see in Office; as tour guides; as shopping assistants; as a means of support—rather than calling in to a support line, you query the support character.

Or the characters could be used simply for entertainment purposes. I've seen a couple of applications for Microsoft Agent in traditional computer games, like Reversi or chess. The difficulty is personifying the computer, so the model is fuzzy. Some of these games have just added an animated character that reacts to your moves. For example, after you make your move, the character scratches its head or displays a disgruntled look because it didn't like your move. But that changes the whole dimension of the interaction. Now you are getting information that you would traditionally get only from another human being. This type of interaction is not necessarily a system requirement, because you could certainly play chess against the computer without it, but it adds an extra, more natural dimension to the interaction. And that's really what Microsoft Agent is designed to do.

We think enhancing the communication channel this way will help us introduce speech into the interface. Several studies show that speech works much better when it has a focal point. I theorize that those results have to do with the mental model users create when interacting with the computer. If you're talking to your computer and all you're seeing on the screen is your normal GUI interface, you build this mental model: "Wow, this is my computer; it's supposed to get everything right; it's the model of precision; it shouldn't make any mistakes." But as with most recognition technologies, there are breakdowns; mistakes will happen. Breakdowns occur in human conversations as well, but we use a variety of different strategies to repair the breakdowns. One of them is social feedback. If I start speaking gobbledy-gook, you'll give me a very puzzled expression that lets me know immediately that you don't understand; you don't have to say a thing. You don't have to put up an invasive dialog box. All you have to do is give me a puzzled look, and I'll know that I'm probably not communicating at that point.

Speech combined with social cues creates a much more natural model, which we learn by communicating face-to-face with each other. From the day we're born, we look up into our parents' faces and try to read them. A number of studies show that children are happier when presented with images of faces as opposed to just any image. Facial expressions are important to us. It's not impossible to communicate without having a face in front of us—we do it all the time over the phone or listening to the radio. And we can create a social presence without necessarily putting a face on the screen. The classic example is HAL from "2001." Clearly HAL was a personality, and yet he didn't have a face. His personality was expressed in other ways: in the way he spoke, in the way his presence was established. But face-to-face vocal communication is one of the highest bandwidth communications that humans have. With Agent, we're trying to create the same high-bandwidth experience.

Character, speech, and natural language understanding are part of the linguistic interface. Some of the decision theory research investigates how to understand user intent. I think as systems grow to have more memory capacity and richer processors, we'll see expanded opportunities to include smart interfaces. The software will be able to model the user's intent, offer to perform tasks on the user's behalf, and learn which patterns of tasks the user will delegate to the software.

You see some of this functionality in the Microsoft Office applications: if you repeat a certain sequence, Office automatically offers the same sequence to you. For example, in Microsoft Excel, when you enter dates into three columns and you tab to the next column, Excel offers to put the date in the fourth column automatically. Or consider the smart spelling capabilities that you see in Microsoft Word: when you type *teh*, Word interprets that you really meant to type *the* and automatically corrects your spelling. If Word's correction is not what you intended, you back up and you change it; Word doesn't try to change it again. I think building a Bayesian belief network about what the user is doing will become important.

THE FUNDAMENTAL THINGS APPLY

The basic principles of user interface design don't change. When designing for interaction, the fundamentals apply. For example, keeping the user in control is important. One of the lessons we learned with Microsoft Bob is users want to be able to control their interaction with characters. One problem with Bob was the ever-present character. Although we are social animals, we need privacy and we need to work on our own. When the character was constantly present, people felt the interface was condescending, because it implied, "You always need assistance, so I'll always be here, and you can't dismiss me because you're not skilled enough to know how to do things on your own." There wasn't enough user control.

Microsoft's three generations of social interfaces: characters from Microsoft Bob, Microsoft Office, and Microsoft Agent serve as the focal point of the user interface.

With Microsoft Agent, we've given the user more control over the interface. If the user doesn't want to see a character ever again, she can click a check box and none of Agent's characters will show up in her face. Users can also control other aspects, too, such as turning off speech input or output in environments where they're not effective. Some people simply don't like that form of interaction. They work better unassisted, without any other personalities around them at all. So users always have to be able to control and personalize the interface.

The principle of consistency holds up for the CE platform just like it does for the desktop platform. Users are most comfortable with things that remain relatively consistent with what they expect. You can allow a certain amount of variation as long as the fundamental principle of interaction works the same. For example, I show you five different designs for a button and as long as each looks like a button, you understand their function and you care less about their differences. But as soon as the functionality of something familiar changes, you get confused.

And this all gets back to why we use metaphors in the interface. Metaphors are intended to provide cognitive bridges from what a user knows to a new experience. As human beings, that's how we learn new situations, by conscious and unconscious comparisons to previous experiences. You don't have to be rigid about staying with the metaphor, but you want to be consistent enough to provide a bridge to a new experience.

THE SINGLE PROGRAMMING MODEL

Edward Jung

When we started the Advanced Technology division, one of our big goals was insurance against sea changes: "What could wipe out Microsoft? In the same way that CDs wiped out vinyl records, what could do the same thing to Microsoft?"

Edward Jung

Certainly one possibility is that somebody's speech interface becomes very usable and takes over, and everyone gears their hardware and tailors their apps to this new speech interface. Everything that we've got today will fade in importance; all the action and innovation will happen somewhere else. That's what will kill us. As a software company, we're so dependent on innovation happening on our platform.

Steve Ballmer's mantra back at the time we started the Advanced Technology division was, "Windows everywhere, Windows everywhere." So we had off-site meetings about how to get Windows everywhere. Certainly one of the form factors that we were thinking about then was the handheld form factor. One of the first projects, Pulsar, was based on two underlying ideas:

◆ A traditional, larger form factor PDA with handwriting recognition.

◆ A wallet PC that would hold electronic money (e-cash). Think of it as a really, really fat smart card.

The wallet PC functions were centered around purchasing and pager messaging. If you went shopping, it could hold your credentials, help you find things to buy, and keep track of all that for you. Some studies that circulated even suggested that the money supply, M1, could be affected if you had e-cash floating around as opposed to dollar bills!

We originally believed that electronic wireless communications would be fairly prevalent and that e-cash was right around the corner. A lot of the early architectural and technical work for Pulsar was based on these concepts, which didn't materialize as fast as we thought they would. And when they did come into play, they were extremely expensive. Even today, widely available wireless communication is measured on a per-minute basis. And e-cash doesn't look like it's going to happen very soon.

(Another area where we really guessed wrong for Pulsar was memory. When we started, memory was cheap and looked like it was going to get really cheap. Of course, as we all know, in the mid-1990s memory actually got quite expensive compared to the other parts of a PC. Now it's cheap again, but it leveled off for a while before it dropped again. So this idea of an operating system that did more than just the bare minimum turned out to be expensive and noncompetitive. That memory price hurt us. Oddly enough, we also guessed wrong when memory prices were high. We embarked on a project called Talisman, which was all about trading off memory for CPU to get amazing graphics and sound. Of course, just about the time we were ready to release that technology, the price of memory dropped through the floor. So that was a case where we bet wrong on one side and then we bet wrong on the other side. It just shows how tricky it can be to try to plan.)

After Pulsar merged with WinPad and became the Handheld PC, and as we got more and more into the project, we had a lot of really interesting ideas that never panned out. Some of the wireless packet radios and pagers were running at roughly the same frequency, so we had this idea that the pager radio would turn on the wireless radio. The reasoning was, batteries for wireless radios last six or seven hours, but the batteries for pagers last a couple of weeks. You would get a page and that page would turn on your wireless radio, and then you could wire some connectivity so you wouldn't eat up your battery.

So all those ideas about the design of the Palm-size PC—its form factor, its size, the handwriting capability—those were all ideas we had at Microsoft back in 1994, and I'm sure those ideas also existed at Apple and a billion other places that we won't know about. In this industry, every idea is basically the same idea over and over again, just in a different context. It's really the timing of the idea that's important. So many things we do today are ideas we had a long time ago, but the timing just wasn't right. If you lay out the history of Pulsar and the H/PC, it's really interesting to see how we change and adapt and remold our initial ideas, and how the infrastructure changes.

When you talk to OEMs about why they were interested in Windows CE, you find out that establishing a standard enables them to get access to a lot of applications that they don't want to write. They want to be experts at their hardware or running their distribution channel. They don't want to write every single app out there. If you open it up for anyone to write the apps, you win. It's that simple.

Of every dollar spent on software innovation by a venture capitalist or by a bank, the largest fraction of that dollar should go into innovation. When everyone spends 50 cents on the dollar for the same work, they're wasting money. Before we created Windows, developers had to write every printer driver and every graphics hardware driver. This amounted to huge development, test, and support costs, which the developers had to pay. It made software much more expensive, and it also capped innovation for printers and graphics and input devices, because the IHVs had to try to sell application developers on writing drivers for their devices. It was inefficient. If innovators have to replicate everything from top to bottom again and again, they never get anywhere. But if you always build up the standard, one layer at a time, and move forward, your innovation wins. Windows gave you a programming model where you wrote to an abstraction and all those drivers were handled for you. Microsoft took on the onus of testing a lot of the drivers and gave people a standard to test against.

The computing experience that really helps augment your choices in life—that's what we want to make as available to you as possible. If you can put it in your pocket or carry it around, and it has enough surface area for a UI, it should be a Windows CE device: a tablet, a notebook computer, a wallet. A wallet makes a lot of sense, if we can make it strong enough to avoid breaking when you sit down. It should be something you can carry around with you at all times.

Windows CE is going to straddle a wide range of user interfaces, and it will also straddle a huge disparity of bandwidth—sometimes highly asymmetric, sometimes symmetric and huge, sometimes symmetric and tiny. You don't want to download your entire inbox over a slow wireless network that costs 15 cents a minute. Notions of priority and importance have to get measured against the cost of moving that message. For example, it makes no sense to send a humongous graphic to a wallet device.

One challenge we'd really like to address in the next several years is how to enable people to develop for these different devices without writing a separate application for each one. Writing a bunch of separate applications will ultimately stifle our innovation. We want to tell developers, "Write to this abstraction." We'll handle getting the code onto devices the size of a wallet and the size of a whiteboard so that developers don't have to hand-code and test every configuration. Ultimately, we want to say this: "Hey, here's one programming model for all those devices."

One example of that single programming model running with in-house technology is Microsoft's *Sidewalk.com*; I think we want to get technology like Sidewalk into our Windows programming model down the line. Sidewalk is built in such a way that an application developer can describe the intention of what she wants to show the user so that it will be rendered appropriately on different form factors. By changing a driver, Sidewalk renders a down-level HTML client, HTML with ActiveX controls, or DHTML, so the authors don't have to change any of their back-end content. That's a big win for Sidewalk in terms of keeping to their editorial publishing schedule and managing their workflow without the worry of how the information is rendered.

Sidewalk was done in SGML, a predecessor of XML, because XML did not exist at the time. XML is certainly becoming the industry-standard for describing your information, and applications will probably continue to use

XML in the future. The developer on the back end describes the capabilities of the application, and a run-time library figures out from those capabilities what you want to show. That information gets rendered in XML, the XML goes across the wire, gets bound to a style sheet, and gets displayed.

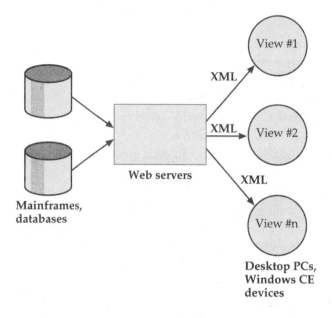

XML and related standards allow you to define tags that indicate the logical role of your data, rather than only its formatting information. Microsoft is currently promoting the use of XML in a three-tiered architecture. Information passes between databases, Web servers, and end users at a desktop or Windows CE device. The XML content can be translated to HTML so that the logical information can be rendered appropriately for that device.

You can do a lot with only XSL or the style sheet languages and binding to logical tags, but there's a limit. Sidewalk, for example, supported a telephony interface. To create an adaptive telephony interface, you have to be very careful. Your rules are based on the length of the utterances and the assumption that the user can remember 7 plus or minus 3 items. The way you navigate through the data using a telephony interface is totally different from the way you would navigate through an HTML page. So a renderer that can handle a telephony interface requires different kinds of information than you would tend to see in style sheets, which are usually geared to visual presentation.

Another interesting challenge involves your schedule and email. How would you convert it from the full size of the desktop display to less than one-eighth of your screen, or even less? You can't just miniaturize it. You have to be smart about what data you throw away. Style sheets aren't usually powerful enough to do that kind of work. They're not good at filtering how much data you want to see.

We're also faced with the challenge of figuring out how adaptable the device really has to be and which markets go for the different form factors. That's what we're doing today. We did the same research with Microsoft Office: we understood which apps were used by whom and we understood their relative importance. That was great input when we integrated it all. It told us what features had to go into our scripting programming language, VBA, and where to emphasize Office assistance. Same thing with Windows— we had several years of DOS under our belts helping us understand graphics cards and what people thought about layered pixels, the color model, and pixel blocks versus true bitmaps. We can learn a lot from the market.

In the next few years, we're going to have a greater understanding of the different form factors and how people use them, and that's going to give us information on how to build this new programming model.

RESOURCES

Topic	Resource
DCOM, COM+, RPC	The Platform SDK, available through the Microsoft Developer Network (MSDN); *http://www.microsoft.com/msdn/*
DirectX	*Inside DirectX*, by Bradley Bargen and Peter Donnelly (Microsoft Press, 1998)
WebTV	*http://www.webtv.com*
Microsoft Agent	*http://inetsdk/workshop/imedia/agent/*
XML, XSL, and XQL	*http://www.microsoft.com/xml/*

INDEX

JOHN MURRAY

John Murray wandered around the American West as a journalist before collecting a computer science degree and working in Utah for five years developing flight simulation software. He has written sample code and programming guide documentation for many Microsoft software developer kits, including Win32, RPC, COM, MAPI, networking, interactive television, streaming media, and the social user interface.

John Murray (left) is congratulated on the completion of Inside Microsoft Windows CE *by the eternal Darryl Rubin, a standup figure of the Microsoft vice president that Brian Valentine and the LAN Manager team created for just such golden moments.*

The manuscript for this book was prepared and submitted to Microsoft Press in electronic form. Text files were prepared using Microsoft Word 97. Pages were composed by Microsoft Press using Adobe PageMaker 6.52 for Windows, with text and display type in Palatino. Composed pages were delivered to the printer as electronic prepress files.

Cover Designer
Tim Girvin Design, Inc.

Cover Illustrator
Glenn Mitsui

Interior Graphic Designers
Kim Eggleston, Barbara Remmele

Principal Artist
Travis Beaven

Principal Compositor
Paula Gorelick

Principal Proofreader/Copy Editor
Roger LeBlanc

Indexer
Liz Cunningham

Register Today!

Return this
Inside Microsoft® Windows® CE
registration card today

mspress.microsoft.com

1-57231-854-6

Inside Microsoft® Windows® CE

FIRST NAME	MIDDLE INITIAL	LAST NAME

INSTITUTION OR COMPANY NAME

ADDRESS

CITY	STATE	ZIP

E-MAIL ADDRESS	( ) PHONE NUMBER

U.S. and Canada addresses only. Fill in information above and mail postage-free.
Please mail only the bottom half of this page.

For information about Microsoft Press®
products, visit our Web site at
mspress.microsoft.com

BUSINESS REPLY MAIL
FIRST-CLASS MAIL   PERMIT NO. 108   REDMOND WA

POSTAGE WILL BE PAID BY ADDRESSEE

MICROSOFT PRESS
PO BOX 97017
REDMOND, WA 98073-9830